Childhood and family life have changed significantly in recent decades. What is the nature of these changes? How have they affected the use of time, space, work, and play? In what ways have they influenced face-to-face talk and the uses of technology within families and communities? What are the effects of race and social class on early and later language development and education and career choices?

Eminent anthropologist Shirley Brice Heath sets out to find answers to these and similar questions, tracking the lives of 300 black and white working-class families as they reshaped their lives in new locations, occupations, and interpersonal alignments over a period of thirty years.

From the 1981 recession through the economic instabilities and technological developments of the opening decade of the twenty-first century, Shirley Brice Heath shows how families constantly rearrange their patterns of work, language, play, and learning in response to economic pressures. Determined to enter the mainstream, parents and children navigate newly desegregated schools, the need for new skills for new jobs, and the realities of compressed and overlapping time demands in family life. In the care of "intimate strangers" – including childcare workers, coaches, music teachers, and community organization leaders – children become closely aligned with peers in their ways of talking and choices of special interests that engage them with play, work, and technology.

Combining social history, language records, and a close examination of community life over many years, this outstanding study is a must-read for anyone interested in family life, language development, and social change.

SHIRLEY BRICE HEATH, a leading social historian and ethnographer of family life, is Margery Bailey Professor of English and Dramatic Literature and Professor of Linguistics, Emerita, at Stanford University. Her previous publications include *Ways with words: Language, life, and work in communities and classrooms* (Cambridge, 1983/1996) and *On ethnography* (2008, with Brian Street).

Words at Work and Play

Three Decades in Family and Community Life

Shirley Brice Heath

LIS - LIBRARY

Date	Fund
11/4/12	e-RIV

Order No
2287249

University of Chester

CAMBRIDGE
UNIVERSITY PRESS

CAMBRIDGE UNIVERSITY PRESS
Cambridge, New York, Melbourne, Madrid, Cape Town,
Singapore, São Paulo, Delhi, Tokyo, Mexico City

Cambridge University Press
The Edinburgh Building, Cambridge CB2 8RU, UK

Published in the United States of America by Cambridge University Press, New York

www.cambridge.org
Information on this title: www.cambridge.org/9780521603034

© Shirley Brice Heath 2012

This publication is in copyright. Subject to statutory exception
and to the provisions of relevant collective licensing agreements,
no reproduction of any part may take place without the written
permission of Cambridge University Press.

First published 2012

Printed in the United Kingdom at the University Press, Cambridge

A catalogue record for this publication is available from the British Library

Library of Congress Cataloguing in Publication data
Heath, Shirley Brice.
Words at work and play : three decades in family and community life / Shirley Brice
Heath.
    p.   cm.
ISBN 978-0-521-60303-4 (pbk.)
1. Language and culture – Piedmont (U.S. : Region)   2. Sociolinguistics – Piedmont
(U.S. : Region)   3. English language – Dialects – Piedmont
(U.S. : Region)   4. African American children – Piedmont (U.S. : Region) –
Language.   I. Title.
P35.5.U6H43   2012
306.4409756–dc23

                                                                            2011025089

ISBN 978-0-521-84197-9 Hardback
ISBN 978-0-521-60303-4 Paperback

Cambridge University Press has no responsibility for the persistence or
accuracy of URLs for external or third-party internet websites referred to
in this publication, and does not guarantee that any content on such
websites is, or will remain, accurate or appropriate.

In memory of Marjorie Martus
and
In tribute to
Jerome Bruner and Courtney Cazden

Contents

Maps, family trees, figures, and tables

Acknowledgments

Since 1969 I have followed the lives of children and grandchildren of 300 families I first met in the Piedmont Carolinas just as the Civil Rights Era was drawing to a close. Individuals from these families and their friends have found my persistent presence in their lives occasional diversion and support, as well as erratic annoyance and provocation. We have laughed and cried together. We have gathered in one another's homes to take in the horrors of accidents, the loss of young and old family members, and to reckon the toll of twists of fate on those we have known and loved. Together we have been to churches and prisons, hospitals and schools, soccer games and piano recitals, and funerals and graduations of sons and daughters, mothers and fathers.

I am deeply grateful to all the individuals whose lives this book reflects in one way or another. Their perceptions and philosophies have given the depth of history and interpretive power critical to social history and ethnography. Though families will recognize themselves and their friends in these pages, none of these individuals can be mentioned by name. I hope they will, in the main, agree with my account and analysis of the values and habits that have shaped the course of their lives.

This book benefits from the intellectual nourishment of scholars who have debated and critiqued the papers and talks that have reported my research over past years. I cannot adequately acknowledge or thank them. My offering of appreciation is this book. As all scholars do, I take full responsibility for the findings and interpretations given in these pages.

Foremost among those whose ideas have advanced this book is Milbrey Wallin McLaughlin, my colleague and friend at Stanford University, with whom I worked for a decade on research funded by the Spencer Foundation. Her wit and wisdom have been with me through many tough spots. She and I spent years thinking together about how social scientists can most effectively study the lives of young people living in under-resourced communities. The approaches I bring as linguistic anthropologist to this methodological challenge have been amplified by Milbrey's expertise in policy analysis, as well as her commitment to a range of qualitative and quantitative methods of research.

Other colleagues at Stanford University in the School of Education and the Departments of Linguistics and English will also see their influence here. Elliot

Eisner graciously joined with me in debates about the lasting influence on children's learning of participation in the arts. Ingram Olkin, my long-term colleague in statistics, listened to my account of tracking from year to year details of language and life in families scattered across the United States. He advised me against excessive use of quantitative records to support the interpretive narrative of this volume. Readers will, I trust, be grateful for his wise counsel. The work of linguists Elizabeth Traugott, John Rickford, and Penny Eckert, all keenly interested in language change and style, has deepened interpretation of the spoken and written language of children and adolescents in their peer interactions. I have also benefited from Andrea Lunsford's longitudinal research on how young adults bring to their ways of writing expertise in the performative power of other media.

Scholars who have followed literacy into community settings will find their ideas on nearly every page of this volume. David Barton, Deborah Brandt, Marcia Farr, Mary Hamilton, Elizabeth Moje, Beverly Moss, and Brian Street have taken ethnographic routes on their own journeys to follow reading and writing in schools, churches, youth activities, and homes. In our explorations of contemporary uses of oral and written language, all of us have benefited from historical portraits of reading and writing. Central in this research has been the work of historians Elizabeth Eisenstein, Harvey Graff, and Elizabeth McHenry.

Several generations of graduate students have kept me alert to nuances of youth culture, language, and media interaction. I am particularly grateful to those who spent several years working with me as "guerrilla anthropologists" in youth community organizations across the United States. Those who have most shared in my desire to keep language at the center of my study have been Nicole Fleetwood, Adelma Roach Hnasko, Elisabeth Soep, Stuart Tannock, and Jennifer Lynn Wolf. Their research and writing, along with their expertise in critique, have been gifts shared with affection, diligence, and good humor.

Shelby Anne Wolf, my friend, sometime co-author, and frequent editor, will see in several portions of this volume the influence of her longitudinal multi-site research on children and young people working in youth theatre. This work has made me think in new ways about children's development of empathy and interpretive skills through both the dramatic and visual arts. We have had many conversations around our mutual interest in how children living in crisis situations at home or in their communities can set aside their fears and distrust when they become full participants within learning environments centered in the arts. I am deeply grateful to her.

Many of the arguments in this book reflect the continuing influence on my thinking of Elinor Ochs, Bambi Schieffelin, and Alessandro Duranti, colleagues with whom I have shared much in common over more than two decades. Among us, we have benefited greatly from younger researchers, such as Kris Gutiérrez, Carol Lee, and Luis Moll, who have continued to examine the sociocentric nature of language use in the complex interdependence of family, school, and community life.

Hall Kelley of Gualala, California, has generously provided advice on design of maps and figures. My thanks go to him for insights that have substantially clarified textual materials.

Jeremy Mynott and Andrew Winnard of Cambridge University Press have waited a long time for this book. Their patience and commitment have made it possible.

Several institutions have provided opportunities for the unending task of organizing and analyzing decades of audiorecordings, transcripts, fieldnotes, and conversational interviews. Chief among these has been the Carnegie Foundation for the Advancement of Teaching, whose president Lee Shulman made possible the first version of this work, in which I kept myself as ethnographer out of the narrative. Though aborted in favor of the current work that admits me into the cast of characters, the first version of that volume made possible in many ways this eventual publication. Lee's faith in my research on learning and teaching has made all the difference at several critical points in my personal and professional life. He has my deepest thanks.

The Center for Advanced Study in the Behavioral Sciences offered a refuge for writing in two critical years. In my 1987–1988 term there, colleagues, chief among them Barbara Rogoff, expanded my understanding of the roles of observation, imitation, and participation in young children's learning. In my second term, 2001–2002, I was fortunate enough to join Mark Turner and an extraordinary set of interdisciplinary scholars to consider what Mark termed the "irrepressibly artful minds" of humans, young and old, past and present. Colleagues at the Center guided me to the value of neuroscience research on visual cognition and language development in the interpretation of longitudinal ethnographic data on language socialization.

Since 2005, scholars within the Science of Learning Center on Learning in Informal and Formal Environments (LIFE) at the University of Washington and Stanford University have brought me as linguistic anthropologist into their vibrant intellectual mix of neuroscientists, psychologists, and learning scientists. Their company has meant several years of steep-curve learning to expand my ways of thinking about nurture, brain development, and ecologies of learning. I am grateful to them for helping me understand how language development moves in close coordination with the human capacity for visual perception and sustained attentiveness to role fulfillment in the environment.

In the final months of bringing to a close a manuscript whose creation has taken too many years, every scholar needs the fresh eye of a patient engaged reader. Paula Little, a wise teacher, has played this role for me with good humor and a discerning wit. She has my deep appreciation.

Retirement is hard to forsake. Yet my dear friend Elizabeth Bailey did just that to help me with the final editing of this book. She knows more than anyone the extent of my gratitude. Sustaining me always through the years of completing this volume has been her friendship and that of Eileen Landay and Andrea Lunsford. These three friends have kept steady their prodding questions and growing intolerance of my travel schedule, along with their readiness to urge long seaside walks. Their support and friendship have given me inspiration and incentive.

Marjorie Martus, my supportive friend and ready listener, was very much part of the early history of this book before her death. I sorely miss her warm and spirited presence.

Jerome Bruner and Courtney Cazden, friends and scholars to whom this book is offered in tribute, have helped me travel across contexts and disciplines. They have kept all of us who have followed them appreciative of narratives, wary of dichotomies and abstractions, and sensitive to the value of modest theories. I hope they find this volume thoughtful and pleasing

The Blue Canoe
Anchor Bay, California

Note on transcriptions

In transcribing the speech of the characters in this book, I have made no effort to provide phonetic representation. Words are presented in an approximation to standard orthography, with as much "eye-dialect" as seems necessary to indicate the varieties of English used, primarily African American English Vernacular and Piedmont Carolina dialect. The children of the two working-class communities of Trackton and Roadville grew up learning local dialect forms. Trackton children who did not leave the community until they were in their adolescence retained more features of African American English Vernacular than those who left before they entered school. The children of the children of both Trackton and Roadville spoke southern dialects only if they grew up in the South. In the interest of saving space, I have not included self-interruptions or expressions of hesitation (such as *uh*). There is no intention to stigmatize any variety, and the modified spellings are used in full awareness that all natural English speech differs from what standard orthography indicates.

Nonverbal behavior during talk and immediately prior or following talk is indicated within closed [square] brackets.

All material in quotation marks or set off from the text in blocks is a direct quotation. Texts of youth in groups and other long text blocks that are multi-party were taperecorded. Long text blocks of my conversations with individuals were also taperecorded. Quotations embedded within the text were either taken from taperecordings or written down in field and interview notes. Detailing of the situational context of the speech was part of the routine of taking fieldnotes. The following transcription conventions are used for long text blocks.

CAPS	Loud volume in utterance of words or phrases
Italics	Heightening of primary stress by vowel-lengthening and raising of pitch
.	Sentence-final falling intonation and a full pause
,	Clause
?	Rising intonation and pause
[	Overlapping utterances (used to mark the point at which an utterance in progress is joined by another interrupting utterance)
=	Contiguous utterances (used when there is no break between adjacent utterances, the second latched to, but not overlapping, the first)

xiv

All is mere breath. That which was is that which will be, and that which was done is that which will be done, and there is nothing new under the sun.

Ecclesiastes 1: 9 [Translation from Alter 2010]

Prologue

"Never ask her to give you a recipe for apple pie. She'll take you back to the Garden of Eden."

A friend once described me in this way. She explained: "Beginning-to-end, start-to-finish: the long run matters to you."

As it turns out, my friend was right. This book proves her so.

Words at work and play is a relay race of then-and-now stories. Across three decades, this book follows families I first met in a Garden of Eden of a sort – the southeastern United States as the 1960s decade of Civil Rights struggles came to a close. Hopes for positive change were high. I first wrote the stories of white and black families of that region in *Ways with words: Language, life and work in communities and classrooms* (1983/1996) after living and learning with them as a linguistic anthropologist for a decade. During that time, my interests centered on children working and playing in their homes and neighborhoods and adapting to classroom life in newly desegregated schools.

In *Ways with words*, I introduced readers to children and adults in four communities clustered within a fifteen-mile radius of one another in the Piedmont Carolinas of the southeastern United States (see Map 1, which reflects primary centers of manufacturing, agriculture, and shipping in the Carolinas during the 1970s and 1980s). Two of these communities, one white and the other black, consisted of mainstream middle-class families who led business, civic, and religious life in the region. These two groups I called "the townspeople."

Two other nearby communities, one white, one black, were made up of working-class wage earners. The first of these I called Roadville, the second Trackton. Small farmers, millworkers, and domestics, the adults made their living as manual laborers unquestioningly living the Protestant work ethic passed on to them across generations and affirmed weekly in their Sunday School and church services. The long run taken by the 300 families of these two working-class communities lies at the heart of this book. Three generations of their families are illustrated in Family trees 1 (Trackton) and Family trees 2 (Roadville).

In the early 1980s, the deep economic recession that devastated the manufacturing economy of the southeastern United States shook the faith and tested the resilience of Roadville and Trackton families. To find work, these families

1

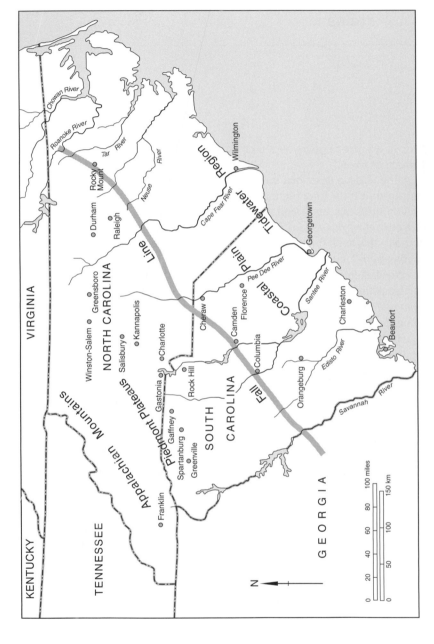

Map 1 Piedmont Carolinas

Trackton original family 1

Lettie Ann Green

Mildred Louise Green
Claudie Riley

Rosa Lee Green (b. *1954*; d. *1987*)
Zinnia Mae Green (b. *1966*)

Jerome Green (b. *1980*)
Lucia Ramirez (b. *1980*)
Donna Green (b. *1983*)
Marcello Green (b. *1985*)
Melvin Green (b. *1985*)

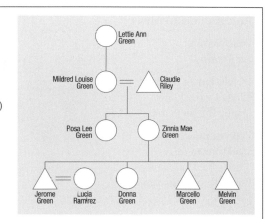

Trackton original family 2

Lillie Mae Clark

Tony Clark (b. *1961*; d. *1988*)
Katisha Anderson (b. *1961*)
Sissy Clark (b. *1966*; d. *1992*)
Red Carranza (b. *1960*)
Benjy Clark (b. *1966*)
Lem Clark (b. *1970*; d. *1988*)

Timothy Clark (b. *1986*)
Denny Clark (b. *1980*)
Tameka Carranza (b. *1992*)

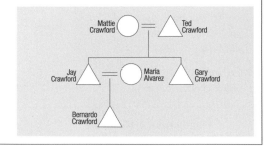

Trackton original family 3

Mattie Crawford
Ted Crawford

Jay Crawford (b. *1968*)
Maria Alvarez (b. *1974*; d. *2002*)
Gary Crawford (b. *1970*)

Bernardo Crawford (b. *1994*)

Family trees 1 Trackton

4

Roadville original family 1

Peggy Brown
Lee Brown

Martin Brown (b. *1970*)
Cindy Dunn (b. *1968*)
Danny Brown (b. *1972*)

Rebecca Brown (b. *1993*)
Mark Brown (b. *1994*)

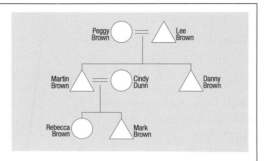

Roadville original family 2

Sue Dobbs
Eric Dobbs

Jed Dobbs (b. *1958*; d. unknown)
Lisa Dobbs (b. *1962*)
Frank Avery (b. *1962*)
Sally Dobbs (b. *1968*)
Bob Ryan (b. *1962*)

Robert Avery (b. *1980*)
Richard Avery (b. *1982*)
Ellen Ryan (b. *1982*)
Anna Ryan (b. *1984*)

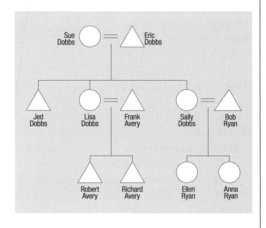

Roadville original family 3

Alice Turner
Jay Turner

Catherine Turner (b. *1962*)
Tom Armstrong (b. *1963*)
Dana Turner (b. *1965*)
Todd Bailey (b. *1960*)

Martha Armstrong (b. *1993*)
Cordelia Bailey (b. *1994*)

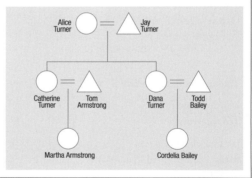

Family trees 2 Roadville

had to scatter well beyond their Eden to strange and new job demands, neighbors, schools, and churches.

The recession squeezed manual laborers in millwork and farming out of the physical, social, and religious spaces that had long shaped their ways of talking, reading and writing, mapping plans and actions, and valuing daily routines. Over the three decades after the double-dip recession of the 1980s, working-class families realigned daily habits, life-choice values, and perceptions of identity. Radical changes came to their ways of thinking about themselves as workers, parents, worshippers, and citizens.

Forced into resettlement in distant places, they struggled throughout the 1980s. Many had barely a secondary-school education, and they could no longer rely primarily on their manual skills and accumulations of common sense in their jobs. Some suffered negative effects of urban life – asthma or other chronic health conditions or a child caught up in gang life or crack cocaine addiction. These families especially felt the absence of an extended family when a child was born with severe birth defects, a spouse turned violent, or a tragic accident cut short the life choices of parent or child. In the prior generation, family members and life-time friends had stepped in to help. Nuclear families were now splintered under the strain of managing crises without a fall-back support system based in long-term relationships in church and community. Their children had to adjust to moving back and forth between dad's house and mom's apartment in either a single-parent or a newly partnered household.

For the majority of families from both Roadville and Trackton, relocation gradually brought them into small-business development and further educational opportunities that situated them to take advantage of the 1990s economic boom. These families resolved to help their children achieve the American dream of university education, home ownership, and mainstream ascendancy.[1] They could no longer separate their skills and values from information technologies. Project development and implementation dictated the pace of their home and work lives. Schedules imposed largely by outside forces shaped daily comings and goings of family members. Community get-togethers for children and adults went on the calendar weeks in advance.

By 2000, the majority of families from both Roadville and Trackton identified themselves as either well on the way to being middle class or already there. In over 80 percent of the families, both parents had checking accounts; 42 percent also had savings accounts. Over 90 percent of the households had at least one credit card, and households with two working parents sometimes had as many as eight different credit cards. Some parents had joined the late 1990s rush to mutual funds and knew about 401-K (tax-efficient retirement) investing. Their children went away to college with checking accounts, credit cards, and sometimes debit cards. In some families, grandparents chose to take early retirement, citing a desire to be closer to their grandchildren and to spend more time watching them grow up. Adults believed the internet bandwagon would take them where they had never dreamed they might go. This uniformity of belief had spread rapidly as the basis for new habits of family and community life and expectations for the future.

With the economic setbacks that followed the attacks on the World Trade Center in New York City on September 11, 2001, the adult children of families across the United States who had been working class when the recession of 1981 hit had to face the fragility of economic opportunities they had believed would go on forever. The foundations of the world they had thought so secure began to crumble.

The harsh recession that began in late 2007 disproportionately hit families whose employment depended on financial markets, new product development, and sustained technological innovation. Many of these families had not fully grasped the meaning of sub-prime or adjustable-rate mortgages. They had assumed their salaries would keep going up and up, and their monthly mortgage payments could always be covered. Cutbacks or job losses came first for fathers, usually the primary wage-earner in two-parent families. Mothers fared better in holding onto their jobs, but significant differences between monthly bills and paychecks mounted. Many of these families had to recognize that the fall in value of real estate had made their homes worth less than the principal remaining on their mortgage. Unmanageable credit card debt, foreclosures on mortgages, and letters of warning from college bursars brought disbelief, shame, strife, and finger-pointing in families who had become accustomed to the comfortable confines of being mainstream and middle class.

Struggles of relocation and joblessness that had come with the double-dip recession of the 1980s had long been forgotten, wiped away by the economic opportunities of the 1990s. Grown children of Roadville and Trackton families only dimly remembered hearing stories of their parents' heartaches and how "things have never been the same since." These children had never absorbed the extent to which the broad financial, social, and geographic forces of the economic hardships of the early 1980s had disrupted relationships, values, and expectations for their parents. Set on the pathway to college, new homes and jobs, and lives filled with material goods and entertainment, these young people had no time to prepare for the changes the new millennium would bring to their sense of security – national, financial, and personal.

In 2012, thirty years after changes in the global economy had pushed their parents and grandparents into building new identities as workers, today's labor force lacks options. Their ancestors did what workers have done for centuries when holding onto a job in the place where they have lived is no longer possible. They left. Today's generation has few geographic frontiers, new lands, or opening economies to look to for a new start. What they must do is plan and build as-yet unimagined kinds of work. As they do so, they will hold in memory bits and pieces of incidents and emotions they and their children may someday sift through to tell stories of sustaining families and communities while crafting the new work critical to national and global economies.

Every tale or tapestry of woven tales should evoke recognition, empathy, and connection. Human beings hold primary interest in two things: reality and telling about it. The latter cannot, however, be taken for the former. Any story differs with each passing moment, new purpose, and favored vantage point. Neither the whole story nor the true one ever exists, however much we may wish for it. If we could achieve wholeness and absolute truth in our stories, we would have no more stories to tell. And tell stories, we must.

1   On being long in company

This book traces families in the United States across three decades from the recession of the early 1980s into the recession that began in 2007. The first generation grew up knowing only the Piedmont Carolinas, the center of the textile industry that had emerged at the end of the Civil War.

Manufacturing and agriculture set the rhythm of their lives. Racial segregation and marked discrepancies in quality of housing, transportation, and education kept black and white, poor and middle class, living in separate worlds. Their families had grown up with a dedication to God and acceptance of "Thy Kingdom come, Thy will be done . . ." Tomorrow would surely dawn very much as today had, and nightfall would come after sundown just as always.

But the tumultuous Civil Rights decade of the 1960s seeded among many a notion of the power of individual agency. The leadership of Martin Luther King and activists from different faith communities who put their lives on the line to end "separate but equal" inspired widespread self-reliance among the working poor – black and white.

In *Ways with words: Language, life, and work in communities and classrooms* (1983/1996), I told the stories of black and white working-class families who lived in the Piedmont Carolinas throughout the 1970s. They saw new laws redefine service relationships and employment opportunities. Blacks became millworkers; desegregated schools promised equity. Front pages of newspapers announced plans for multi-family housing projects and suburban developments. Automobile dealers previously known to welcome only white customers held lot sales for which flyers were distributed in black communities. Loan officers of local banks met with black church leaders to make clear their openness to black clients. The Federal government cut back social services, reduced taxes, and promoted individual business initiatives. Hard work became a national mantra, even as the oil embargo of 1973 led to a drastic reduction in the availability of fuel across the nation. In parallel with these changes in the national economy, less visible shifts in the regional economy of the Southeast were taking place. Agricultural exports were declining. Foreign investors were gradually taking over control of mills long owned by local families. By the end of the 1970s, as textile mills began their closures and cutbacks, effects rippled to manufacturers who produced the machinery used in the mills. Widespread unemployment followed, and in the Southeast, blacks who were the most recently hired were the first to lose their jobs. By 1982 unemployment rates in the Carolinas topped 11 percent; for blacks the rate was double that for whites, with rural and small-town areas most affected. Within these figures are the realities that hit families who bounced between hope and promise and despair and desperation from the end of the 1960s through the 1990s.

The stories behind these realities began for me in 1969 when I lived in the Piedmont Carolinas and played a part in the lives of 300 black and white families who were trying to make sense of what desegregation and "equal rights" might mean for them. Trackton was a black neighborhood of sixteen families whose extended kin included just over 130 families living within a twenty-mile radius. As a friend of a long-time matriarch of the community, I was first welcomed into their churches and homes. In the years that followed, my young children and I helped with cooking and gardening alongside the women and children. We sat on the front steps of porches in Trackton and heard women's stories and occasionally those of the men only recently allowed to work in the textile mills.

A little over three miles away was Roadville, a cluster of nine look-alike mill houses. Home to twelve white families whose extended kin included 146 families living nearby, Roadville consisted of men and women who had known no jobs other than those of the textile mills. Each family kept a garden and sometimes a few chickens. Introduced into Roadville by the wife of a local minister, I fell easily into church and home life there and provided an extra hand with childcare, household chores, and garden tasks. Women asked my advice about their children's homework, and I consulted them about dressmaking and canning vegetables.

In *Ways with words* (1983/1996), I had recounted the decade of the 1970s. The book ended with an epilogue forecasting that the economic recession hitting the United States in the early 1980s would alter the life course of both Roadville and Trackton families as I had known them. In 1996, a new epilogue for the book pointed to ways in which closure of the mills and realignments of job types had remade patterns of time and space usage in families and communities. Language uses, as well as types and roles of interlocutors, had shifted in tight relationship with schedules of work and play, choices of childcare, and modes of transportation. With the dispersal of families from the Southeast throughout the United States during the 1980s, individuals had reshaped their intimate relationships, beliefs and values regarding family, and expectations of debt to God. I closed that epilogue with the reminder that "what seem limits or losses can be beginnings as well as endings" (p. 376).

This current book has two purposes as it details life for those who described themselves as poor and hard-working in the early 1980s and within the next decade came to think of their families as middle class.[1] My first purpose is to demonstrate how the nature of self-identification of individuals and families morphed in relation to when, where, and how they worked and played. Closely tied to this first goal is the second: illustration through the voices of parents and children of how their uses, structures, styles, and models of language moved in synchrony with their values surrounding work and play. In particular, I want to relate the vital role that community activities and organizations played in the pacing and quality of time for children and parents.

Questions follow from these two purposes. Who and what have the working poor of the local communities of the Piedmont Carolinas become over three decades? What do their children understand today about changes that resulted when the economic pressures of the 1980s created the need for both parents in the household to work full-time? To what extent do today's young see material goods, spectator entertainment, and their after-school organizational life as criteria for judging the worth of their parents? How have individuals in each generation claimed the power to imagine and plan their futures rather than to let the future just happen to them?

While the cases of individuals whose lives are recounted in this book go some distance toward answering these questions, neither they nor I claim that their cases are "typical" of other descendants of families who were among the working poor in the 1970s. They would insist, as I do, that readers keep in mind that all the reports and generalizations that appear in the following pages come from the lives of descendants of Roadville and Trackton and not the general populations that readers may think they represent. Their parents and grandparents had a particular history of rural and small-town life in southern farming and manufacturing before being forced to rearrange their lives, many of them to urban areas, during the double-dip recession of the 1980s. In these relocations, they were very much affected by changes in attitudes and access that resulted from the Civil Rights Era. In every case, the individuals of this book, if asked directly, would be quick to argue that they are unique. Being so may well be the moral they would attach to all the narratives in which they play leading roles.

Working for wages

In the late 1960s, when textile mills accepted black applicants, most started out on the third shift from midnight until eight a.m., allowing them to work their gardens during the day or hire themselves out for any available day labor. Whites, especially the relatively few women employed by the mills, worked the day shift from eight a.m. until four p.m. Their husbands generally took the second shift from four p.m. until midnight, giving families the benefit of double incomes and children the presence of their mothers during the after-school and evening hours. Farmers, black and white, who had long worked small farms, did "double time," maintaining farms they owned or rented while simultaneously working in the mills. Elders and children pitched in to help out in the kitchen and garden and with household chores and house and farm building repairs. In white and black working-class families alike, the 1970s in the Piedmont Carolinas was a decade of coordinated hard work involving all family members and bringing neighbors together for sandlot baseball and softball games, Sunday church services, and Bible School and revivals as well as special suppers and seasonal events sponsored by regional churches.

Roadville parents, dependent primarily on mill work and occasional seasonal farm work, planned their family times carefully. Habits of talk, respect, work in and around the house, and between adults and children reflected a firm sense of needing to "make do," to stretch everything seen as being in short supply as far as possible. Money, time, and the life of the family automobile, water pump, refrigerator, or kitchen linoleum had to "hold out" until some windfall of financial resources somehow happened.

Even young children always knew when pay day came. Mothers and fathers saved up to repair or to buy household appliances, purchase school supplies and clothes, and put on layaway (purchase on installments) surprise gifts for family members. Grandparents who collected Social Security pitched in to help when unexpected expenses came up for their children, and mill workers tried to keep savings accounts in the mill's credit union. A piggy bank, teapot, or shoebox was usually somewhere in the house, ready to be offered up in a crisis or as a surprise windfall for ordering a special birthday cake. Families kept chickens, planted gardens, and bartered fresh eggs and produce in exchange for fresh meat when family members living in nearby rural areas killed hogs each fall. Grocery store purchases were kept to a minimum, reserved for staples and special seasonal purchases, such as tangerines, nuts in the shell, or the occasional grapefruit.

Children grew up with a keen sense of the need for them to learn how to do things. Roadville parents believed they had to teach their children to talk, and they began early to respond to babies' babbling sounds by revoicing these as nouns or verbs selected from the local environment. Families, often including several generations and extended family members, lived in homes lined up along several adjoining roads. Female family members held infants and toddlers on their laps, guiding their hands to clap, point, and hold objects such as small kitchen tools. They offered running commentary on babies' actions and encouraged them to play peek-a-boo and patty-cake. Adults told babies and toddlers the names of people and objects in the immediate environment. They asked teaching questions, often with deictic gestures pointing to the person or item of focus: "Where's Daddy?" "Where's your ear?" "Is that your spoon?" "Is momma making you a cake?" They told stories about their children, casting them in current settings and actions: "You're gettin' to be a real little cook. You know how to roll biscuits, don't you?" Spaces had purposes, and things "belonged" in their places. Children generally slept in a crib until they were old enough to have a bed. They had a box for toys, a shelf for books, and a yard for play.

Roadville parents, grandparents, and extended family members read to children from books that often came from their churches or checkout stands at the grocery store. They asked for the names of pictured items and the main characters in the stories. They took their children to Sunday School and church on Sundays, Bible School in summers, and homecomings and family reunions held in the church hall. They said grace or blessing at meals, and children said their prayers each night after their bedtime story.

Roadville children yearned to go to school and did well in their first few years. They enjoyed the games of matching letters and sounds, and they did well with comprehension questions that asked them about what happened in stories and who the characters were. As they advanced in school, they struggled when they met texts and tests that asked them for more than comprehension. They puzzled over questions of interpretation, and they felt uncomfortable when asked to imagine possible outcomes of stories or problems and to explain emotional responses of story characters.

Trackton families lived in clusters of duplexes (two-unit dwellings). From the small three-room units and large front porches, residents lived very much open to what went on in their neighbors' lives. Trackton babies were born into a world of talk. The double porches that fronted the duplexes served as stages for family and neighbor talk, and babies were handed off from one person to another, as individuals interspersed their chats with household and garden chores. Babies slept with other family members, and as they grew older, several children near the same age slept together in one bed. They played with kitchen pans and spoons as toys, shared rides on tricycles and make-shift scooters and wagons, and teamed up for ballgames, jump rope competitions, and games of marbles. Toddlers began talking by picking up the ends of sentences they heard in the play of older children and the conversations of adults around them. They seemed aware of sounds and voices and often imitated these, to the delight of adults who rewarded their performances with gales of laughter.

Trackton children saw print in the world around them and heard talk about what people had to read and write in their daily lives. They watched older siblings do homework, they knew logos of television programs, and they read labels on cans and boxes. They told stories, and adults questioned them about where they had been and what they had done or where their stories came from. They teased one another as children and were teased by adults, who played a variety of roles and encouraged children to animate their stories by taking on the roles of individual characters or animals.

When Trackton children entered desegregated schools and faced white teachers for the first time, they found their ways of talking did not match what they had known at home. They found it perplexing to be asked questions to which they knew their teachers already had the answers. Trackton children were used to giving information, not repeating it. In their communities, they expanded meaning, entertained adults, and enlivened stories. They lived in a world of communication, cross-age roles, and improvisation. They remembered stories well; they did not do as well with separate letters, single words, or step-by-step sequenced reading programs. Their first few years of primary school came hard to them. Many turned their attention to friendships, special interests, and daydreaming by the time they reached the final years of primary school.

By late 1979, economic change was very much in the air. An economic downturn from January to July 1980 was soon followed by the deep recession that lasted from mid 1981 through all of 1982 and came with double-digit inflation. Unemployment in the United States went above 10 percent, caused largely by widespread closure or downsizing of manufacturing plants. Outsourcing was beginning.

For households of both Roadville and Trackton with one full-time wage earner and two or more children, the annual income over the past decade had rarely exceeded $24,000, with an average of $11,000 in the leanest years. Saving money, except for layaway items, never entered the realm of possibility. Families shared the use and maintenance of the few automobiles and trucks in both communities. Only a few white families owned their homes and had checking accounts. Some oldtimers had handwritten wills. Most black families had neither savings nor checking accounts. They owned no real estate and generally rented their homes on a month-to-month basis.

The closest big city to Roadville and Trackton was Alberta, an entrepreneurial center that developed in the 1980s first as a regional and then as a national financial hub. The sprawl of bedroom communities and shopping centers for the burgeoning urban population began to erase evidence of the 1970s landscape of Roadville and Trackton. Both neighborhoods were cleared away by 1986 to make way for new construction – in the first case a housing subdivision, in the other a highway. More and more developers from outside the region came south as construction engineers for new housing subdivisions and shopping malls. National chain stores replaced family-owned hardware and department stores. A nearby lake was developed as a resort area, with lots available for those who wished to build second homes.

Mainstreamers, black and white

However, only mainstreamers of the region stood in line to benefit from these changes. The working poor did not. The economic changes of the 1980s laid the cornerstone for the divergence between the rich and poor that was to become the national norm over the next three decades. While the working poor found it necessary to leave Roadville and Trackton and similar neighborhoods across the Southeast, mainstreamers, black and white, stayed put. During these difficult years in the South, mainstreamers watched what was going on around them and stayed alert to new investment possibilities. These families owned property and stood in line to inherit land elsewhere in the region from parents or grand-parents. Moreover, they were professionals, business owners, and civic leaders who saw economic promise for them in the changes coming to their region. Even as state school reforms put school districts into upheaval, these families felt secure that their ways of providing for their children would outweigh any alterations in classroom instructional and testing practices the state might impose. Their children were headed for college, and these parents accepted as given a secure future for their offspring.

In addition to their home, many middle-class white families also had a small place on a regional lake or on one of the oceanfront beaches of the Carolinas. Some also had a "homeplace," a farm with a sprawling late-nineteenth-century house where their parents or another older extended family member lived. They had checking and savings accounts, and though they often had mortgages on their primary home, they held deeds for land or housing located elsewhere in the region and leased to sharecroppers.

In general, it was the men who led small businesses in regional town centers and along the strips of highway leading into town. Often their fathers or grand-fathers had established these businesses during or just after World War II. Holding public office tended to run in families, with the same names appearing year after year on ballots. Businessmen held public office, belonged to the Chamber of Commerce, and debated zoning laws and hiring practices. Their wives were teachers, nurses, or stay-at-home mothers. Each Sunday, and often during the week, the family attended churches with large sanctuaries (area of the church in which the altar and nave are located) and numerous extensions that housed libraries, offices for ministers and their secretaries, and meeting rooms for Sunday School. Families kept one or two cars at the house in town and a truck or recreational vehicle at the beach or at the country homeplace. Lawns and flowerbeds in front of their homes were meticulously maintained, and the whir of lawnmowers filled the evening air on long summer days. Forested backyards had cleared areas, often for vegetable gardens as well as spaces reserved for badminton, croquet, or storage of recreational boats between visits to the lake.

Parents and grandparents were alumni of one of the regional universities and maintained active involvement as sports team enthusiasts for their universities. Families traveled across the Southeast for football games and weighed in heavily with praise or scorn for coaches at state universities. Children of many white mainstream families attended Christian academies established when desegregation became inevitable. Some white mainstream children went to local public schools undergoing desegregation. Their parents took active part in parent–teacher associations and closely monitored homework assignments, textbook choices, and administrative appointments. Families were forward-looking and deeply committed to being good citizens and to keeping the national turmoil of Civil Rights from disturbing local patterns of interaction. Members of mainstream white families who spoke out urged tolerance and counseled patience along with vigilance. They expressed the view that their long-standing friendly relations with black workers on their family farms and as domestics in their homes could ensure their ability to "work for the good of the community" across racial and class boundaries.

Planning ahead was an integral part of family life. When parents and grand-parents gathered in front of the television to watch college football games, they reminded children that they were expected to attend the state university favored by family members. Mothers hired tutors for children who fell behind at school and issued poorly veiled threats to remove privileges if children had either academic or discipline problems at school. Printed materials held a place in every room in the house, and most kitchens included desk areas, as did upstairs hallways between bedrooms. Devoted times for homework, as well as after-school athletic practices, piano or guitar practice, and choir rehearsal, filled the calendar pinned to the bulletin board above the kitchen desk. Making posters, banners, nametags, items for sale at school carnivals, and Sunday School and Bible School materials involved children and mothers in art projects, as did summer neighborhood sales of lemonade in makeshift front-yard stands.

Nightly bedtime reading involved multiple choices of books and readers. Activities across the state, such as carnivals or circuses, were cross-referenced in books, news articles, and television advertisements. Dads were often instrumental in bringing traveling circuses to their local region, and these plans got top billing during dinner conversations with children casting their votes for favorite acts or musical groups. Family vacation travel, as well as car trips to visit relatives, attend reunions, or hold meetings related to professional positions of either parent, offered hours for word and letter games, stories, riddles, and family narratives.

In one small town after another in the Piedmont Carolinas, white mainstream middle-class families lived on one side of the town and often on one side of the train tracks, while their black counterparts lived on the other side. A large portion of black mainstream middle-class families were professionals – ministers, teachers, attorneys, pharmacists, and doctors, whose training had been in historically black colleges. Some had inherited farmland they rented out to rural black families, often relatives. They had accounts with local banks that also held the mortgage on their homes. They had safety deposit boxes for deeds to their property, birth certificates of family members, and wills they had drawn up with local attorneys. Some entered commerce, managing small grocery stores, auto repair shops, and feed and garden stores located within black residential areas of the town. Some owned businesses that provided services such as insurance sales and funeral arrangements for black families.

Many retired black veterans of the Korean War had returned home to the South after serving twenty years of military duty. Educated and experienced in living in other parts of the United States as well as in Europe and Asia, these veterans had a keen sense of possibility that the future in this region would open for them and their children. Many had earned the rank of master sergeant in the military, taken specialized training, and held deep respect for order, discipline, and strong leadership. By the late 1970s, several had successfully run for local office, worked in small-town city halls, and served on the school board.[2] Loyalty to the military and faith in education and a promising future ran high.

Their wives had grown up in families of long-time school teachers and ministers. During the Korean War and throughout the 1950s, historically black colleges throughout the South enrolled a preponderance of young women from such families. Most of them trained as teachers or nurses. They joined sororities while in college and continued active participation in regional chapters through-out their lives. These holders of a Bachelor of Arts or Bachelor of Science degree were among the first graduate student applicants when desegregation opened enrollment in the formerly all-white state universities of the South.

Active in church life and gospel music groups, families encouraged their children to study music, lead Sunday School classes for younger children, and take part in summer camp-like gatherings for adolescents. Families traveled all over the Southeast for college reunions, sorority events, and church home-comings and revivals. Family reunions held at the homeplace of grandparents drew regional families as well as relatives who had migrated to northern cities in the 1940s and now returned annually for reunions.[3] Children of these families visited back and forth, with children from up North sometimes spending the entire summer with relatives in the South. Mothers and fathers held professional positions that often meant working hours were somewhat flexible, and blocks of time around holidays and during summers were open for one or the other parent to take the children on short visits to family members or to entertainment in the state capital.

Located in housing subdivisions whose entryways had open gates that carried names such as Creekside Villas, homes of black mainstreamers were generally single-story with three bedrooms and two bathrooms. In the driveway were two sedans, one late-model, the other older. Boxwood shrubs, azaleas, and roses filled borders across the front of houses and along driveways. Small floral and vegetable gardens shared backyard space with swing sets, children's bikes, and plastic above-ground swimming pools. Magazines and books, reflecting the special interests of husband and wife and a range of children's choices, filled at least one living-room bookcase, lay scattered in the family room, and competed with recipe books for space in the open shelves of the dividing wall between dining room and kitchen. During times of preparation for Bible School and revival meetings, educational materials could end up anywhere, with children and parents working together to clear the table for dinner, leaving the living-room floor for arriving guests.

Regular hours for evening meals, with rigid rules for table manners and order of distribution for desserts or other special treats, brought parents and children together. Talk circled through activities of parents and the children's day at school or play excursions with neighboring families. Adults and children took turns talking, though children joined in only after being asked opening questions, such as "How many were in your Bible School class today?" Dinner conversations often turned to future events, especially those related to church and school activities, and, in the summer, to upcoming opportunities for traveling, visiting relatives, and planning musical performances for revival meetings. Levels of choir, each outfitted with distinctive robes, involved children and adults alike in a graduated hierarchy of performers, musical directors, instrumentalists, and soloists. Pending purchases of big-ticket items, such as a freezer or desk for a child's bedroom, entered dinner-time talk as givens, with family members planning the trip to the store to make the selection, taking part in measurements, and weighing in on the height of a needed desk chair. Such items were usually bought through store credit, with a down payment and monthly installments, though furniture for children's rooms often appeared around birthdays or holidays, having been on layaway at the store for several months.

Evenings were for homework, project planning, travel mapping, writing thank-you notes for birthday or holiday gifts, and special television programs. Children of different ages had to observe strict times for baths, bedtime preparation, and choice of bedtime story Either parent could be the designated reader, though, during summer months, older cousins held this honor, testing from year to year the younger child's progress in reading.

In 1981, I did a round of interviews with teachers who had remained in their classrooms even as desegregation brought immense uncertainties to their professional lives. These teachers, black and white, were respected mainstreamers who knew that their property ownership and educational backgrounds would provide them with the insurance to protect against significant economic or social setbacks. They wanted to take part in ensuring that children of this post-1960s generation could have the same assurances. In the early years of desegregation, they innovated, created, collaborated, and celebrated classroom successes that took place in spite of continuing strife and protest sometimes occurring on the streets surrounding their schools. Busing orders brought increased tensions and, in some regions, violence kept schools closed for weeks at a time.

In the end, however. it was not these disruptions that led mainstreamers to decide to leave their teaching careers. By 1981, news headlines affirmed that all teachers would soon have to pass accreditation tests that most Southerners saw as culturally biased.[4] Moreover, teachers would have to install standardized curricula and assessment measures in their classrooms. Mandatory accreditation tests and curricular programs with strong cultural biases became the final push toward exit for a large number of highly experienced teachers, black and white. Education policies questioned teachers' competence and reached into their daily classroom, social, and academic life. Legislators and state education departments demanded new ways of teaching and testing as the 1980s decade opened. They argued these changes had become necessary because of the region's increase in information-based businesses and specialized service industries.

Such demands took away the heart of the innovative practices black and white teachers had been left alone to create in the years immediately following desegregation. Policies from the state level now insisted on initiatives with sequenced standard reading programs and mathematics curricula, formalized lesson plans, and prescribed arrangements of classrooms based on children's performance levels. Literacy would no longer be *reading to learn*, to tell and illustrate stories, and to forge ahead to satisfy curiosity. Each classroom now had to transform literacy into *learning to read*, level by level. Talking, drawing, and writing shrank in relation to the ballooning of time that now had to go to learning to read. New education initiatives drained away the professional pride that innovative teachers had taken in handling the early pressures of desegregation and the resulting relocations of both black and white teachers.

By the late 1980s, these teachers began to look beyond their classrooms for professional career choices. The majority of those who had stayed in their classrooms through the first decade of desegregation now explored careers that were opening for the first time to women. Management, finance, small-business development, and advanced education welcomed black and white women of determination, creativity, and change-making spirit. They were on their way to lucrative jobs and leadership in government, commerce, and service industries. Within a few years, they found it easier and easier to forget the names and faces of the children who had sat in their classrooms.

Schools, families, and community life

In the following chapters, I have emphasized families and communities and changes that they have experienced and accommodated in their ways of seeing and talking over three decades of play and work. Several reasons lie behind my choice to omit from this book extensive coverage of children's lives in schools and classrooms.

Most important among my reasons is acknowledgment of the unique benefits that have come from my having maintained contact with so many families through the triumphs and tragedies of their relocations from Trackton and Roadville. My audiorecordings in family life enable me to compare how the same family across two, sometimes three, generations spent Saturday mornings with their two-year-old or twelve-year-old. My data allow me to answer questions that open up the degree and kinds of differences that marked children's learning environments over three decades. What were adult members of households doing with their adolescent children during family vacations in 1981, 1991, and 2001? How did their activities generate different demands on close attention to visual details, fine-motor control, improvisation, and explanations of cause and effect? Such information can be available only through sustained longitudinal contact and non-judgmental observation and participation with families in activities of their choice.[5]

A second reason for the attention I have given in this book to families and communities comes from the increasing importance since 1980 that families have attached to their children's out-of-school activities. Parents recognized that community organizations in visual arts, dance, music, drama, environmental projects, and sports could give their children experiences for which moms and dads had neither time nor talent. Parents justified their commitment of their children's time to community activities as necessary to build résumés (CVs) for college entry and to prepare for the highly competitive "real world." Over three decades, how did these organizations shift in their missions, modes of operation, and involvement of professionals as guides for the young? To what extent did coaches and directors expect the young to play roles other than those of child or student and to use language and strategic thinking to match responsibilities that came with being a member of a team or community organization?

A final reason this book takes readers into families and communities rather than classrooms comes from the fact that tens of thousands of studies describing school environments already exist. These cannot follow the same learners over as much as a single decade. They generally detail single classrooms at a particular point in time with a specific teacher or curricular approach, or the impact of a particular aspect of school reform over an academic year. The majority of such studies come from primary schools and children in classrooms where they spend most of their school day. As students move beyond primary school to middle and secondary school, researchers have to focus either on target youth or on teachers within particular subject areas. All studies of the institution of schooling have to take as starting point the fact that school attendance up to a certain age is mandatory. The role of student is not optional and it has varied little in its interactional demands over the past century.[6]

We may well say that the role of being a family member is also not optional for children. However, since the 1980s, older children of families identifying themselves as middle class have made many of their own choices about learning environments. Moreover, it has become increasingly evident that definitions, contexts, accountability, and quality of life make it extremely difficult to pinpoint actual parameters of *family*. Within a single neighborhood, variation in family life – toys, schedules, eating habits, furniture arrangement, and location of electronic gadgets and entertainment centers – will be much greater than is likely to be found across thousands of classrooms over a broad geographical range. Families and schools, religions and governments, are *institutions*, sustaining entities essential to the continuation of human society. However, families as individual units present much greater variety than do other institutions. Schools, not only within the United States but also across nations and cultures, remain highly stable in their physical arrangement and assignment of strict roles for instructor and learner.

The composition of families, as well as their frequency of geographical relocations and economic adjustments, heavily shapes the intangibles of daily life such as degree of stress and coping skills, as well as tangible features that can be easily measured – number of bedrooms, size of living space, number of books and toys, and types of furnishings. These come together to mold ways that parents nurture their children and value artifacts and attitudes that add up to *caring* – for physical needs and through emotional support. From the 1980s forward, as more and more adults entered and remained in the work force full-time and faced childcare needs that had to be dispersed to individuals outside the family and to places beyond the family home, options of environments to meet these needs came to matter more and more. How they did so embraced aspects of childcare previously thought of primarily in terms of families – ways of instructing, praising, and scolding, as well as the extent and nature of experiences provided. Older children and adolescents played significant decision-making roles within families, much more than they did within their schools. The range of optional environments of learning open to children increased as they grew older, had more independence, went where their friends were, and learned to recognize and express their particular likes and dislikes regarding the caregivers and activities for which their parents paid.

Of emphasis in this volume, along with families, have been *organizations* such as sports teams, youth groups, community arts programs, libraries, and environmental groups linked with museums, parks, and community gardens. Unlike *institutions* that must remain relatively predictable and unchanged, *organizations* must be highly adaptable. They originate in response to contemporary needs, and they fade out of existence when society no longer needs them. Businesses, support groups, arts programs, and sports teams are organizations that adapt to shifts in public interest, financial conditions, technological developments, and consumer and audience demands. Organizations appeal to the young primarily for their ability to stay in tune with current interests. Yet they also give participants the sense of being linked with something bigger than the moment.

Toward the after-years

This book is meant to ensure that, for the children of Roadville and Trackton, we do not "quit [these] young lives after being long in company with them, and not desire to know what befell them in their after-years."[7] All narratives are beginnings, even when they may appear to end. Their characters live on in our minds, and so does our curiosity about what happens to them as their lives unfold.

Thus we begin with a look back to 1980 and the birth of a baby boy in Trackton. His introduction establishes the comparative perspective that will move us back and forth across the stories of both Roadville and Trackton families. Subsequent chapters give micro perspectives on how changing economic and demographic landscapes affected play, work, and communication in individual families within the widely varying types of communities in which they lived after Roadville and Trackton.

Zinnia Mae Green became pregnant when she was fourteen. No one knew who the father might be, and Zinnia Mae would not talk. Attention centered on who was available in Trackton to care for the baby boy. Zinnia Mae's mother, severely crippled by diabetes, was blind, and her grandparents who lived near Trackton were elderly. Within weeks after the birth, Zinnia Mae's older sister, Rosa, took the baby boy into her family. She and her husband lived twenty miles away on the outskirts of Alberta. Her mother-in-law lived with the family and took care of the baby and Rosa's two older children while Rosa worked as a nurse's aide in Alberta's hospital.

Zinnia Mae went back to school, but soon after she turned sixteen, she dropped out. Within a few months, she and a girlfriend went to Atlanta. Zinnia Mae never returned. Within a year of leaving Trackton, she had a baby girl and in the next two years, twin boys. When she was pregnant with the twins, she met a social worker who helped her find placement in a high-rise inner-city public housing project. Her welfare check was their only means of support when I located her and arranged a visit in mid 1985. As had been the case during the 1970s, I came as both friend and linguistic anthropologist, bringing along books for the children as well as my audiorecorder and notebook of transcripts.

We talked about the "old" Trackton, and my audiorecordings and transcripts gave her an audiotour of her childhood home and neighborhood. Because her diabetic mother was blind, Zinnia Mae's grandmother had spent much of each day taking care of both Zinnia Mae and her mother. From the time she was a toddler, Zinnia Mae had worked alongside her grandmother as they cooked and cleaned, tended the garden, and helped ensure that Zinnia Mae's mother left the house every day to visit with neighbors. Most of my recordings had been of her grandmother talking with her in the kitchen of the tiny Trackton house. When Zinnia Mae listened to the tapes in 1985, she heard talk of foods she had not eaten since childhood.

The audiotapes reminded us that her grandmother had been a talker. For Zinnia Mae's benefit and that of her blind mother, her grandmother kept up a constant stream of commentary on anything happening around them. Through my audiorecordings made periodically in her Trackton home well into Zinnia Mae's middle-school years, she re-envisioned her childhood.

In 1985, Zinnia Mae began making audiotapes of her talk to her own children. She could now hear these recordings along with those I had made of her when she was a toddler back in Trackton. She commented most about the role of food and its preparation in her talk with her grandmother. She noted how much she had learned by having to take care of her mother. She also remembered how isolated she felt from other children when she was growing up. Now she lived on her own with her children in a tiny fifth-floor apartment in an urban housing project.

By this time, Zinnia Mae suffered from severe diabetes exacerbated by obesity, and she thought of herself as almost entirely trapped. The elevator on the fifth floor worked erratically. Her nearest relatives lived more than 300 miles away, and those whose whereabouts she and I knew were either elderly or had young children of their own. Infrequently, she was visited by a kindly social worker who was also from the Piedmont Carolinas. Zinnia Mae and her children went outdoors only when she needed to go grocery shopping or managed to keep medical appointments for her or the children. She had long ago given up going to church. She had no friends or family members to call on to watch her children or to offer their homes as alternative play spaces to the concrete barren spaces between the blocks of public housing in which she lived. She counted on the fact that as her children grew older they would somehow find ways to get away from the crowded, dangerous public housing projects and "to have opportunities I never had back where I used to live."

2   A boy finds his mama(s)

On an early winter evening in the mid 1990s, a young man on a Chicago bus pulls the cord for the next stop. As the bus slows, he studies his reflection in the darkening bus window. His smooth brown skin, long eyelashes, and thin lips go well, he thinks, with his cropped hair. His fingers run along the side of his head, tracing the design his uncle's barber sculpted last week.

Jerome jogs from the bus stop to the front steps of the two-story brick building, an old elementary school in years past and now home to one of Chicago's youth theatres. Heading into the large bare room, he throws off his jacket and backpack and joins a group of friends.

"Lose the accent," Jerome remembers his Puerto Rican friend Eduardo telling him the first month after Jerome started middle school in Chicago. Eduardo had said to Jerome a little too loudly: "Man, you sound like you from somewhere in the South. Then some other time, like, you know, you talk like one of them cops from the Bronx on TV! Where'd you come from anyway?" A popular seventh grader, Eduardo liberally tossed out insults, many of which had a mild but persistent polemical thrust. Jerome knew within a few weeks after entering middle school that Eduardo was worth watching. He noticed that on some days Eduardo left school early, announcing to anyone around: "Gotta go outta town." One day, Jerome overheard Eduardo talking about the bus trip he had taken with "a bunch of my friends, 'cause we act 'n stuff." That afternoon Jerome followed Eduardo after school. Within a few blocks, Eduardo shouted over his shoulder: "Got any money? Wanna soda?"

Jerome learned that Eduardo was heading to meet friends at "my theatre." They walked along together to an old brick school building that seemed abandoned. In the entry way, a security guard nodded at Eduardo and asked: "He with you? Everything okay?" Eduardo answered: "Yeah, okay, no worries," and he took the steps to the second floor two at a time.

A man carrying a drum under his arm spotted Jerome on the landing just ahead of Eduardo: "Come on into the studio. You speak Spanish?" There Jerome found himself swept from the full group's warm-ups into reading lines with a cluster of three other boys. Jerome followed along, watching and listening. At break, Eduardo introduced him to some older boys: "A new guy at my school – name's

Jerome." He nodded toward Jerome: "Tell 'em where you come from." Jerome laughed, as did the other boys. Without losing a beat, Eduardo launched into one of his exaggerated imitations of the arts director, who had opened the warm-ups that day with a loud sequence of Middle Eastern drumming followed by his announcement: "Pretty good, huh? Only my tenth lesson last night."

By the end of his first day at Liberty Theatre, Jerome knew most of the other young people by name. As he left the studio, he figured out that some lived in nearby housing projects, while others came by subway or bus from other parts of the city. Several spoke Puerto Rican Spanish.

A few weeks later, Jerome took Eduardo home to meet Tia Maria, the matriarch of the household where he was staying now. Eduardo and his girlfriend Lucia reminded him of some of his friends back in the Bronx. There he had gone to several different schools before taking off from New York for Chicago when he was eleven years old. He had lived with Tia Maria ever since. He figured that having Tia Maria meet Eduardo might help him wangle her permission for him to travel out of town with the theatre group, once he had been with Liberty long enough to qualify for the touring company. Tia Maria did not want him making friends with just anyone, and she also had to know where he was and what he was doing after school every day.

Jerome knew Tia Maria would throw him out if he ever broke her basic rule about how he should pick his friends: "If you can't have 'em come 'round here to this house for Sunday dinner, then they're not gonna be your friend." Not sure at first what Tia Maria meant by this rule, Jerome moved cautiously in thinking about who among those he met at school and in the neighborhood might pass Tia Maria's Sunday-dinner test of acceptability.

Experience had taught him that any time Tia Maria met someone new, she wasted no time in finding out who they were and where they came from. Jerome had first met her back in the Bronx, when she had come to visit his last foster family there. He remembered how she had watched him then and, like Eduardo, had asked about his accent and where he came from. When he pretended not to hear her question, her eyes followed him as he quietly slipped away from the table to take his plate to the kitchen. At the end of her first visit to the Bronx, she announced: "You got southern manners; you show respect for ol' folks."

Several years later when he arrived in Chicago with nothing in his pockets but a scrap of paper scrawled with her address and phone number, she had taken him in.

Sometime back before he started first grade, Jerome, born in the Piedmont Carolinas in 1980, had moved to New York City with his mom's sister, Rosa. Soon after the move to New York from South Carolina, Rosa had gotten sick and died within a year. Social workers, unable to trace his birth mother's location, had put him with one foster family after another. He counted himself lucky, for after a series of tough situations with these families, he had landed at age eight with a good Puerto Rican foster family in the South Bronx. The oldest boy in the family was a drummer, lots of kids came and went in the household, and his foster mom was tough but not mean. They ate well. She worked part time helping in a restaurant owned by her cousin, and she brought home lots of leftover food. His foster dad worked as janitor and handyman for several Catholic churches. Each Sunday, anyone who was around was marched off to mass and several times a week besides if his foster mom's church groups had meetings.

All this had come to an abrupt end when his foster dad fell down a staircase at work, broke his back, and could no longer work. His foster mom had to move back to Puerto Rico where her family could help care for her invalid husband. Jerome could not go, and social workers told his foster mom they would place him in another family. He had previously had stints of living on the streets to escape violent households, and he did not want to take any chances of doing that again. Though only eleven years old now, he was old enough to know that he needed to take charge of where he was going to live.

Jerome bought a bus ticket for Chicago. He remembered that Tia Maria had said each time she left from her visit to his foster family in the Bronx: "Come to Chicago sometime; you'll like it." Going back to South Carolina was not an option. When he was just starting school in New York City, one of his social workers had told him her office had not been able to locate his real mom. She no longer lived in the little town where he was born and where he had lived with Rosa before she moved up north. His grandparents were dead. Jerome did not know whether or not he had brothers and sisters.

Once in Chicago, with the help of a map and some newsstand vendors, Jerome made his way to Tia Maria's apartment on the third floor of the biggest housing project he had ever seen. When she opened the door, Tia Maria cupped his chin in her hand and announced to no one in particular: "I figured you'd end up here. Now put your things down, and help me with dinner."

Jerome had barely said a word during his entire fifth and sixth grades in the neighborhood primary school near Tia Maria's. By the time he started middle school in another part of town, he still preferred listening to talking. Life at home with Tia Maria and her older children meant living by her rules, helping with laundry, errands, cooking, cleaning, and preparing every Saturday for the Sunday family get-together. This was always a feast, and music blared. People stood around all over the apartment and out on the balcony with their plates; there were lots of jokes, occasional dancing, and dressed-up babies and toddlers for everyone to fuss over.

When he was barely thirteen, Jerome got a job cleaning a bodega (corner grocery in a Puerto Rican neighborhood) down the street from where Tia Maria lived. On his way to work every day, Jerome passed by the Catholic church with the tall bell tower. Sometimes he stopped in just to look around; he liked the lingering smell of candles and incense. But no one in Tia Maria's family went to mass on Sunday. In New York, his last foster mom had wanted him to become an altar boy. Now he sometimes slipped away to attend the mass in Spanish the priest held on Saturday afternoons.

Connections across miles and years

I found Jerome quite by accident. I knew that Zinnia Mae, daughter of the Green family in Trackton, had had a child when she was fourteen, and the child had been given over to her older sister Rosa. Their mother suffered from severe diabetes, and she was nearly blind by the time Zinnia Mae entered elementary school. Zinnia Mae and her mother lived just up the road from her grandmother who, though crippled with arthritis, was an energetic lively woman – a favorite of all the Trackton children. I had seen Zinnia Mae's son, Jerome, a few times before Rosa moved to New York City in the mid 1980s. A handsome child with a winning way, he seemed keen to please adults and adored Rosa. When they moved away to New York, I lost touch. A few years later, I heard that Rosa had died. I often wondered what had become of Jerome. His mother and grand-mother had no idea.

In Chicago, during the mid 1990s, when I was studying youth organizations there, a fourteen-year-old in a theatre group where I spent a lot of time seemed oddly familiar to me. He was fluent in Puerto Rican Spanish. When he spoke English, pairs such as *pen* and *pin* carried the same vowel, and he had a very Southern way of saying "a whole 'nother." Several weeks after meeting him, I asked if he was from Chicago. He quickly said, "No." When I asked how he came to be in Chicago, he met my query with a laugh and shrug: "Just lucky, I guess." He went after the drums that day with what seemed to me a special vengeance.

Months later, when I was driving some young people from Jerome's theatre group to a Chicago suburb for a performance, we were all talking about places we had lived and our favorite music. I mentioned growing up in the South and liking country music. A series of groans came from everyone in the van. On the way back downtown that same day, Jerome sat in the front seat with me. While the others were talking among themselves, he leaned over and asked: "Where in the South?"

When I told him: "Sort of all over, grandmother in Virginia, foster family in North Carolina, high school in Florida, and finally back in South Carolina and North Carolina by way of New York." He grew quiet. "Me too," he said several minutes later.

I did not get what he was saying and asked: "In the South – where?"

He explained that he had been born in South Carolina, lived there for a while, then New York, and now Chicago. "Lots of places, my mom, then my aunt, couldn't take care of me, so I went with foster families and now here."

We said no more that day, but eventually I pieced bits of his story together and learned that he was Zinnia Mae's lost son.

I had kept up with Zinnia Mae over the years after she moved to Atlanta in 1982 at age sixteen, two years after Jerome was born. She lived on welfare and disability checks in a high-rise public housing unit in Atlanta with her three children, a girl born in 1983 and twins born two years later. I saw Zinnia Mae and the children a couple of times a year, and she had kept records of the language of the three children from the time they were about two years of age. On my visits, she heard tapes of herself as a child, along with my questions about the recordings she had made of her own children's language. She had asked first in 1985 if I could bring her a picture of her first child who had gone to live with her sister. I had once gotten a photograph of Jerome from Rosa, just before they moved away to New York. Jerome was emerging from toddlerhood, standing tall and looking straight into the camera. For years, Zinnia Mae kept Jerome's picture tucked into the edge of her bathroom mirror.

Now in 1994, Jerome was fourteen and living in Chicago with Tia Maria, a caregiver he had found, more or less, on his own. His birth mom and half-siblings were in Atlanta, and I had the bizarre fortune of being able to connect them. The next time I went to Atlanta, I got Tia Maria's permission to buy Jerome's plane ticket and take him with me. None of my audiorecordings included him as a child, but they gave him a glimpse into Zinnia Mae's life as a child and the home life of his half-siblings in their early childhood. By 1994, Zinnia Mae and her three children had been living for several years in a small single-family home, happy to be away from the high-rise apartment she had moved into when she first came to Atlanta.

After the initially strained and gradual reunion of mother with the child she could not remember ever having seen beyond the photograph, Zinnia Mae took me aside. She asked if I would drive them all back to the housing projects where she had lived during her first years in Atlanta. Puzzled, I agreed, and later in the weekend, we drove slowly back and forth along the streets near her old high-rise apartment building. Zinnia Mae's younger children, Donna and the twins, Melvin and Marcello, remembered the place well, and Donna told stories about cockroaches "the size of a mouse," and she and the boys giggled their way through the song played by the ice cream truck that came through the housing projects every afternoon. Jerome looked around and asked his mother where she went shopping back then. She was still obese and walked with difficulty, having had two toes amputated because of dia-betes. I could sense that Jerome was trying to imagine his mother with three babies making her way down and out of that apartment building and through the neighborhood to a grocery store.

Jerome asked Donna, who had just turned eleven, what she did for fun. I wondered how she would answer, for I knew she was already hanging out with kids who played truant, shop-lifted occasionally, and stayed out later than her mother thought she should. Donna shrugged.

I interjected: "Have you thought any more about doing stuff at the YMCA?" I knew the twins, Melvin and Marcello, now nine, spent lots of time there, having figured out through a friend at school that by being at the YMCA, they could play games, have access to a swimming pool, and take lots of out-of-town fieldtrips on the YMCA bus. Zinnia Mae had no car and had never learned to drive. Every day after school, the twins took the public bus to the YMCA, but Donna almost never joined them, preferring to be with her friends. Her mom now worked at their neighborhood church's daycare program as receptionist, and she wanted Donna to come be with her after school, an option Donna flatly rejected. Donna told her mom she had to go to friends' houses to do her homework. Once Donna entered the sixth grade, Zinnia Mae almost never saw her except in the mornings before school and during summer months, when she came home from her girlfriend's house to get some clothes, tease her younger brothers, and then head out again.

Jerome was quiet on the plane back to Chicago.

But several weeks later, he asked: "How come I'm different?" We talked about how much he had moved around, all the options he had seen, and the fact that he had the good fortune of being bilingual, musical, and a clown in front of audiences. "And my skin color?" He didn't wait for me to respond; I knew he had noticed how light-skinned he was in contrast to his half-siblings. He laughed and said: "Maybe gettin' tossed around from place to place and not havin' a real family ain't all that bad after all?"

Conversations for now

Jerome's on-the-go life at fourteen meant that he thought a lot about what was coming up soon, where he had to be today, and what he needed to do. Early in our acquaintance, when I asked him where he would be next month or next summer or even next Christmas, he shrugged and looked puzzled. His talk with friends, as well as around the bodega where he worked, focused on the present, the immediate short term. In the theatre, the group talked incessantly about what was coming up over the full season, how they had to plan, and when they needed to do what. Jerome listened. What he heard made him realize that his friends at Liberty looked ahead farther than the next few hours or the upcoming weekend.

After Jerome and I went to Atlanta together, he wanted to know more about how the audiotapes of his mother's life had come about. We talked about what "linguistic research" was, how I found it useful in my teaching, and how his mother had become a paid partner in my research when she agreed to record Donna and the boys during their preschool years.

Soon thereafter, Jerome came to me with six of his friends ranging in age from fourteen to sixteen, some from the theatre and others from his block.

He announced: "We want to do linguistic research." Their intent expressions told me they were serious – at least enough to listen to what I might expect of them. I began: "It's not as easy as it might look."

After explaining the ethics, permission forms, and explanations necessary before recording anyone, I went over procedures that followed the actual audio-recording. Each boy would receive the same type of briefcase I used; it contained taperecorder, notebook, permission forms, and log for keeping track of who was taped when and where. They would have to fill out a Script Time Data Sheet and log the language features for each recording on the Linguistic Research Chart. Figures 2.1 and 2.2 are prototypes of these two documents, which the boys changed slightly from year to year. We reviewed the steps several times and practiced recording one another, filling in the Script Time Data Sheet and logging features on the Linguistic Research Chart. I could see their enthusiasm waning.

I continued with further step-by-step instructions. Once they had completed their recording, they would need to log and transcribe each occasion, taking care afterwards to fill in the Script Time Data Sheet. Once this was done, they logged the language features on the Linguistic Research Chart. We met weekly to review their work either in person or by phone. The boys asked about payment. I reviewed the terms: $5.00 for each full page of annotated transcript with accompanying tape plus the Script Time Data Sheet. They would have to decide who did the transcription for each tape. Only the individual who signed off on all the pages for a specific tape would be paid. If two individuals worked on a tape together and both signed off, they were to split the pay. For each hour of bi-weekly sessions in which we reviewed transcripts and checked logs, each participant would be paid $5.00 an hour. The seven boys agreed to a two-month trial period in which they would record conversations among themselves and with close friends three times a week at different times of the day and only during their out-of-school hours. Each person who stuck to these terms for two months would receive $20.00 and the opportunity to sign a contract for the next six months.

At the end of the trial period, Jerome and three of his friends signed contracts. We began our bi-weekly sessions at the theatre in which we reviewed transcripts. We talked about what was in the tapes they had made and what was not there. We had the Linguistic Research Chart as our check-list of items to look for – different tenses, words of more than three syllables, connectors such as *because* and *when*, and different kinds of questions, such as those that began with *what if?* The boys endured the grammar lessons that became necessary: "What's past tense?" "How come that's a coordinating conjunction?" "What's a syllable?" Over the next six years, from 1994 until 2000, the original four boys, including Jerome, grew to ten, with younger friends, including some females, joining each year. They called themselves the "Script Team" and named our sessions together "script times."

30

```
                    SCRIPT TIME DATA SHEET

Recorder's name: _____

Code # (Recorder's initials plus date): _____
[For example, a recording that Shirley made on May 22, 1997 would
have the code # SBH 5/22/1997.]


Setting (location): _____
Number of speakers under age 18: _____
Age range of speakers: _____
Number of speakers over 18: _____


Time at start of recording: _____
Time at end of recording: _____


Has the recording been logged? ___no ___yes; date _____
Has your digital recording file been put on Shirley's computer?
___no ___yes; date _____
Has the recording been transcribed? ___no ___yes;
transcribed by (name) _____ on (date)_____


Write a sentence or two to tell those who listen to your recording
what the situation was when you recorded this session (e.g. friends
standing around waiting for the coach to show up; friends on the
subway heading to a concert).
```

Figure 2.1 Script Time Data Sheet

College students who worked as "guerrilla anthropologists" with me during these years provided added attraction for Jerome and his friends.[1] In their usual circle of peers, they rarely had opportunities to hang out with young people who had not only successfully enrolled in a university but had stayed to complete their studies and to receive a degree. Any of the older teens they knew who

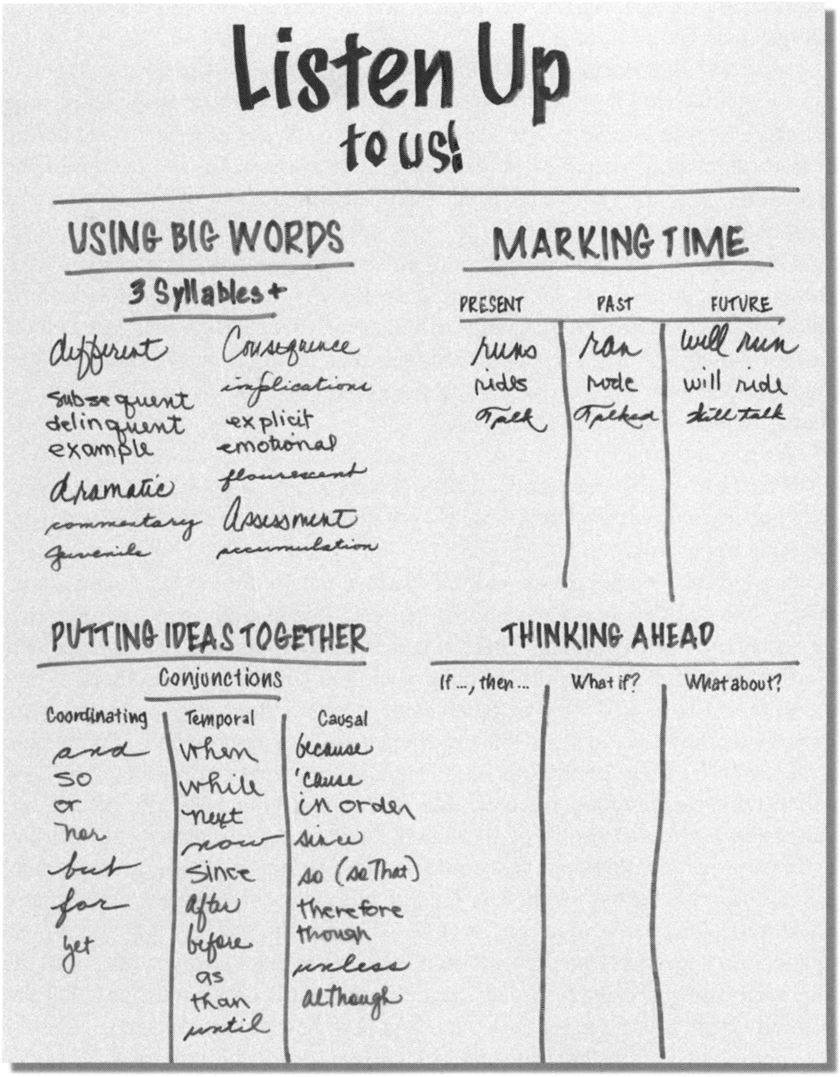

Listen Up
to us!

USING BIG WORDS

3 Syllables +

different	Consequence
subsequent	implications
delinquent	explicit
example	emotional
dramatic	fluorescent
commentary	Assessment
juvenile	accumulation

MARKING TIME

PRESENT	PAST	FUTURE
runs	ran	will run
rides	rode	will ride
Talk	Talked	will talk

PUTTING IDEAS TOGETHER

Conjunctions

Coordinating	Temporal	Causal
and	when	because
so	while	'cause
or	next	in order
nor	now	since
but	since	so (so That)
for	after	therefore
yet	before	though
	as	unless
	than	although
	until	

THINKING AHEAD

If ..., then ...	What if?	What about?

Figure 2.2 Linguistic Research Chart

started college had come home within a year discouraged by having to take remedial courses. The jobs they found were no better than the ones that high school graduates could get. "College sucks," they were fond of saying. The theatre's artistic director and I quietly agreed that showing would always persuade better than telling. When the script team worked shoulder to shoulder with college students in their research, they might rethink what college could be.

In our marathon script times, we transcribed and analyzed recordings, entering our tabulations on the language chart in order to keep track of speakers' uses of specific words and language structures. Each year, the team, often led by the senior members, changed some of the categories as well as the design of the chart. They wrangled over categories, changed arrangement of data entries, and decorated each new chart.

Into every session came questions of ethics and interpretation of usage: "Can we write that down?" "He not 'posed to say that." As the team spent more time talking through transcripts, arguing over the need for accuracy, matters of ethics and careful counts, members observed their own language usage change. They talked about what they were hearing themselves say and why they might be changing their ways of talking.

"We travel so much."

"We talk to all different kinds of people who've got jobs we never heard of."

"They always want to know how we got into theatre, why we do it, and what we think about it."

Through their theatre work and out-of-town theatre travel, the young actors talked with people who had a range of interests, occupations, and backgrounds. As representatives of Liberty Theatre, they had to explain their work to several kinds of audiences – from other young people to curators and directors of city museums. Often asked what being an actor meant to them, they had to tie what they were doing now to ways this experience might play into their future plans.

When Jerome and his friends were "hangin' out and doin' nothin'," as they called their social times together, their lively talk contained lots of teasing, performing incidents known to all of them, and revoicing segments of talk they had overheard as commentaries on girlfriends, boyfriends, sports, and teachers. Topics switched often. Talk was loaded with present-tense statements and questions, along with numerous prefaces of "and she's all . . ." or "he go" as openers for segments that revoiced text they had heard. During script times, as they analyzed such talk recorded among their friends, the team found that the column titled "present tense" filled quickly, and they had to add a new page for this item well before they had moved halfway down the columns for either future- or past-tense verbs. We talked about the need to consider the raw numbers for each item in relation to context, topic, turn exchanges among speakers, and length of recording time.

They asked: "Does it matter that this column fills up so fast?"

My irritating answer to them was always: "What do you think?"

For a long time, they ignored the question, but one day, within a year after Jerome and I had come back from our visit with Zinnia Mae in Atlanta, he blurted out: "It's like a time warp, only we're warped in one place and that's *now*."

I looked quickly to be sure the taperecorder was running and held my breath waiting for the others to respond.

Segments of that conversation follow:

RAOUL: If that's happenin', where are we?
MARLY: We can't stand outside and just say that kind of stuff
                              [
JEROME: but we're not outside
CARLO: I just wanna say I can't think about bein' some time but now, we're talkin' reality here, 'cause most of us ain't goin' nowhere but here=
MARLY: =not goin' anywhere? I'm goin' to Minnesota next week.
                              [
ALL: laughter and guffaws
RAOUL: Look at this column [pointing to the past-tense listing, which was much shorter than the present-tense column]. So what does that mean – we don't think back?
MARLY: Now is about the same, same as then, same thing over and over, nowhere to go, nothin' to do. It's a communication problem.
DEIDRE: I think this is great, all the stuff you guys are sayin', but I KNOW where I come from and who I am. You just talkin' crazy.
JEROME: That's what we all hear in school, but who really thinks about that stuff, and what's that got to do with where we go, 'cause that's what we're talkin' about here, isn't it?
JULIE ANNE: Who's got somebody who's really gone anywhere, who went from where they were to somewhere different? Our kids gonna grow up just like us – stuck in NOW.
MARLY: I just wanna say sump'n. A friend of mine, Erica, got to know this kickboxing expert – yeah, I know she's a girl and all that – but she wanted to go into the military, and she started thinkin' about gettin' fit and ready for the Marines, and all that. She decided she had some place she wanted to go in the future. And she got there; she's off in some camp in the South right now=
JEROME: =she figured out what she had to do NOW. Maybe if other people see what we're doin', they'll start that way too.
DEIDRE: Yeah, and she's sure to be killed too. She gonna die in some battle in some foreign country. She be goin' nowhere fast NOW.

The conversation broke off at this point, when the theatre director came through to call time and ask the transcript group to clear out.

Deliberative talk

I had an idea. What if we recorded the young people in the theatre taking part in an upcoming city-wide youth conference when teens from neighborhoods across Chicago were getting together to talk about crime in their neighborhoods and what they could do about it? The year was 1998, and racism, poverty, violence, and drug dealers in neighborhoods were topics never far from the minds of teenagers.

Together we pulled off this idea. When we sat down to go over the data we had collected, the team worked feverishly and grew increasingly quiet as they worked. These transcripts did not look like their recordings of peer conversations.

Announcements of the conference had been distributed in schools, parks and recreation programs, and after-school projects. Flyers described the conference as a time when young people could talk about making their views on crime heard by city, state, and national policymakers. The only basis for selection to participate was at least one year of sustained experience in a sports, community service, or arts organization, either after-school or as an extracurricular activity with their school. Most of the teens who came to the conference were under eighteen years of age, not yet old enough to vote. A big concern they expressed in the survey handed out as they convened for their first session was the need to hear what their peers were thinking about how to make "things in our neighbor-hoods better and how to control drugs and violence." Next in importance to them was racial profiling and how this reflected the deep racism they saw in American society.

One young man started the conference session on racial profiling by asking if the others thought racism could ever "really go away." Several participants interpreted the question literally and threw out simple "yes" or "no" answers. Other individuals talked over one another on the issue of whether or not laws could "outlaw" racism. The transcript below picked up just after one of the older youth participants had made the point that he thought city politicians and the police had recently shown improvement in "working together" with youth of color. He ended his comment by noting that a huge remaining problem was "the number of poor people, the poverty."

JANINE: I think that the laws that need to be made are laws that will save people from poverty, 'cause I think that's one problem that sometimes transcends racism. That people stay within their own economic class and don't venture to meet people of other economic classes because they act differently. Because, and, uh, if we could take more from the rich and give more to the poor people and support people and find new jobs, then maybe something could happen [voice trails off].

FANELLE: I'll have to disagree. I agree that we need to work on the poverty in the United States, but I think racism is a total skin color issue. I mean regardless if you are a rich black person, then you can still be discriminated against. So it has nothing to do with your poverty level when it comes to whether you are Latino or African American. It's the way you look that's the problem.

FRANKIE: I think one of the main causes of racism is lack of exposure. I mean if you look at the people who've been exposed to, the, uh, take African American culture, what it has to offer in music and everything, they are usually not the people who are going to be racist. But if you look at people who are living up on a hill in a predominantly white neighborhood that are secluded, they are, 'cause they haven't experienced what all these other races have to offer them in culture and things like that, so we could make laws to have everyone get some exposure to see all these other things they're passin' up and that they're missin' out on. I think that would help a lot.

RAOUL: I say the only thing about racism is that the only way to end racism is to make everybody equal, and if you make everybody equal, then the world would be borin'.

A murmur of agreement follows, and one member offers a resounding, "I agree."

Then a young man stands and turns to the group: "How can we get all these Asians to stop treating us African Americans like shit?"

Someone else follows with another question: "Yeah, and how can we learn to work with people from other groups if they're not like us?"

Several other young people then jump to their feet to report that they have known, dated, and in one case "married an Asian," and "I can tell you they're not all like that."

Another member says: "Yeah, they're as different even if they do all look alike as people who are African American. We're not all alike either."

The group goes on to deliberate their ideas after one person's question: "Yeah, how different are all the races anyway?"

They wrestle with views of the future asking: "How can we?" and "Could we?"

They express the possibility of mandating values as well as outlawing behaviors that discriminate against "people who hurt our neighborhoods – like the drug dealers." They seem to want to ensure astute tolerance while avoiding blind impartiality.

In the ensuing months, one or another of the theatre group members referred to this conversation as they worked on their next play. Though they did not see their current play as centering on the topic of racism, issues of discrimination, choice of friends, and "being different" always figured in one way or another in the plays they wrote collaboratively. In their writing workshops during the opening months of each season, theatre members wrote their ideas and pieces of dialogue and narratives that they wanted the group to consider working into the next play.

Mad Joy was the title they gave to the first play that Liberty Theatre did after the conference. The work begins with a woman dying and ends with her birth.

The play opens.

NARRATOR: This is a story; it's like any other family story. Some of it I lived through, some of it I was preached to, some of it I had to figure out on my own. This is a story. It's just like any other family story. You want to make sure you know it well, so your son or daughter knows who your grandmother was.

The dying grandmother says to those assembled for her passing: "Look at the gentle skin of a rough life. A dried-up life, a life filled with misplaced dreams. Maybe if I was born here like these people [looking around at children and grandchildren assembled around her], my name would mean beauty, hope, and love. I dream of a new name."

A voice from the chorus breaks into the dying woman's reverie: "Maybe if you had talent to go with a new name, you'd have one by now."

A pastor shouts out: "I think the world should start back over . . ."

From two sides of the stage, the chorus sings: "Let's start back over and leave the world as it was."

Near the end of her dying scene, the old woman cries out: "I'm sick of people lying; I'm sick of people talkin'; matter of fact, I'm sick of talkin'."

The narrator steps forward from those assembled around the woman's death-bed and speaks directly to the audience: "Time really begins with death. You accumulate time as you live. Time is artificial until you die. Then time is real. Time is real to the point when you can touch it. You can almost put time in your pockets." [The narrator nods toward the deathbed in the center of the stage.] "See, her time is bass-ackwards [backwards]. Her memory is bass-ackwards too. She can vaguely see her youthful future. She is already forgetting her past. She had a happy ending first. But unfortunately . . ."

The growing-forward-from-dying central character of the play looks out at the audience: "If I could see my future, I'd change it."

In *Mad Joy*, the theatre group made clear that seeing the future meant they had to plan for it. If they planned, they could change it. Past and present went a long way toward making the future.

What the script team learned from their analysis of the conference talk and conversations around creation and production of this play reflected the teen-agers' concern with their roles and the purpose of their artistic and linguistic work. In the conference talk as well as conversations around the creation of their play script for *Mad Joy*, they heard adolescents moving easily back and forth from past to future in their talk. They heard them raise hypothetical scenarios and question consequences that might come from specific actions. Their talk lined up temporal sequences for these actions as well as causal outcomes. As we analyzed these data, our analysis of the transcripts of this purposeful deliber-ative talk filled the columns marked *past tense, future tense, if–then* proposi-tions, and temporal and causal conjunctions.

Counts of the number of instances and the frequency of turn-taking among interlocutors revealed an increasing degree of participation as the newcomers who joined the group at the beginning of each season stayed on with the script team throughout the year. As they talked, listened, and read and wrote texts, a sense of membership in a collaborative venture put them in multiple roles – deliberative, dramatic, and organizational.

Each year, by early January, the young people working on the script team tried to convince me to give up noting instances of words of more than three syllables. Those who had been members of the script team in prior years argued that any individuals with at least one year of experience in the group now used such words "all the time." I argued that as the years rolled forward, we were documenting not only change but also the rate of change of certain language features. Thus we would for each feature need at least three points in time to do so.

The script team pointed out that the same technical terms in the theatre that were at least three syllables came up every year. Jerome quipped: "Yeah, kids like us who work in the theatre get to use these words like we know what they mean."

I asked: "Yes, but how soon does a new kid learn to throw these terms around, and do they keep them from year to year?"

The script team ignored me and continued talking about whether new terms came up in their writing workshops and, if so, did they ever get used in the actual scripts of the plays they produced.

Another context that added new words as well as different kinds of syntax was "all those critics and what they write about us." The theatre staff expected the young actors to read reviews of their productions written by theatre critics and to figure out the meaning of expressions such as "logistically complex," "semantically vague," "tantalizingly mature." In rehearsals of later plays, the young actors sometimes inserted phrases from the critical reviews into their discussions around production details. I often heard young actors who had been around the theatre in prior years jokingly tell the cast either to avoid or to embrace situations their critics had identified in their reviews of plays from earlier seasons.

Contending forces

When the young actors worked in the theatre, their job was to pose problems collectively in their writing workshops. They wanted to sort out for themselves possible ways to solve societal issues related to discrimination, crime, and poverty. Within six weeks or so of work in the theatre, even the shyest, most reluctant speakers joined in the group's deliberations over play content, staging, casting, and setting times for rehearsals. The young actors seemed to take to the idea that none of their theatre directors expected them to reach consensus, come up with pre-scripted answers, or debate one position or viewpoint in opposition to another. Some newcomers floundered for weeks, confused by the rapid give-and-take of the group's conversations around decision-making. Several told me that at school and with most adults in their lives, they found themselves usually reaching for answers other people wanted them to give. They were not supposed to set up hypothetical situations or to pose problems.

"How about when you're with your friends?" I asked.

"Then whatever we say, one person has to win out over somebody else. That's how we get in fights. We disagree. And one person's gotta win."

Raoul, who had been a friend of Eduardo's since kindergarten and was now a third-year member of Liberty, jumped in: "Before I came here, I would always run toward a fight. Now, for the first time, when I see a fight, I wonder why everyone is runnin' toward the fight instead of walkin' away. It feels good to be writin' a play about violence that teens from all over Chicago can see. Maybe I can help other kids understand that we all have a choice when we see bad stuff."

Like Raoul, many of the young people who found their way to collaborative project-oriented community organizations had close friends and family members who were either villains or victims. Liberty wanted them to see that navigating life on the streets and at home meant finding a way to stand back and move on rather than to fight back or jump in.

But Liberty had its own interests in mind as well. The theatre's existence depended on young people creating, producing, and critiquing collaboratively. The young writers and actors had to do shows, or Liberty's revenue dropped. This reality was never far from the minds of the young actors. On the wall of the office where they hung out after practice and talked to office staff, the young people saw charts of income and expenses that changed each week. They knew they had work to do, and the adults around them left little doubt that once the rush of the season got under way, no one had time to "mess around." Disagreeing and wasting time arguing one point against another meant that other ideas got cut out of consideration. The arts director told every entering group: "Around here, ideas are what make us happen. Keep 'em comin', and we'll keep goin'. Otherwise, we're history."

Liberty could also be "history" if the writers and actors did not monitor their work in order to make it acceptable for public performance. In their writing workshops, they could write whatever they wanted – "just get it out there." As they began to work through their writings to select pieces toward a narrative, however, they had to become censors.[2] The realities of adult powers, as well as their sensitivities to what teenagers "should" be thinking and saying thus came to help shape the selection of particular lines of dialogue. These debates raged around hypothetical and posed situations in which audiences might be "offended." At some point during this period of script production, the arts director usually asked a selection of board members to sit in with the young writers and hear their concerns about being "muzzled." Representative of corporate life as well as education, city government, and the medical profession, these adults had become accustomed to hearing the young direct toward the board their indignation at being censored. The outcome each year, painful and often protracted, left the young people with a clear sense that no organization dependent on the good will and patronage of the public can vent their complaints about society's authority figures. Taking the perspective of others and being shrewd editors could bring them in line with what the American mainstream arts audience would tolerate.

Young actors, particularly those like Jerome who wanted to work in media, music, and theatre, struggled to come to grips with their multiple positionings. They railed against the hypocrisy they saw in themselves when they "let" audiences "manipulate" Liberty's representations of the real struggles of inner-city youth. No topic created as many occasions for deliberation as "censorship" of their written materials that would be included in the final script. In the process, they persisted in calling out to one another the biases they saw come up in their edits. As they did this, they found their ideas of justice, equality, and tolerance shifting, becoming more ambiguous, attenuated, and situated.

Long-term members of groups such as Liberty Theatre, especially those located in urban centers, tended to draw recently immigrated youth as well as African Americans and Latinos whose families had been in the city for decades. In groups such as Liberty, the young people portrayed in their writings, theatre, music, and visual arts their worries about not being themselves. They asked questions: "What does freedom mean?" "Whose freedom?" "Who decides?" In most years, they ended their debates and moved forward toward production by agreeing to some version of the idea that "if you call yourself liberal, tolerant, outraged, angry, or repressed, that does not mean you can say anything and everything just anywhere ... match your words for the right time and place."

By the late 1990s in Chicago, in addition to the often angry questions the youth deliberated in their community organizations, they reported that in school courses they were reading and talking about these same issues. Friendships made during out-of-school activities put concepts such as "multicultural," "diverse," and "special needs" into active interpretation of theories the young people heard about in school. In community youth organizations, openness of group participation meant that everyone had a voice in mediating what they wanted their productions to mean. Everyone had to be aware that they could not offend their funders and those who supported youth arts.[3]

Jerome's place

Jerome finished secondary school in 1998, graduating with his friend Eduardo. By now, Jerome had started work at a warehouse to supplement his earnings from the bodega. He was saving money to go to the local arts college. He wanted to study music and theatre, but Tia Maria, who seemed happy enough for him to stay on at her place, had heard about college loans and warned him against debts he could "never leave behind." She urged him to enroll instead in a two-year college.

He followed her advice. Soon after he began coursework at the college, Jerome ran into his favorite high-school English teacher, Mr. Martinez, at a coffee shop near the community college. Their conversation led to what Jerome planned to do after he completed the current year of coursework. He was planning to transfer to a four-year university. Mr. Martinez asked: "To study what?" Jerome hesitated: "I'm thinkin' I wanna be an English teacher." His teacher's face broadened into a big smile. Hardly taking a breath, he launched into all the possibilities in teaching for someone like Jerome, who was bilingual, had been in theatre, knew the music kids loved, and thought nothing of being the clown in front of a group.

Four years after this conversation, Jerome graduated from the University of Illinois in Chicago, having gone through their bilingual education program and been certified in elementary education. He had acted in the college theatre and occasionally helped out the arts director at Liberty Theatre. He also kept working as clerk at the bodega.

Jerome's first teaching placement put him in a school with many Puerto Rican students who lived in housing projects and nearby neighborhoods of single-family homes. Jerome organized an after-school theatre club in which the children collected Latin American folktales and songs from their parents. Trained in using digital recorders, the children recorded their parents, transcribed their words in Spanish, translated the pieces into English, and each year put together a printed program of their materials and a dramatic performance.

On the Sunday nearest the date of his twenty-fourth birthday, Jerome went to Tia Maria's house. Now in her seventies, she still ruled over Sunday dinners with great fanfare. During a rare quiet moment, she called Jerome to the kitchen and said: "When you gettin' married? I'm not gettin' any younger, and I'm gonna dance at your wedding."

"Funny you should ask," Jerome said with a twinkle in his eye.

He and Lucia, Eduardo's girlfriend from middle school, had just become engaged, and they wanted Tia Maria to help them set the date for the wedding. Lucia had gone to art school and was a set designer for several theatre groups in Chicago, so her calendar was planned far in advance. Jerome's teaching and his summer professional development seminars meant that he also knew his schedule well into the next year.

The wedding was scheduled for the next June in the Catholic church with the tall bell tower. Eduardo, now married with two children, was the best man. Tia Maria sat in the front row of the church next to Zinnia Mae and Donna, who had flown in from Atlanta. I sat next to Marcello, one of the twins, who now lived in Chicago.

After the ceremony, while the guests gathered in the church hall for the reception, Jerome and Lucia stepped aside, and Jerome whispered something to the priest. The three of them came over to Donna and me. Jerome motioned for us to follow him, while Zinnia Mae, Marcello, and Tia Maria made their way to the reception hall. The priest led the four of us to the second floor and from there up the narrow staircase to the bell tower. Now I knew what Jerome's secret request of the priest had been. We looked out over the immediate world of Chicago, a city that had become Jerome's place. He put his arms around Lucia and Donna and smiled at the priest: "I never thought about how a place you know so well from down there could look so different from the top." Ever the performer, Jerome now had his very own family as audience.

3   The closeness of strangers

Martin Brown grew up in Roadville, barely three miles away from Trackton. Born in 1970, four years after Zinnia Mae, Martin was the son of textile mill workers Peggy and Lee Brown. During early childhood Martin and his brother, Danny, two years younger, stayed with their mother at home during the day, and their father at night. He worked the day shift at the mill, she took the second shift. Peggy's sister and her husband lived just down the street. Children played in one another's yards and were quick to collect at the back steps of any kitchen from which the smell of fresh-baked cookies came. Teens took over carports and driveways to work on one another's bicycle, motor scooter, or the family power lawnmower.

Church events took up several chunks of family time each week, and by the time they were six, Roadville's children took pride in the number of Bible verses they knew and the books of the Bible they could name. Reading in preparation for Sunday School or Bible Study activities and the writing of recipes, thank-you notes, or grocery lists took place while family members sat around the kitchen table. When children did their homework, they sat at the table, working while an adult prepared meals or cleaned the kitchen. Before children started school, either mom or dad obeyed children's demands for a bedtime story, usually drawn from books given out in Sunday School or bought from stands near the checkout counter in grocery stores. Every Sunday for dinner, family and friends gathered, adults at the dining-room table, children at the kitchen table with the eldest child in charge of the younger ones. The eldest male offered the prayer of thanks, including blessings of the week and special needs of loved ones who were sick or facing unusual hardships. At the adult table, gossip, family news, information about changes at the mill, and incidents from recent fishing trips circulated. The children's table went unnoticed by adults, unless the laughter and noise got "out of control." A word of warning issued by a male voice from the dining room was followed by muffled giggles. Once the children cleaned their plates and put their dishes in the sink, they escaped outside to play or to resume a softball game.

On Saturdays, holidays, and often during vacation weeks, the entire family spilled out of the house into the outdoors. Men and boys went fishing, played ball, or worked on refurbishing the family boat that could be towed to the nearby lake in the fishing season. There was always the tool shed to be cleaned, the lawn and garden to be cared for, and painting and "fixin'" to be done around the outside of the house. "Keepin' things up" was a family mantra in Roadville. As a consequence, girls and boys grew up knowing how to work with their hands. The craftsmanship of boat-building, carpentry, and fence-building seemed to come easily to the boys, while girls learned to take care of the garden, freeze and can vegetables, cook, sew, knit, and crochet. Hiring someone from outside the circle of family or neighbors to do repairs or maintain property was unheard of. Someone always knew a friend or family member who had a knack for plumbing, fixing cars, and finding ways to get rid of wasp nests lodged in difficult places. Grandparents, cousins, aunts and uncles, or friends stepped in with the needed knowledge, tool, or building material. Garden and yard work presented consistent chores, small plots of ground in a corner of the backyard for children's own planting choices, and new discoveries each year of different kinds of insects, weather conditions, and mildew and fungi. In the larger family garden, as children worked along-side their elders, the young absorbed vocabulary along with concepts and causes behind changes in plant and insect life. A Swiss chard patch in need of harvest was "bolting," "rust" had taken over the garlic this year, and the unusually wet summer explained the mildew on the zinnias in the flowerbed across the front of the house. The children lived in a world of practical roles, household and yard projects, and regular enlistment to help out and pitch in on whatever had to be done.

Chores and jobs at home, rituals of church life, and family get-togethers came with stories, jokes, and instructions that assumed children as listeners and imitators first and reluctant commentators or questioners last. Children were expected to remain in the room for a polite period when family or friends of their parents dropped in to visit. Visitors were expected to address the children and engage them in a brief conversation. These generally included lessons, pointers, and stories that opened with "When I was your age . . ." or "I remember when . . ." In their talk and work with children, adults named tools, utensils, foods, seeds, and plants involved in the task and expected children to know this vocabulary. Verbal instructions came in the fewest words possible. Demonstrating by doing the work of the kitchen, garden, backyard, or carport driveway prevailed, and children were expected to observe and to be ready when the chance for trial and error was offered. In shopping malls, church services, or backyard projects, adults pointed out to young children people and objects in terms of what they did and why: "See that man over there. He's a security guard who watches the stores and helps people when they need directions."

Martin and Danny grew up immersed in words and actions of family and friends ready to help out and to offer advice or to show off what they knew. Because Martin was older, family and neighbors expected him to show Danny and younger children not only what had to be done in chores but also how to do the work.

One day, as his uncle watched from the kitchen window, five-year-old Martin tried to lead three-year-old Danny through their mother's instructions about how to know when spring onions were ready to pull out of the ground.

MARTIN: [pointing to the base of several onion tops as they poked through the soil] See, it pulls back, the ground, I mean. Loose, like this. It comes up when you pull. [Martin pretends to pull on an onion, while Danny takes the lesson literally and grabs the upper tips of an onion plant.]

MARTIN: No. See, it breaks, and that one's not big enough. Look. [Martin mocks the action of pulling up an onion again, this time placing Danny's hand on the onion down near where the plant meets the ground.]

Later that evening at dinner, Martin's uncle asks Danny what he knows about how to pull up spring onions. Before Danny can answer, Martin jumps in to perform again his somewhat failed lesson given earlier to Danny in the garden. The family laughs, enticing Danny to imitate his older brother and to expand on what he knows about onions. At every possible opportunity, retold accounts of children's developing skills and knowledge slip into family conversations.

Tied to mill vacation schedules that gave mill workers only the week of the Fourth of July off each year, Roadville families stayed close to home. They used each year's vacation for chores, extra church events, and sometimes a special trip to the shopping mall. Families rarely ventured far from home except to visit relatives in the region. Peggy and Lee kept a map of the United States pinned to the wall of their back porch. Whenever the boys had to learn the names of the states and their capital cities for school assignments, they drilled them on how to find locations on the map. Whenever they heard of someone they knew who visited a distant state, they worked that narrative into their talk at home around the dinner table.

Martin and Danny loved school, and both succeeded in winning academic prizes as well as playing baseball for their high school team. Both went on to college, Martin to the University of Michigan and Danny to the University of South Carolina where he planned to go on to law school. Martin went to dental school at Tufts University in Massachusetts, where he met his wife, Cindy Dunn, a software engineer. They married in 1992, and after graduate school, Martin joined a practice in a downtown Boston clinic. Cindy worked as a consultant for a software firm and traveled out of town several times a month. Once a year, they went back to South Carolina to visit Martin's parents. When Lee had a heart attack and died in 1995, Martin tried to persuade his mother to move north. But she had already moved in with her sister and brother-in-law and did not want to be uprooted again or to go so far away from home.

Full schedules

When their first child, Rebecca, was born in 1993, and a baby brother, Mark, came along a year later, Martin and Cindy reluctantly made the decision to leave their condominium in downtown Boston. Cindy's parents helped them buy what they jokingly called their "country place" in a suburb outside Boston where they knew the children could attend good public (state) schools. Cindy hired a nanny to live in the small guest apartment attached to the garage of their suburban house. Etta, an older German woman whose grown children lived in the next suburb, came to work for the family when Rebecca was sixteen months old. She remained with the family until Rebecca graduated from high school. Etta spoke almost exclusively German to the children and insisted that Cindy buy children's books in German. By age two, both children went to church nursery school half of each day; at four, they went full days; at five, they began public kindergarten. Their schools overflowed with books, puzzles, puppets, educational toys, volunteers, and ecological fieldtrips to nearby farms. Their suburb included families from all over the United States, and several children, like Rebecca and Mark, were growing up bilingual, though most were learning Spanish, because their nannies were from Mexico or Puerto Rico. Each day when Rebecca and Mark came home from nursery school, Etta made sure the children took naps. As they grew older, she insisted on a "quiet time" each day when the children spent time in their separate bedrooms with books and toys. During meal preparation, she told stories from her German childhood, explained German fairy tales, and involved the children in preparing food and clearing and setting the table.

Whenever Cindy or Martin came home from work, Etta retired, leaving the parents to take charge of the children, ask about their day, plan excursions for and with them, and read with them at bedtime. Etta prepared evening meals most weekdays and then went to her apartment, but if the parents were not home, she fed the children, made sure they did their homework, and put them to bed. She resisted any involvement in homework. Knowing this, Martin and Cindy checked in on homework whenever they could. They were on constant lookout for events and activities they could do with the children on weekends, and the family went to their suburban town's Presbyterian church nearly every week.

As Rebecca and Mark grew older, Martin took one afternoon off each week to pick them up at school so he could spend some time with them before dinner. Both children joined in on what had become Martin's passion – cycling and building custom bicycles. When the children were secure on their own bikes, the three of them explored their suburb and quiet roads through surrounding rural areas. Together they studied maps, catalogues, and websites, calculated times and distances, and followed cycling competitions. Though Rebecca's interest in cycling dropped off as she became interested in visual arts and environmental sciences, she continued to take part in the lively conversations between Martin and her brother about their trips. Father and children kept alert to new sources of information, making, "Did you see . . .?" or "Did you hear . . .?" a frequent opener in their talk with one another. Martin valued Mark's opinions on purchases, routes, professional riders and races, and questions about athletes' use of steroids. Once when Mark was twelve, he and Martin put their bikes on the family car and went to South Carolina to see Martin's elderly mom and to cycle some of the back roads in the Piedmont.

Once Rebecca and Mark started primary school, they began taking part in Scouts and church choir. Etta did the driving and kept close tabs on the tight after-school schedule of each child. By the fifth grade, they were involved in after-school activities, having friends over, or visiting friends' houses almost every day. By seventh grade, summer camps took them to other parts of New England, and their school started information sessions on summer trips abroad. During middle school, Rebecca and Mark traveled with Etta or by suburban train an average of ten hours a week in connection with their scheduled after-school activities.

In secondary school, they increased the number and frequency of their after-school activities. By 2008, each of them averaged more than twenty committed time slots each week of the school year. During their particular season, sports teams – soccer, tennis, and swimming – consistently required as many as five slots of time each week. The children's work commitment in an organic farm group at a nearby agricultural center and sometimes in an urban garden in Boston took three to five time blocks each week, except in the middle of winter. After-school clubs and events, such as chess club, science club, the school play, or choral recital, required three afternoons on average. Church choir, the arts cooperative in downtown Boston, and the spring leadership club associated with the organic farm group called for different levels of commitment depending on the time of year, but these rarely exceeded twice each week.

Maps as territories

On a typical September afternoon, Rebecca and Mark rushed home to change clothes so they could catch the train into one of the inner-city communities of Boston. When their organic farm group, Mac's Farm, met in the city to plan the next week's work at the soup kitchen, the commute by train took half an hour. At the soup kitchen, the young people helped cook and serve food made from vegetables harvested on Mac's Farm located in the suburb where Rebecca and Mark lived. The Farm had been started in the early 1990s by a local enthusiast for young people's direct connection with agriculture and the food system. Even more important to the mission of Mac's Farm, however, was the founder's faith in the power of collaborative ecological work to bring teens from the suburbs together with their inner-city counterparts.[1]

LIBRARY, UNIVERSITY OF CHESTER

Once in town at the soup kitchen, the assembled young people from different suburbs around Boston and several inner-city neighborhoods gathered in the kitchen to listen to the soup kitchen's director and employees from the city's Department of Health. The adults asked the dozen or so assembled young people to check out the kitchen equipment, to be sure they knew how everything worked, and to review the routine to be followed when clients arrived at the soup kitchen next week. After these chores, the director and young people sat around and assigned responsibilities for the next week and charted the travel schedules of all group members. Everyone was to work in the soup kitchen each week throughout the fall into November, as long as the produce from Mac's Farm held out. The soup kitchen director and Department of Health employees went over health and safety regulations the young people had to follow and reviewed the security regulations, inspectors' responsibilities, and clients' legal rights to privacy. "No screwin' up!" the director snapped at the end of the session, then smiled as he waved the group out the front door.

During harvest season, Rebecca and Mark worked at Mac's Farm one afternoon a week to sell the produce that customers had paid for through their Community Supported Agriculture (CSA) fees. Each fall, families paid a set fee that entitled them to weekly boxes of vegetables, herbs, and flowers at the Farm. Twice each week, Mac's Farm also ran farmers' markets in downtown Boston, one near mid town and the other in an inner-city area. The young people from Mac's Farm worked at these markets, setting prices, arranging displays, collecting recipes, and serving customers.

On a Saturday late in September, 2007, Rebecca was ready before Mark and shouted for him to hurry. He called out: "Did you call the art center? Some joker called you last night at 11:30. You better be glad I picked it up and not Dad." Rebecca gasped: "Oh no, I forgot to call Randy to tell him I can't be there today to lead the tour. Hang on a sec' and I'll give 'em a call. My cellphone's [mobile phone's] dead; I forgot to plug it in last night."

Rebecca still belonged to a Youth Arts Collaborative in Boston that she and a group of her friends first visited when she was ten years old. Through secondary school, she worked there several times a week during the winter when Mac's Farm was not in full swing. The Collaborative did entrepreneurial work with its art and brought in professional artists to help the young members, ages twelve to eighteen, learn design and various techniques in painting, woodcutting, and sculpting. Visitors often came for scheduled tours, and once a term, each young artist had the responsibility of acting as tour guide, taking visitors through the artists' studios and the gallery. Rebecca was supposed to play that role on this particular Saturday, but as was often the case, her schedule was double-booked.

Mark played soccer in the local league from the time he was in elementary school. During middle school, he loved being the star, but his position as goalie became more challenging during secondary school. When he twisted his ankle for the second time in the season, his coach told him to stay away from practice for a few weeks. Mark increased his time working at Mac's Farm. Martin and Cindy encouraged Mark and Rebecca to work at the soup kitchens and farmers' markets in the city and to develop a wider range of friends than those in their suburban school and neighborhood. On the train in and out of the city, the two sat together and did their homework.

By middle school, Rebecca and Mark had scheduled practices each week for sports teams and church choir. These commitments came in addition to work at Mac's Farm and the Youth Arts Collaborative, participation in school plays or debate teams, and attendance at special school or church events. Each of these activities involved a different face-to-face network with slightly different levels of access to cellphones and services. Text messaging worked with some, but not others, and only some of their friends had the kind of access to unlimited cellphone usage and up-to-date computers and programs they had at home. Thus they kept several levels of social networking at play, with frequency and density of contacts on these networks varying by season and level of activity of their after-school groups.

Mark had a group of friends who cycled, and they sometimes planned trips on Saturdays, but Martin made clear that the primary cycling commitment was with dad. They spent time almost every week of the year cycling or working on their bikes in the garage or studying websites and catalogues to assess what their next need might be for equipment and gear. From the time Mark was eleven years old, each summer he and his dad studied maps of the Northeast and scheduled a week of biking together. Rebecca thrived in science and literature classes; Mark excelled in mathematics. Rebecca and her friends worked on computer graphics in their spare time, while Mark spent his spare time with friends kicking soccer balls around or hanging out at the local sandwich shop exchanging news about the latest cellphone services and applications.

Intimate strangers

Though more actively engaged in mutual interests with their parents than most youngsters over the age of eleven, Rebecca and Mark still spent at least thirty hours each week with "intimate strangers" in youth and community organizations.[2] Leaders of these groups guided the young people under their charge into understanding concepts related to time, respect for the property and privacy of others, and appreciation for rules and their sources and enforcers. Intimate strangers for Rebecca and Mark during their middle and secondary school years included Etta, soccer coaches, choir leaders, Mac's Farm agronomists and youth leaders, Youth Arts Collaborative studio artists, science camp directors, Scout leaders, and summer camp counselors.

Cindy and Martin entrusted these individuals, many of whom they had never met, with their children. They counted on the organizations with which Rebecca and Mark were affiliated to hire adults who knew how to keep the children committed to high performance, clear-headed judgments, and the kind of behavior expected of "good kids." In almost all instances, the youth organization leaders with whom Rebecca and Mark spent more and more time as they moved through secondary school had less formal education than either Cindy or Martin.

In the 1990s, communities across the United States experienced a dramatic increase in the number of non-profit organizations that put academic content into action in socially attractive after-school activities. These groups met several times a week during most of the year, involving youngsters in activities centered on environmental sciences, arts, community service, or sports.

Some city governments helped support enterprising artists and environmentalists who worked with young people. Civic-minded adults wanted adolescents to avoid the allure of drugs, gang life, and association with peers at risk for trouble. They wanted to harness what they saw as the promising potential of teenagers as mentors and models for younger children.[3] Organizations without city government sponsorship or national affiliation relied on donor support, grants, and dedicated volunteers to keep their operations going and their doors open. Directors of these grassroots organizations sometimes held professional positions that gave them flexible hours. They enlisted volunteers, often parents, to help out, working during after-school hours and on weekends and sometimes securing *pro bono* help from friends at the office when their organization needed legal, accounting, or insurance advice.

At times the values, skills, backgrounds, and interests of intimate strangers expanded and tested those that young people brought from home. When Mark and Rebecca worked with Mac's Farm, they got to know the agronomist there. He also worked with the County Extension Agency and as special advisor on research projects under way at the University of Massachusetts. Their church choir director taught organ at the music conservatory and gave concerts in Boston churches. She had a background in music ministry from a seminary in New York City. At the Youth Arts Collaborative, Rebecca worked shoulder to shoulder with visual arts professionals who had their own studios and worked under deadline and with critique from curators, dealers, and clients.

These intimate strangers believed in the cultural capital they contributed to the lives of young people. They also appreciated the flexible work hours and opportunities to supplement their incomes. Those who volunteered, often the case with sports team coaches, wanted to play out their own interest in the value of sports, environmental sciences, music, or visual arts to the future of young people. Coaches, artists, musicians, and gardeners who worked in communities provided contacts and opportunities for adolescents unavailable through schools. They passed on information about internships, apprenticing jobs, and summer camps to the teens. By watching these professionals at work, young people saw the craftsmanship, self-discipline, time and space management, language, and world views that differed from the talents, interests, communication style, and contacts of their parents.

The intimate strangers who populated the childhood and teenage years of Rebecca and Mark stretched their language, interests, values, and contexts far beyond those that Martin and Cindy could offer during their available family times. The children's many roles outside home and school socialized them into appreciating what was meant by having a professional identity in community organizations and taking part in public events. Equally important was the exposure the children had to the federal, state, and city laws under which service organizations had to work. In one or another of the organizations in which they took part, Rebecca and Mark heard something each week about new regulations in health and safety, changes in liability insurance, and restrictions on travel. They worked alongside and had the chance to question professionals who represented areas of specialization unfamiliar or unknown to either their parents or teachers. They took part in tasks and talk that circulated around calculations of pounds per bushel, rate of absorption of water in different types of soil, and variation in the meanings of "biodynamic agriculture." They learned about different philosophies of curators in local museums, and they traveled with the organizations to places their parents had never heard about. They tasted foods they never saw in their homes, met people who would never cross their parents' paths, and gained a sense of confidence not only in what they knew but also in how they could find out what they needed to know.

Table 3.1 delineates the frequency and types of interactional patterns that characterized youth organizations dedicated to either the arts or science-based activities. In both types of groups, adult professionals (for example, artists and curators or agronomists and biologists) interacted in close hand-to-hand work. The delicate work of planting seedlings, weeding, thinning, picking, and packing shared with art the precision of craft work. The artists and scientists in community organizations operated with a moral imperative to be within a community and to work with intellect and imagination as well as with the hand. Technique was everything for the success of the young people, for their products, performances, and exhibitions had to meet the needs and norms of their customers and uphold the standards of the artists and scientists with whom they worked. Their work demanded that they slow down, take care, pay close visual attention, do the tasks called for at each stage correctly, and help newcomers learn to do the same.[4]

The experts who guided the young people called for attention to demonstrations, used technical vocabulary in verbal explanations, told stories to help them

Table 3.1 *Interactional patterns of individual attention in youth organizations**

Frequency	Interaction	Purpose
60	Directives to look, feel, imagine, listen	Instrumental guidance
14	Spontaneous demonstration by expert adult or peer of what a performance or product can look like	Call to imitation and creative adaptation
13	Uses of vocabulary specific to techniques	Inclusion
12+	Verbal illustration or explanation of a routine, technique, or movement	Inclusion and instrumental guidance
6+	Portrayal or reflection, serious or playful, on current or past events familiar to participants	Humor and role-modeling
4+	Suggestion for rethinking or reworking application of a specific technique or conception within a project	Critique
3+	Playful re-enactment and retelling of incidents within teller's life	Humor and inclusion
1–2	Small-group talk to work up ideas and to plan for an exhibition, performance, conference, or market	Collaborative creativity

* Data are drawn from longitudinal studies of twelve youth organizations in different regions of the US. Frequency counts represent occurrences during a two-hour period of work that took place at least six weeks after each organizational season began.

remember specific points, and elaborated on possible approaches to particular steps. No one talked about what the young people did as anything other than *work*. They were creating products for discriminating markets, and theirs was serious business.[5] Yet playful talk, diversionary breaks, and travel allowed time for valuable social bonding. The types of interaction within youth organizations devoted to artistic and scientific pursuits centered on building a sense of inclusion through instrumental guidance, critique, and humor.

Through experiences in their out-of-school organizations, Rebecca and Mark grew up with a strong sense of the hierarchical nature of responsibility in relation to experience. The same pattern worked in food bank kitchens, on retreats with Mac's Farm youth, and in the Youth Arts Collaborative. Experience moved individuals up in the hierarchy of roles, put them in line to be mentors, and provided opportunities to assess the leadership skills of others around them, including adults.

Rebecca and Mark and other Mac's Farm youth felt the repercussions of careless financial transactions at the farmers' market and in distribution of produce boxes for the customers of the CSA program. The teens' supervisors expected them to make correct change, weigh vegetables accurately, and keep track of the names of vegetables and their prices. When accounts came up short or customers were given incorrect information or were responded to with disrespect, consequences followed from organizational leaders.

Sports teams offered some of the same lessons in building responsibility. Their learning context differed from those in the arts and sciences mainly because of the pre-scripted rule-governed nature of sports. Discipline, regimen, and attention to the game dominated over originality, imagination, and creative artistry. Talk within and about sports covered a more narrow range of topics, genres, and vocabulary than talk in projects dedicated to art or science. Like these activities, however, involvement in sports called for a communal spirit and individual responsibility. After having been with the soccer team for over a year, Mark knew more than the newcomers. His coach expected him and others who had been on the team to guide, mentor, and model for novices. Moreover, the coach expected players with more experience to assume responsibility for taking younger players to task when they broke rules, showed anger, cursed, or showed up late for practice. His coach had strict rules about cellphone use, and he had no hesitation about benching anyone who broke those rules. Older members such as Mark came in for public censure by the coach when they did not take seriously that maturity meant keeping the full group in line through following the rules and being role models. Mark and his friends on the soccer team alternately loved and hated their coach, judging him "too harsh," "mean," and "sometimes unfair." At other times, they had nothing but praise for his leadership in winning a game or at the end of a championship season.

Both Rebecca and Mark suffered the public humiliation of goof-ups in choir performances, tour guiding, time scheduling, and missed saves in soccer games. They and their friends did not like to "mess up." To avoid doing so, they learned that staying focused on what they were doing made a big difference in outcomes. They figured out the value of planning and thinking ahead, not just for each day or week, but for an entire season. They kept school calendars in their backpacks and duplicated that information on their cellphone calendars. Because cellphone usage was banned in school, at sports practices, and during certain activities at Mac's Farm and the Youth Arts Collaborative, they did not give up scheduling on paper. Their phones were useful also for some of the calculations and data tracking they did as a matter of course at Mac's Farm. Rebecca and her friends could plot the location and production of particular seed crops in relation to climate, soil testing, and time of year planted. At home, they played around with ideas about presenting this information in different graphic designs. They shared their designs with adults who had to give talks to funders, leadership organizations, and national conferences. Their lives in their youth organizations had built in a sense of possible territories to explore. In mapping their futures, they received wide-ranging, sometimes contradictory and occasionally complementary, guidelines from intimate strangers.

Real life roles for the future

In 2006, when Rebecca was thirteen and Mark was twelve, they helped me plan and analyze a random selection of twenty hours of audiorecordings we had made in sites of their activities outside of school. At that time, what they called their "real life," their time not spent in school, had three distinct features:

1. Their youth organizations worked in cycles from beginning to end of a season, term, or project. The language of the young people at the beginning of each year did not sound the way it did at the end. As each season moved forward, the young people grew more assertive, declarative about their ideas, and forceful with their questions.
2. Rule distribution within the organizations related primarily to manners, time, dress, school grades, and job expectations. The young had to turn in report cards to organization leaders in order to keep all privileges intact. They also had to follow sports and organizational rules related to foul language, weapons, drugs, and discrimination. They learned the need to heed county and state laws related to insurance regulations, privacy protection, and requirements that certain pieces of personal information (e.g., name, address, Social Security number, emergency contacts) be on file at the organization.
3. The life of organizations depended on individuals knowing their roles and how to play them. The children heard themselves reminded often of their particular roles and responsibilities for maintaining not only smooth personal relationships, but also standards of achievement and accountability for the good of the group as a whole.[6]

Martin came home early one afternoon when Rebecca, Mark, and I were tabulating counts of language evidence for each organizational feature. We were debating whether particular kinds of utterances should be listed as characteristic of only a single feature or of all three.

Martin listened to our vigorous debate while he made peanut butter sandwiches for a bike ride he hoped he and Mark could take later. Finally, he asked us to explain what we were doing. He listened quietly for a long time before he commented: "But that's how *all* organizations work. I don't care whether it's my dental office or your soccer team or farm project. We're talkin' about the realities of the labor market and life in a litigious society here. This stuff is not for kids; it's for everybody."

Mark looked as though he wanted to rebut, but Rebecca broke in: "Dad, you don't get it. That's just the point. Adults never think kids can do what they do. We *can* and we *do*. But we're always havin' to prove stuff, like we really *are* responsible."

Mark left the table: "Dad, come on. I hear a fight comin'!" The two headed out the back door.

As Rebecca and I cleaned up our papers and packed my computer, she told me about a big fight she and her dad had last summer. He had refused permission for her to go with friends to a Vermont farm for a week. He thought she was too young, her friends were immature, and next year would be better, so she could plan ahead. As Rebecca walked me to the car, she mused: "Why is it easier to convince anybody but your parents that you won't always screw up, that you can do some of these things they never think you can do?"

Parental allies

Rebecca's comment went to the heart of a view commonly held by young people who worked within community organizations: the adults there trusted them more than their parents did. Moreover, these organizations *needed* the young. From the late 1990s forward, children in families whose economic fortunes had been boosted during the decade's strong economy expected their parents to provide camps, travel, clothes, technology, and accessories the young chose for themselves. In other words, children expected parents to meet their *needs* by fulfilling their *desires*.

The opposite held true in community youth organizations, such as Mac's Farm and the Arts Cooperative. The modest budgets of these organizations did not permit hiring as many adults as were needed to manage the life of the group. Young people were vital human resources. They were needed to guide and mentor younger children, monitor life within the group, plan and lead activities, and keep the organizational memory alive. The young were expected to carry out these responsibilities by following what were specific norms of behavior governing good sportsmanship, property maintenance, and respect for others. Consistency in upholding such rules often exceeded parental expectations. Furthermore, children might rationalize their failure to follow their parents' rules by saying: "What are they gonna do? They're not gonna throw me out? And, hey, my parents don't even do what they tell me to do, so why should I?" Such was not the case in youth organizations: persistent flouting of rules brought direct confrontation and a request to leave the group. Young people who wanted to belong demonstrated in their adherence to group rules that they wanted to stay.

Across the country from the suburb in which Rebecca and Mark Brown lived, Bernardo Crawford shared the view that Rebecca expressed about parents and intimate strangers. Bernardo's father, Jay Crawford, had grown up in Trackton. He had joined the Air Force after he completed secondary school, and he had made a career of military service. Jay had been stationed in Texas when he met Bernardo's mom, Maria Alvarez, who was from Mexico. She was attending a community college when Jay came to her physics class to fill in for the instructor for a few weeks. Struck by Maria's interest in science, he remembered her. A year or so later, when he was giving a guest lecture on aerodynamics at the state museum, he noticed her in the lecture hall. They dated for a year and married in 1992. Bernardo was born in 1994.

Maria spoke only Spanish to Bernardo, his dad only English, and Bernardo attended a bilingual primary school. His mom and dad insisted that he read, write, and speak Spanish and English, and he grew up immersed in children's books in both languages. He loved school, and he and Jay played math games on long car rides, waiting in line at supermarkets, or waiting to pick up Maria from work. His mom had introduced him to comics in Spanish and encouraged him to create his own.

Bernardo had sketched since he was five, and he and his mom went to art galleries and museums together. The ones Bernardo liked best were those that included sections on natural history. Skeletons were his favorite things to sketch, and his first winning piece in an arts competition had been of a steer's skull on a dry barren landscape. Maria trained to be a science teacher, and she tried out on Bernardo science activities she was thinking of using in her class-room. She was diagnosed with acute myeloid leukemia in 1998 and died in 2002, when Bernardo was eight.

In 2006, Jay was due to retire after twenty years of service in the Air Force. The family had looked forward to a long vacation that year exploring national parks in the Southwest. Jay kept that trip in mind when he retired and accepted a job in an engineering firm in Colorado. In the four years between Maria's death and Jay's retirement, Bernardo showed signs of getting in trouble. He did not come home after school, refused to tell his dad where he had been, and began playing truant. Jay spent long days at his job, and Bernardo refused to have anyone else in the house after his mom died. By the time Jay retired, he was desperate to be a better parent and to recover the relationship he had with his son before Maria died. Within six weeks of Jay's retirement, the two set out to Colorado. On the way, they camped and hiked, toured Grand Canyon and Bryce Canyon, and talked for what seemed the first time since there had been only the two of them as a family.

Jay bought a house in Highland, a town of 40,000 in the Rocky Mountains. Gradually, Jay and Bernardo adjusted to the seasons and the long winter months of snow. They went snowshoeing, and they learned to ski.

Bernardo and Jay began to rebuild their relationship in Colorado, but Bernardo still had outbursts of anger and resistance. He tested Jay at every turn by getting in trouble at school and hanging out with friends Jay distrusted. A colleague at the engineering firm told Jay to get Bernardo involved in after-school activities. He suggested the Catacombs – a local youth organization that offered kickboxing, soccer, and chaperoned club nights with music and dancing for kids as young as twelve years of age. The place had a strong reputation for putting young people at the center of management. Their motto was "We're run for kids by kids."

Bernardo liked the idea and agreed to try out the place. But he continued to hang out almost every day at a fast food restaurant with his friends from the soccer team, and homework never seemed to fit into Bernardo's schedule. He did begin to spend more time at the Catacombs, but he never talked much about what he did there and why he and his friends disliked school so much. Within a year, this attitude seemed to change. Bernardo began working as a junior youth coordinator at the Catacombs. One night every weekend as well as every Tuesday afternoon, he was the designated manager for the part of the youth center where sixth graders could come. He and the other youth managers took charge of sections of the center at certain times of each week. They met once a week to plan activities for specific areas of the center for young people of different ages. They reviewed budgets, rules, and security and discipline issues. They heard cases of individuals who had been formally reprimanded three times for refusing to follow the center's rules. Bernardo was the only member of the board who spoke fluent Spanish. Therefore, he had major responsibilities for handling orientation, rule explanation, and case hearings for a new group of kids who had recently come to the area from Mexico. He got along well with them, on the whole, and occasionally ran into them in the hallways or at lunch time at his middle school.

Jay gradually felt that he could stop worrying about having to entertain his son all on his own, and he appreciated the sense of responsibility Bernardo seemed to be taking from his duties with the Catacombs. Bernardo's girlfriend, Regina, was in a beginners' Mexican dance academy. Regina and some of the girls from the academy sometimes came with their boyfriends to the Catacombs on those Saturday nights when the center was open to middle-school students.

When I first visited them in Colorado, Jay asked me if I still had any audiorecordings of him when he was a child back in Trackton. Ted, Jay's dad, had been in construction work, and his mom, Mattie, involved their two boys, Jay and Gary, in everything she did – housework, household repairs, gardening, shopping, and visiting on the plaza. Bernardo was intrigued by the differences between the Carolina accent and the Texan talk he had grown up with. He and Jay had gone back to the Carolinas only once that Bernardo could remember, and his grandparents seemed very old to him then. On the tapes, he heard Jay interrupt his mom's storytelling on her neighbor's porch. He laughed when he heard his dad tease Gary, his uncle, Jay's younger brother. Gary had followed Jay into military service, but he had joined the Marines, and he was now close to retiring after twenty years. He never married, and he came often to Colorado to ski and hike with Jay and Bernardo. When Bernardo heard the tapes from Trackton, he asked Jay to translate the southern African American Vernacular English and the local idioms. Bernardo picked up on the big-family atmosphere of Trackton's front porches and the teasing and chatter in which children and adults often exchanged leading roles. When Bernardo heard the audiorecordings of Jay and Gary, he said: "We tease a lot too, Dad. Now I know why."

Occasionally, I persuaded Bernardo to audiotape times when he and his friends were hanging out, but their conversations were generally quite short and markedly performative, making recorded words a poor substitute for what actually happened in their interactions. Though I knew my presence in the group would flatten their usual ways of behaving and talking, I got Bernardo to let me treat at the fast food restaurant when he went there with his friends.

One afternoon, Bernardo and three soccer team members went for tacos after soccer practice. When we talked about the audiotapes, I asked boys who were from Mexico how their soccer team in Colorado was different from their team back home. Bernardo's friends looked at one another and shrugged. One of them said, "What do I know?" "¿Qué sé yo?" another repeated.

"Why don't you think you know?" I asked. I must have caught the boys on a good day, for they talked about their feeling that nobody wanted to talk to them or cared about what they knew. The teachers "hate us and hate it when we talk Spanish." Bernardo said nothing.

Later I asked Bernardo about what the boys had said. I was puzzled that he just listened when the other boys presented themselves as knowing nothing. He identified with them in part, because he saw himself as Mexican much of the time, though at lunch time at school, he often sat with African American friends. In response to my question about what the boys at the restaurant had said, Bernardo laughed and replied: "I never see lots of those kids from the soccer team at the club events at the Catacombs, and they don't go to my school. So I totally try to be like them when we just hang out. We know the same music. We play soccer. What else is there?"

When he was with the younger African American members at the Catacombs, Bernardo's body movement, language, and demeanor aligned with theirs. When he was with his soccer team, all of whom were from Mexico, his behavior was largely indistinguishable from theirs. When he sat among the honors students on the school science club board, he played the role of a comic until the business of decision-making and planning came to the table. In the hallways of his school, his dress, slouch, and hooded jacket gave little hint that he was on his way to an honors science or mathematics class. He could assume the "gangsta" look as well as any of his friends, but on the days of board meetings at the Catacombs, he traded his droopy jeans for khaki pants, and a canvas jacket replaced his hooded sweat shirt. Bernardo never complained about the challenges he faced in fitting in at a new school and figuring out all the places and people that called for his different identities.

Bernardo still daydreamed about going to the rodeo with his dad back in Texas. Jay had taken him to the stables at rodeo time, and he had met some of the best riders. One day at the Catacombs, he overheard several boys talking about a local rodeo champion. Bernardo asked if any riders from Texas ever came to Colorado rodeos. Most of the boys shrugged their shoulders.

BERNARDO: Didn't you read about the other one that's comin?
SHANE: No, I just ask my uncle. He knows 'em all.
BERNARDO: What's the stables like? Kids ever work there? You know anybody there?
SHANE: Sure, lots. But they don't hire kids.
                                                  [
PABLO: My cousin was there.
                                                            [
BERNARDO: Workin'?
SHANE: There's a kid comin.' I'm gonna beat the shit out of him if I catch him in my uncle's place. He's been stealin', my uncle knows it, just can't catch him.
BERNARDO: Didn't you ever steal? It's easy if you know how
                                                  [
PABLO: um, I know, a kid was walkin' in the aisle in the 7–11 near me, and then he bends down to tie his shoe, 'n when he stands up, he grabs a couple candy bars. See? [he re-enacts the scene]
RENATO: Yeah, totally. It's already made up, so, see, it goes the one guy in there, 'n the guy behind the register watches him, but when two or three of us are there, it's easy to go – [he imitates Pablo] 'n one time back where I used to live, this kid just came from nowhere up to the back of the store, and he just keeps walkin' around and around like he's lookin' for something. The register guy goes: "You lookin' for something?" This guy said his dad took a wrong turn, and they were lost, so he asked for a map. When the register guy bends down to look under the counter for the maps, this kid grabs a bunch of gum in one hand and candy in the other, heads out the front door, 'n he's gone, just like that before the register guy comes up. When he sees the kid's not there, he comes out the front door yellin' for the cops [laughter].

The boys understood now that Bernardo knew about rodeos and also might know about stealing.

When I asked Bernardo about this conversation, he explained that some of these boys had just started coming to the Catacombs and were testing the rules at the Catacombs. A few had already come before the board for rule infractions. He knew several had only recently come from Mexico, and he identified with what they faced in their new location. During one visit to the Catacombs, I was sitting in the office when some of these boys dropped by to talk while Bernardo was on management duty. I asked Renato, a particularly talkative boy who carried a huge backpack bulging with books, how school was going.

He replied: "Okay, I guess, but I just don't talk much." The other boys and Bernardo laughed. Renato continued: "Hey, totally. Who's gonna listen to us? Just a bunch of kids? No adult wants to hear what we gotta say. Besides they just wanna see us get into trouble."

Bernardo cast a knowing smile in my direction, and I moved on: "But what about soccer, and the music you listen to, and the rodeos? You know lots of stuff."

Pablo broke in, speaking in English and Spanish: "We don't talk to nobody. Who cares? Yo la verdad no sé nada. [Really, I know nothing.]" The others laughed.

Jay very much wanted Bernardo to maintain his fluency in Spanish and to put to good use his interest in management of resources, human and environmental. Within a year after moving to Colorado, Jay found several ranches that worked in collaboration with inner-city community gardening programs in neighborhoods of Denver populated by recent immigrants from Mexico. The ranchers met several times a year with the adult and youth managers of these city gardening programs. They sought to find ways to inspire inner-city Spanish-speaking youth to an interest in environmental sciences. The state Agricultural Extension Program supported the collaboration through a Spanish blog that covered topics such as beekeeping and composting, reviews of summer internships on organic farms, and conferences and workshops welcoming student participation. Jay and Bernardo began volunteering with the program and helping with the blog.

When Bernardo was a sophomore in secondary school, he enrolled in a community college course on international agricultural development, and he and his dad began planning for Bernardo to go back east the next summer to work on an organic farm in Vermont. Jay planned to take his vacation at the end of Bernardo's internship so they could visit several universities on their cross-country drive back to Colorado.

Bernardo's internship convinced him that he wanted to be a farmer. Already, his top choices for university study were Cornell University in Ithaca, New York, and the University of California in Davis, California. Bernardo had never spent time on the east coast or on a farm, and the summer in Vermont had won him over. He wanted to support an organic gardening farm and cooperative and manage a dairy. Jay was pleased his son was branching out beyond what his dad knew, and he could ask his son real questions about topics which Jay knew nothing about. Bernardo talked for hours about his experiences in Vermont with his dad and friends at the Catacombs and in the Denver program. Bernardo had seen the CSA satisfy mail-order customers as well as local residents. While he was in Vermont, his penchant for management led him to spend as much time as possible studying ways the small towns in some regions of the state pooled their specialties for marketing as a collaborative. With just one click, customers could order honey, cheese, baked goods, and vegetables – all from different towns but drawn together by sound economic management of rural resources.

Moving on

After 1980, the family and community life of individuals whose grandparents and parents grew up in Roadville or Trackton evolved through patterns of work and play that depended to a great extent on the geographic location in which they settled. As Table 3.2 indicates, by the end of 2009, the 154 Trackton

Table 3.2 *Approximate number of Trackton and Roadville original and descendant households,* * *1969–2009*

	1969	1974	1979	1984	1989	1994	1999	2004	2009
Trackton	154	165	183	209	225	226	239	254	279
Roadville	146	142	160	198	218	209	218	239	296

* *Original* households are defined as those physically located in Trackton and Roadville plus those of family members living within a 50-mile radius of either community. *Descendant* households include not only those established by the children and grandchildren of original Roadville and Trackton families but also those individuals living in nursing facilities, foster families, prison and college housing, or serving in the military.

households of 1969 had become 279 households; the 146 Roadville households had grown to 296.

As the narratives of Jerome, Zinnia Mae and her children, Martin and his children, and Jay and Bernardo illustrate, children of the original households of Roadville and Trackton scattered widely, and some moved several times. Map 2 portrays the distribution of destinations of the first wave of relocations that took place from Roadville and Trackton between 1981 and 1990. The South, including Texas, and the Northeast were the primary sites of opportunity in this first wave. Map 3 portrays destinations favored during the second wave of moves between 1991 and 2010. In the early years of this time span, families were motivated to move by new and better job opportunities, particularly in developing technologies. After 2001, moves tended to come about when retrenchments and business closures forced families to look for work elsewhere.

Turns of fortune, good and bad, as well as concerted planning for further education and career advancement determined timing and distance of moves. National economic trends that favored small business development as well as multinational corporate expansion also influenced choices that individuals made. Young couples, such as Martin and Cindy, went where they saw the greatest potential for their future; they were fortunate enough not to have to move again to find employment. Others who initially worked in finance had to relocate. Those whose jobs were linked with the computer industry followed the industry's evolution wherever new possibilities sprang up. Those in robotics, biotechnology, and software and hardware innovations went primarily to California's Silicon Valley; Boise, Idaho; the environs of Seattle, Washington; and regions with dense clusters of higher education institutions and corporate research centers, such as Boston, Massachusetts, and Austin, Texas.

Table 3.3 indicates the approximate distances of relocations between 1984 and 2009. In the first decade after the recession of the early 1980s, the majority of descendant households from both Roadville and Trackton stayed within 500

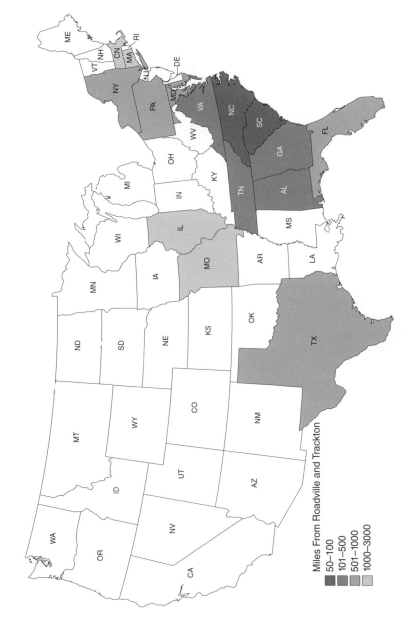

Map 2 **Destinations of first wave of relocations, 1981–1990**

Miles From Roadville and Trackton

50–100
101–500
501–1000
1000–3000

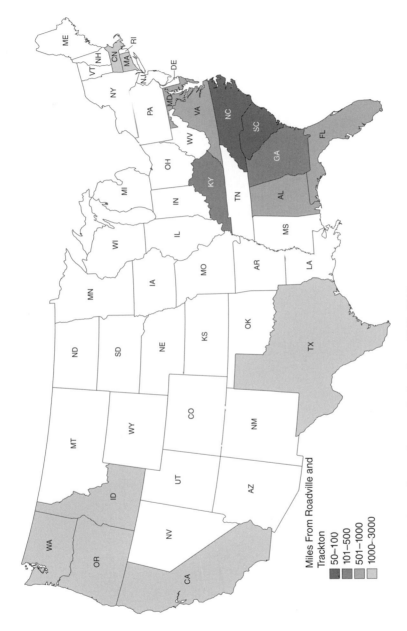

Miles From Roadville and
Trackton

- 50–100
- 101–500
- 501–1000
- 1000–3000

Map 3 Destinations of second wave of relocations, 1991–2010

Table 3.3 *Approximate relocation distances of original and descendant Trackton and Roadville households,* * *1984 – 2009*

Miles from Alberta	50–100	100–500	500–1000	1000–3000	Military service abroad	Total
Original and descendant Trackton households						
1984–1989	65	47	16	18	3	149
1989–1994	54	42	37	23	1	157
1994–1999	51	59	43	54	9	216
1999–2004	62	40	59	52	6	219
2004–2009	43	38	59	80	8	228
Original and descendant Roadville households						
1984–1989	52	47	19	18	6	142
1989–1994	33	19	48	19	10	129
1994–1999	18	13	54	33	14	132
1999–2004	32	31	53	40	12	168
2004–2009	18	51	70	71	14	224

* These figures include *only* those households that relocated more than 50 miles from the Piedmont Carolinas. Note that these figures *include* those individuals in nursing facilities, foster families, prison and college housing, or serving in the military, as well as sequential moves of some households.

miles of what had been "home." The dot.com era of the 1990s drew them farther and farther from home. Individuals who joined the military scattered not only in the United States but around the world. Many served twenty years and retired to start new careers in line with the training and experience they had gained during their military service. These individuals favored parts of the South near military bases or regions that offered leisure activities, such as fly fishing or skiing, available only in particular areas of the country.

The original Trackton and Roadville communities and their ancestors had always moved as *families*, viewing with sadness and suspicion individuals who went far away from family. However, with the first moves away from Trackton and Roadville in the 1980s, *individuals* as well as families moved. Some of these individuals did so to take advantage of small-business opportunities in the rapidly expanding cities of the Southeast. The first generation who went off to college rarely came back to live near their parents. As grandparents grew frail and unable to remain in their own homes, their children could not, as generations before them had, take their elderly relatives to live with them. Both parents worked full-time, and the specialized care and medical interventions that extended life spans meant that the elderly had to be placed in care facilities or assisted-living centers. Though households multiplied, they often included only one person – a situation unknown in Trackton and Roadville in prior generations. Some households, such as those that college students entered, included strangers – a situation rare to those who had grown into adulthood before the 1980s. As the strains of the double-dip economic recession of the 1980s pulled families apart, divorce and separation created single-parent households and dual households, sometimes located in the same city, sometimes elsewhere. During the decade of the 1990s, many young couples lived together, at times in sequentially monogamous relationships with different individuals, and occasionally in the same household with other young couples. Therefore, though Tables 3.2 and 3.3 indicate number of households, those figures after 1984 represent only what can best be described as "guesstimates" made at one point in time during the years indicated. The shifting compositions and definitions of both *family* and *household* created by descendants of Roadville and Trackton caused the numbers in Tables 3.2 and 3.3 to change often.

Across descendant families that I followed from the 1980s forward, parents' meaningful involvement with their children's activities and interests emerged as the most critical factor in their children's development. The demands of such involvement escalated as children grew older. Lines of communication within families had to be kept open, and both parents and children had to set boundaries on what they asked of one another. Reciprocity between young and old went a long way toward having an inclusive family that could hold sustained conversations about their current interests. Caregivers Tia Maria, Zinnia Mae, Martin,

Cindy, Etta, and Jay listened and learned with the play and work of their children. They found common interests that enabled them to show that they regarded young people as co-experts, doing and finding out about things that adults did not know, as well as what they did know. This communication channel increasingly mattered when technology sent work-related tasks home on parents' laptops and when older children grew increasingly involved in school and community sports teams, after-school programs, and arts and environmental organizations.

Tia Maria expected Jerome to learn to cook, serve, clean, play host, and manage his role as man-of-the-house at Sunday dinners. She expected him to get and keep jobs in the community from the time he was an early teenager. She insisted that whatever he did after school, she had to be part of the action and know who his friends were. Once Eduardo passed the Sunday-dinner test, Tia Maria became a fixture at dress rehearsals and performances at Liberty Theatre. When she saw something she did not like or understand, she questioned Jerome and Eduardo about how young people talked and acted in their theatre pieces. She listened to their recounts of the many hours and hot debates the young writers and actors had about what could go into the final scripts. While she did not change her judgment of what "should" be, she listened and took in what Jerome and Eduardo had to say. Later Jerome heard her tell her friends about his accounts of how youth theatre worked, how the set designs came about, and what the schedule might be for the coming year. Once when Jerome took Tia Maria to a play created by a youth theatre that included gays and lesbians, she was silent on the way home. Several weeks later, she asked Jerome to answer some questions about how that theatre had come about, where the young people came from, and what his assessment of their work had been. Such conversations of give-and-take did not come about suddenly or around only one topic. The two of them had a long-standing deep respect that went back to Tia Maria's visit to the Bronx. As they both grew older, this respect remained, and each valued what the other thought and said.

Zinnia Mae had little of this kind of consistency with Donna or the twins until she herself had work and a community sense of belonging. Neither of these had been available to her in the apartment. Once she was in her own house and taking part in church and library life, she had something to share. Though her limited knowledge and understanding of technology embarrassed Melvin and Marcello, Zinnia Mae persisted on her own time and enrolled in a continuing education course at the local library on internet communication technologies. As her children developed interests, Zinnia Mae showed them that she wanted to stay in close touch with what they were doing.

Each parent had a different way of keeping up with the children. Tia Maria allowed no technologies in her house that she did not know how to use. Jerome went to the library or worked in friends' houses when he needed the computer for homework. Because Tia Maria proscribed cellphones in the house, Jerome learned to turn off his phone as he entered the apartment building. His friends knew they had to call him on the house phone at Tia Maria's.

Rebecca and Mark had strict rules from Etta about when they could watch television and when friends could call them on their cellphones. Though Etta knew she had limited ability to monitor what the children watched on their computers, she insisted they keep the doors to their rooms open. Aside from sports events, Cindy and Martin generally proscribed watching television on weekends. Unless the entire family was involved, no one watched DVDs at home. These parents were aware of the powers of technology to divert the allegiance of their children and to distract their visual, verbal, and cognitive attention when they were at home.

The stories of Zinnia Mae and her children, Martin and Cindy and their children, Jay and Bernardo, along with those of others from Trackton and Roadville in the following chapters, give us more than the usual broad outlines of child development and language socialization. They reveal cross-generational changes in arrangement and uses of family time, household and yard space and furnishings, and types of adult–child projects. Rules and routines impact how children and parents spend stretches of time free from school or employment.

In the 1970s, family and neighborhood life had generated multiple opportunities for talk and action centered on need, ready tools, local open spaces, and close-up models. But with each new decade, families did not generate the human resources to provide the quantity and quality of talk and experience necessary to socialize children for adaptive competence. Formal schooling did not keep up with the rapid increase in scientific discovery or the accelerating interest of young people in technology, arts, and design. State and federal guidelines, as well as school budget cutbacks, reduced creative approaches to school subjects. Preparation for standardized tests dominated calendars from elementary through secondary school.

Informal groups and organizations made up of both peers and caregiving adults had access to stretches of time, after school and during summers, necessary for children's development in the talk and tasks of creative play and work. In these settings, young learners had the time for extended conversations, interactions with individuals of different backgrounds, and ongoing practice in honing skills related to the arts, environmental sciences, sports, and community service. These settings called on the young to join in planning, implementing, performing, and critiquing projects and programs over months and sometimes years. Here it was possible to move with adult guidance from beginning through intermediate, and sometimes advanced levels of expertise, often with the possibility of becoming a mentor to others.

Through the 1990s, families as divergent as that of Zinnia Mae, Martin and Cindy, and Jay shifted their ways of interacting with their children. Intimate strangers became a dominant force. Zinnia Mae, once she moved out of her apartment in the public housing projects, saw the offerings of the church, YMCA, and library as vital to a future of hope for Donna and the twins.

For Jerome, his keen survival instincts and good fortune in finding substitute mothers enabled him to rely on becoming "street-wise" wherever he could. In New York City, he had started early to hang out on the edges of the square where old men played chess, break dancers developed their styles, and musicians played. In Chicago, his love of drumming and dance, along with his propensity for showing off, making others laugh, and acting the fool paid off when he found his way to the youth theatre.

For the young people in coming chapters, life in community-centered organizations that operated outside of their homes and schools multiplied their strategies for mapping the future. Each one of these young people created a unique way to get around, accommodate, or reconcile their outside interests with their identities in families and school life. All of them learned to take advantage of the time and physical space the organizations provided for adults and the young to immerse themselves in joint talk and action and coordinated planning toward the same goal.

Children master the miracle of human language, so long as they are neurologically sound, their physical needs are met, and their caregivers give them a modicum of consistent love and respect, as well as give-and-take talk and shared action. Yet children's language fluency depends on their having opportunities to map themselves outside their home and school and to play roles beyond those of child or student. This kind of mapping happens in roles as performers, artists, and scientists who put their craft into public spaces, whether these be theatres, galleries, or organic farms and markets. In all of this work, responsibilities incur risks, whether performing in a controversial production for local theatre critics or making change for customers at the farmers' market. Community youth organizations widen children's sense of where language, curiosity, and imagination can take them. As they make these journeys, they face critics whose primary interest is in young people as neither child nor student but as performer.

4   Embracing talk

Robert woke to the sound of trucks backing and the loading chute scraping against the tailgate. He jumped out of bed, grabbed his jeans, struggled to put his boots on, buttoned his shirt, and reached for his hat. He and his brother were members of the local youth development group, 4-H (head, heart, hands, and health) Club, and they were to help out at the big rodeo today in Big Valley, the county seat. He had almost overslept because he had been up late last night preparing a new case for his Teen Court appearance.

Robert was the prosecuting attorney this month in Teen Court, and he was determined to get it right. His friend Ralph had been the prosecuting attorney last month. Judge Hammond, the only adult allowed in the room during the trials of youth offenders brought up for misdemeanors, had been so impressed with Ralph that he had given him a summer internship in his law office. Robert, now fourteen, was hoping for the same offer for the coming summer from this month's judge. In Teen Court, teenagers with misdemeanor offenses were tried by a jury of their peers who went through six months of training with attorneys and a judge. First-time youthful offenders, ages ten to eighteen, came before Teen Court to be tried and to accept the sanctions imposed by the jury. Teens acted as defending attorney, prosecuting attorney, bailiff, and court clerk, as well as jurors. Sanctions included community service, jury duty with Teen Court, and skills training on topics such as mediation, decision-making, anger management, and financial literacy.

Robert's mom, Lisa Dobbs, who had grown up in Roadville, ran the local theatre program for the Boys and Girls Club. She was thrilled that Robert, her shy and studious son – not at all like Richard, her younger gregarious and musical son – seemed to be happy in situations where he had to talk to people. Robert lived in his own silent world most of the time. He had been especially inclined to retreat there since Lisa's traumatic divorce in 1984 from Frank Avery, the boys' abusive alcoholic father. Once, in a fit of temper, Frank had thrown two-year-old Richard against the bedroom wall. That happened back in South Carolina when Robert was barely four years old. Richard's resulting brain damage meant that he was language-delayed and had trouble with coordination. He spent his early school years in classes for children with special needs. In his second year of elementary school, an enterprising young teacher had introduced the children to percussion instruments and musical recordings as background for their play with puzzles, blocks, and art materials. Richard developed a passion for the drums, and he soon imitated rhythms and beats of recordings he heard in class. Lisa filled the house with music, and she provided each boy with an audioplayer, music tapes, and earphones; when they came to the theatre to wait for her during rehearsals, they had their own entertainment. Richard started to talk when he was five, and within a few years, he was the most gregarious boy in his class. He left special needs classes and had only an hour of help each day from a reading specialist.

After the divorce, Lisa moved with the boys to Texas and enrolled in the local community college, where she studied speech therapy and theatre. Throughout college, she worked at a local protection center for abused women and children.

"The college classroom was the scariest place I'd ever been. The first few months, I couldn't talk to anybody and certainly didn't ever raise my hand. The paper the professor gave us the first day – he called it a 'syllabus,' something I had never heard of – made no sense to me. It looked like we had to read a book every week. I'd never in my life read a book all the way through. I failed my class that first term, but they told me I could try it again. And I did. Three years later, I started at the university."

Lisa supported herself and the boys by cleaning offices at the protection center during the night shift. The boys slept at a neighbor's house until Lisa got off work at midnight and took them home.

"I was determined to study anything that might tell me how to help Richard. That's how I ended up in speech therapy and theatre. Whenever I had the chance to act, to play a role, I could talk. Everybody else said they lost their voice when they had to get up in front of an audience. I had no trouble talkin' as long as I didn't have to be me. I was happy to be somebody else."

When Lisa left community college to attend the local state university, she took the boys with her to night classes. They sat in the back of the class with their tapeplayers, earphones, and coloring books. She worked her way up at the protection center, and when she earned a Master's degree in social work, the office hired her as a full-time caseworker. Every afternoon and on most week-ends, she worked as an assistant arts director for the Boys and Girls Club that ran a theatre program in which Richard excelled.

"There nobody ever thought of him as a 'special education kid.' Robert really admired Richard for being able to step out with his drums in front of audiences. By the time he was in middle school, Richard had bit parts in plays and mentored younger students who wanted to play drums. Everybody always talks about older kids influencing the younger ones. In my case, it's Richard who inspires Robert to come out of his shell. I don't think anyone else could do that."

Robert often went to the theatre with Richard and Lisa. He listened and clapped louder than anyone else at performances. But he never took part, in spite of Lisa's urgings. When Ralph introduced him to Teen Court, Robert saw the intricate processes of the Court and the attorneys' and judge's legal explanations as a big jigsaw puzzle. Robert wanted to find all the pieces and put them together.

When he was twelve, Robert started going with Ralph to Teen Court every week. The first few weeks, he came home discouraged, unable to understand much of what the attorneys said. Lisa suggested he keep a list of words: "Spell 'em best way you can, and we'll figure it out. Ralph will help you, I'm sure." Robert had done that and now had a small notebook almost full of words and phrases he had come to associate with legal work. He disliked having to speak in front of audiences, but he was determined to put his best effort into getting through this month's role as prosecuting attorney.

Lisa had put a down payment on a small run-down ranch twenty miles out of Big Valley when she and the boys came to Texas. Every day as she went to her work or college classes, Lisa drove them to school in the nearby town. She racked up sixty miles a day in the car. She and the boys talked, the boys read aloud to Lisa, and they spent what Lisa called the boys' "spot-on" time in planning weekends, talking about sports and 4-H Club events, and sorting out disagreements. Lisa coined this term in her counseling work, advising parents that only with time to talk, listen, think, and plan could they "spot" potential trouble in their children's lives.

The boys grew up helping Lisa raise vegetables and take care of the chickens. In 1990, when Robert was ten, the boys came home from a 4-H Club event one Saturday to find Lisa out by the barn grooming a horse. Today, Lisa told the boys, they would start learning to ride: "No point livin' in rodeo country if we can't be part of the show."

Seeing differences

Lisa Dobbs remembered a lot about Roadville. She especially remembered her mom, Sue, who had raised her three children alone after her husband died from lung cancer when Lisa was eight. Jed, her brother, was four years older than she, and Sally six years younger.

"Mom always had a way with kids; she worked in the school lunchroom, and even the rowdiest boys minded their manners when she was on the serving line. She never went to school past the eighth grade. But she put her heart and soul into pushing the importance of schooling on us kids. I don't know why her dream that we'd finish high school and go to college never took for Jed. When he quit school at sixteen, it nearly broke her heart. He was her baby boy. Sally and me – we were just her girls."

Jed had gone to work in the local garage, married and had his first child before he was nineteen. Both Lisa and Sally had finished high school, and both had Master's degrees by the time they were in their thirties. In 1990, just months before she died of breast cancer, Sue had come to Texas to see Lisa get her Bachelor of Arts degree. Three years later, Lisa completed her Master's degree.

Sally became a teacher. After she married Bob Ryan, a lawyer whose specialty was environmental law, they moved to Minnesota. Sally and Bob had two girls, each two years younger than Lisa's boys, and the two families got together at least once a year. Lisa and the boys drove to Minnesota where the families stayed at the Ryan family's cabin on a lake. Both of Sally's girls learned to read before they started school and remained inveterate readers. Ellen, the older daughter, bonded with Richard, and they emailed often about their work in local drama groups. The younger daughter, Anna, started ballet when she was four and was convinced she would someday dance in New York. Robert and Richard went fishing, teased the girls, and entertained them with stories of rodeos, rattlesnakes, and dust storms. After the visit each year, the girls retold stories from their cousins to their friends and won the coveted peer appraisal of "Awesome."

On those occasions when I joined the two families during their joint holiday, Lisa and Sally talked about how far away their lives were now from how they had grown up in South Carolina. Both women joked that they had become workaholics and "mother hens," influenced, no doubt, by the non-stop scheduling and energetic personality of their mother, Sue. Neither girl knew what happened to Jed who, in their words, had been "a disaster." They were certain that if their father had not died so early, Jed's future would have been very different. Whenever the conversation turned in this direction, Lisa said firmly: "My boys have to know that I am both mom and dad in their lives. It's just not about being male or female. It's about the kind of guide and model you can be for your kids."

When Lisa and Sally heard audiorecordings from their childhood, they laughed and told one remembered story after another. Their mother had believed in spanking, stern discipline, and strict family time at the dinner table. She had given them many adages to live by, especially about the need to "respect your elders" and "take care of things." Sally remembered waiting until she finished college to throw out some toys she had had as a child: "In my head, I could hear her saying, 'But there's still some good in that. Some child would just love to have that stuffed animal.'" Sue never understood fashion changes in toys. She never saw a videogame.

Sue died in 1990 when Robert was ten and Richard eight. Sally's girls were eight and six. All the children remembered their grandmother and the big family reunion they had back in South Carolina the year before she died. That was the year it was clear to everyone in the family that Jed had really disappeared.

No one had heard from him in years. After Jed's wife divorced him and took the kids, he went from one job to another, with alcohol and drugs in between. A sheriff in some small town in Georgia once called Sue, but the phone call was cut off before she could get any information about where Jed was or what he had done. No one in the family ever heard again from him, his former wife, or his children.

Any talk of their mother led Lisa and Sally to remember how Sue had always compared their stages of development with what she thought they should be doing at certain times: when they were "supposed" to crawl, walk, talk, and answer questions and read books. The two sisters joked that they had no idea of any such "stages" with their own children. Sally did remember the years when her daycare providers had changed schedules or raised prices. Sally had returned to full-time school or employment six months after each one of her girls was born, and both had grown up in daycare programs from the time they were infants.

Our audiotapes of the rare times Lisa and Sally had at home with their preschoolers prompted them to compare these recordings with those I had made of them at home with Sue when they were toddlers.

SALLY: Mama would always talk for us. She never let us decide what we were gonna talk about at dinner. She talked: she asked us questions; she wanted to hear what we did, what our friends did, and what our teachers did. When my family, all of us, sit down together at the table, we try to get our children to talk. We don't get as much out of them as Mama got out of us. We ask them about what they do at school, but they just shrug and look bored. I really try to follow their interests though, so I can get things at home that will interest them. Mama never did that. She just did what had to be done, and it was up to us to go along and get in the swing.

LISA: You're so right, Sally. When Mama went shopping, she looked for what we needed, not what might interest us. You know, like, when I go shopping, I'm always looking for things the boys need or will like.

SALLY: Yes, it's like with ballet and all the activities we put our kids into. They have to have more opportunities than we did. Their world will be so different from the one we had as kids or even the one we have now as adults. Look at how much change we've seen in our own adult lives. All that change is speeded up for our kids, and things are getting faster and faster. They get so much more through technology than we ever did from just being around the house and in and out of friends' houses. My kids watch TV, have all these videogames they share with their friends, and the music – first tapes, then CDs, downloads from the internet, and who knows what's next.

LISA: And both my boys, like, they actually know how to work the projection equipment and amplifiers and turntables, and all the stuff at the theatre. The music director depends on some of the kids to tell *him* how some parts of the sound system should work. They tell him when he needs to replace some piece of equipment. Young people know more than the adults who work backstage. They're always tellin' the guys that come in as sound engineers how to do things, but then I see the teenagers asking the sound crew about stuff too.

SALLY: Well, I think our girls don't get that kind of techie stuff in dance. I wish they could, but they know more about different kinds of music than we ever did, or than I do now, for that matter. And they love being with their friends, and when they're off at dance or soccer, I always know where they are and that some adult will be around. Thank goodness, I get out of school on most days about the time they do, and if I can't, then Leila, from church, takes them where they need to go, and I pick them up. But we talk all the time in the car about what they've been doing and what's coming up next. The only downside of all this is that scheduling is a nightmare. I have to think ahead for every day of every week, and now that they're older, for months ahead. Their schedules run my life more than their lives. I have to think about when I'll need time for extra grading [marking of end-of-term papers and special projects], end-of-year meetings, and parent nights plus back-to-school nights. I keep a calendar in the kitchen for them and one for me and one for Bob.

Lisa and Sally attribute the differences they see between their parenting and their mother's to their need to work and to the unknown demands of their children's futures. When they compare transcripts of audiorecordings and activity logs they made for their children during the preschool years with the occasional few they made after the children started school, they jump immediately to discuss how it is for family members to find time to talk together now. Sally is especially worried, because Bob often works late and goes out of town for several days a month. She and the girls have such hectic schedules that they eat "on the run." Sally says: "Sunday dinner? We sure talk about it, but we almost never do it. Instead, we often end up eating breakfast out on most Sundays, if we can get dressed, get to the restaurant, and still get to church on time. That means we have Sunday afternoons to do what we all have to do to catch up on what we didn't do during the week, unless, of course, the kids have something scheduled, and we have to drive them or chaperone or go watch an event. Even when we're all in the house, we scatter, each one of us to our own room, our own computer, and our own music. The girls are on their cellphones all the time, doing homework and scheduling sleepovers, visits to the mall, or get-togethers at someone's house to work on school projects."

Lisa gave up the Southern tradition of Sunday dinner when her marriage fell apart. She and the boys had hours together each week in the truck on the way to and from school and into Big Valley for special activities. On Sundays, Lisa and the boys went to early service at the church down the road and then came home to chores on the ranch. On weekends, she and the boys caught up with jobs that did not get done during the week: cleaning stalls, planting, weeding, staking plants, doing repairs at the house and barn, and grooming their horse Rosie.

Several months after one of my conversations with Lisa and Sally about what they remembered of their childhood lives and how they compared their mother's ways of raising children with their own, I asked Robert how he would feel about my sharing with his mom parts of the activity log he kept for me. Robert loved to write, and soon after he started school, he kept a log of his activities for which I paid him a small monthly allowance. He could pick and choose the pages he wanted me to read, and we talked about them during quiet time in the garden, out at the barn, or whenever I drove him back and forth to Teen Court. Robert agreed that I could show Lisa a selection he chose of entries in his activity logs.

Lisa and I sat around the dining table, drinking coffee, as she read the parts of the logs Robert had selected for her to see. When she finished, she went to the sink and stood looking out the window at the barn for what seemed a long time. "You know, really, the only part of this I think I actually already knew is the part where he talks about stuff that we have to do together to keep the ranch going and some things about events and stuff we do because his brother does music at the theatre. I do know his homework stuff, because we work on that together a lot, but not really all that much, because we're both always trying to help Richard with his homework."

She looked through Robert's log again and turned to me: "What happens, though, when parents and kids don't have something like a ranch or a farm or 4-H or when parents don't really get into what their kids like and do, you know, like Richard's theatre stuff or Teen Court or even 4-H Club? When do parents and kids talk if they never *work* on something together and end up feeling like they've played and had fun?[1] I just wonder if they ever have anything to talk about?"

Home at work

On the ranch, Lisa, Robert, and Richard had the garden, chickens, a goat, and Rosie, their horse. When Robert was thirteen and Richard eleven, Lisa bought another horse. They also boarded a horse for a neighbor down the road. From the time Robert was eight, Lisa insisted that he would get half the money from boarding the horse only if he kept the records of expenses and income related to the neighbor's horse. For a 4-H project, Robert had ordered and put together a tiny greenhouse in which they could raise seedlings for vegetables they planted in the garden each spring. Lisa helped him plan, order what he needed, and put it together. Lisa taught Robert how to order seeds, and when the 4-H Club did a special project on organic vegetables, Robert became one of the first students in his classroom to know the pros and cons of "going organic." After they bought the goat at a 4-H Club fair, the boys had to build a fence around the garden.

When Robert was placed in the class for gifted and talented students his fifth year in school, Lisa was proud and curious. The teacher commended Robert for his organizational skills, writing talent, quiet way of helping others, and conscientious approach to homework. She said Robert did not talk much in class, but he was "very articulate" in his writing.

Lisa was surprised that anyone would ever describe Robert in this way. He said little at home, especially in contrast to Richard, who kept getting in trouble at school and in the theatre for talking too much and listening too little. Lisa asked me if the transcripts from audiorecordings of youngsters their age looked any different from those recorded of her boys. After removing all identifying information, I showed her four transcripts from families that, like Lisa, described themselves as "pretty much lower middle class, and tryin' to get to be *really* middle class."

Lisa had once said of herself: "Maybe I should just say I'm poor-middle class, if there is such a thing. I say this, because I don't want to describe myself as low class or actually really poor. I've been there, and that's not where I am. Money's always tight, that's for sure, but not like it has been in the past. I know what it is not to have a roof over your head or food on the table. We have a mortgage and all the usual bills, sure, but when I think about those years when the boys were little and we were with Frank back in the Carolinas, I KNOW I'm not poor now, and I never want my boys to know what poverty is really like."

As a social worker whose clients included children from families with an abusive spouse or parent, few prospects for a future, and a child with special needs, Lisa had sensitivities that made her especially loved by her clients. Many of them had children who got into trouble repeatedly – shoplifting, playing truant, and ignoring the local county curfew placed on all teens for school nights. Parents told her all the time that they had no idea where their children went after school. Lisa lamented that young people "get no respect, no attention – all they know is to get into trouble. Then some adult *has* to pay attention to them."

Though we had often reviewed my audiotapes together over the years, it took a particularly troubling incident in the life of one of Robert's good friends at school for Lisa to reflect with me "just what showing respect" might mean with children. Robert's friend was picked up by the sheriff for driving and drinking when he was fourteen. When the news got out at school, Robert had come home that day unusually agitated, yelling and behaving in ways Lisa had not seen since their lives had straightened out once they got to Texas and away from Frank.

I happened to be there that day. The boys had asked me to come for a rodeo event that week. Richard and I were out in the barn when we heard Robert shouting at his mother. Richard put down the pitchfork, went to the door of the barn and listened; a look of terror spread across his face. He began to whimper; soon the air was still and quiet. We walked hand in hand to the kitchen door. Robert and his mom were sitting at the kitchen table. Lisa nodded and asked us to join them. She put her finger on the side of Robert's cheek: "Just a minute, love."

She turned to Richard: "Robert's friend has had a bad time, and we're talking. Can you sit here and listen with us? Do you want to, or do you and Shirley want to check on Rosie's saddle part? Mr. Lee brought it back from being repaired today."

Richard looked at Robert, who had his head down on his arms on the table, then at his mom. He turned to me: "Let's go see Rosie."

An hour later when we returned, Robert and his mom had a pan of cornbread in the oven, leftovers from last night on the stovetop, and the table was set. After dinner when the boys were in bed, Lisa filled me in on what she had learned from listening to Robert. They had ended up talking about Teen Court and why Robert had been so angry when he learned that his friend might not have his case go to Teen Court.

Lisa pulled out the transcripts I had given her as samples of the talk of other families with their older children and adolescents. "As Robert and I talked, some of these transcripts were running in the back of my mind. There's not much here for some of these kids. These can't tell the whole picture. When do these families do stuff together? They're probably not recording those times. For me and my kids, we talk most of the time while we're workin'. We talk about work on the ranch, things that happen in the community, and what's coming up at the Club [Boys and Girls Club], theatre, and soccer season. These families must do that kind of stuff too, but that's not here – they do lousy data [do not keep regular and accurate language data recordings and logs]!"

I agreed that families differed greatly on the care and attention that went into their audiorecordings, but said that the ones I had shown her were pretty typical of single-parent homes or families in which both parents worked, in some cases, two jobs each. All those I had shown her were from families that lived in either houses or condos in urban or suburban areas, and they hired cleaning and gardening services to clean their houses and to take care of their yards. Adults and children had few occasions to plan and work together and to believe that they had joint investments in the family.

Lisa thought a minute or so before telling me the story of one of her young clients. She called him Andre. Lisa had brought the boy to her ranch one day when she came back to pick up something she needed at the Boys and Girls Club. Andre's probation officer had recommended that the twelve-year-old be assigned for community service to the Club after he was charged for a third time with vandalism for spray painting street signs around town. Lisa took Andre to the barn, where she had baskets of potatoes she and the boys had dug last fall. Andre asked, "What's that?" Not knowing at first what he meant, she followed his gaze to the potatoes. She learned that he knew potatoes only as French fries or "jackets." Andre picked up some of the potatoes: "They so small, they can't be jackets you put stuff in."

As Lisa told me this bit of story about Andre, her line of reasoning came through as she puzzled aloud: "This means he probably doesn't know that 'green onions' [spring onions] have any relationship to those onion slices on his burgers at McDonald's. He's got no idea about baby chicks, what kind of grooming the horses need in winter and summer, and lots of stuff about how things that are alive grow up, develop, and do different things at different points along the way. My boys, even Richard, get this every year, just by all the things we have to do around here on the ranch."

Andre's accidental visit to the ranch gave Lisa a new philosophical take on what had previously been to Lisa and her boys simply the work that came with the repetitiveness of seasons, chores, and the work of the ranch, along with their respective dedications to Teen Court, 4-H life, and Richard's music and theatre. Lisa now saw some connection between all this work and features that had come to characterize the boys' ways of relating to the world. She said she understood now where Robert's organizational skills might come from, and she looked with new appreciation at Richard's ability to size up the situation at the kitchen table on the day Robert blew up about what might happen to his friend. Richard read the scene as he might have one at the theatre and realized that the dramatic peak of the crisis had passed. Robert did not need to go over his friend's situation again in front of us.

Lisa was now seeing a new side of both boys' skills and talents. She knew she depended on them and what this dependence meant to her life. Responsibilities at home, in school, and with their chosen after-school activities increased each year. Every new project brought an increase in the number of roles in which the boys had to make quick judgments, strategize, coordinate what they had to do with the amount of time available, and figure out how to ask for help from adults they trusted and who trusted them.

Being together

The move out of the housing projects that Zinnia Mae had wished for came in the spring of 1990 when her daughter Donna was seven and the twins five. In downtown Atlanta, an interracial church and two community organizations had joined forces to renovate small single-family homes and to anchor what the biracial church hoped would be a model plan for turning around highly troubled inner-city communities. Zinnia Mae's social worker helped her get one of the houses and buy used furnishings for it. She also introduced her to an older woman in the neighborhood who knew a lot about planting flowers and gardens. Zinnia Mae and the children slowly began to attend more activities, religious, social, and entrepreneurial, at the church. She enrolled the boys in "Johnny Jump-ups," the creative movement program for preschoolers that met at the church three times a week.

Her first summer in the neighborhood, Zinnia Mae started working a few hours a week at the church's second-hand clothes closet. She enrolled Donna and the boys in Bible School. Several times that summer, a church member gathered children from the church for an afternoon visit to the local library. Librarians, hoping to attract parents whose children would be entering Head

Start preschool soon, helped the children choose books, read aloud with them, and showed them how to make puppets from brown paper bags.

Soon after Zinnia Mae's move to the neighborhood, I arrived on a sweltering Tuesday afternoon just as she and the children were setting off together for the air-conditioned library. That day, Mrs. Zimmer, a Head Start teacher Zinnia Mae had met at the church, was volunteering, and she asked each of the children to pick a book. The children knew this routine by now. Marcello took his mother's hand, and Melvin grabbed my hand and headed for the section on cars. Melvin chose a book after closely examining three. When Mrs. Zimmer called, the children, clutching their books, gathered around her. They knew she would choose three of their selections to read aloud to the group. Adults sat in an outer circle around the children. Mrs. Zimmer sang in the choir at church, so I should have anticipated the captivating quality of her voice, shouting out orders as a pirate captain or whispering softly as a baby bird in search of its mother. Occasionally, she would reach down by her side and pull a puppet or prop from what she called her "bag of tricks," a wooden framed basket with an embroidered cover. She called wiggling, restless children to her lap from time to time. She let the children hold the book she was reading up high so that others could see the pictures. For books with repeated phrases, she stopped to ask one of the children to lead the repetitions.

Before we left the library that day, Mrs. Zimmer asked all the children to choose one book to take home with their parents and then to choose another in secret while their parents sat with their eyes closed. The children had five minutes to make their choices, and each "secret" choice went into the paper bag that Mrs. Zimmer had for each child with his or her name carefully written across the top. The last event of the afternoon was the ritual of checking books out. Then Mrs. Zimmer and the children did a "reading" of all the names on the bags lined up at the doorway. As each child left the library, Mrs. Zimmer stood in the doorway, identified one letter in the name, circled it in red, and asked the child to repeat after her: "This is an A [or any vowel], and it is the third [or correctly ordered] letter in my name."

Walking home that day, Zinnia Mae asked me if I had brought any of her childhood tapes. I had no tapes that day, but I had some transcripts, which were much less interesting to her. She asked: "Did I ever get to do that?" I asked what she meant. "Talk books and do puppets." I reminded her that her grandmother's life was busy in the garden, kitchen, neighborhood, and she was already three years old when I first went to Trackton in 1969. We both kept silent about the fact that, so far as we knew, no one in her family had ever learned to read or owned a book other than the Bible. Both of us also knew that during her years with the children in the housing projects, Zinnia Mae almost never introduced books to the children or talked to them about anything except what was on television.

From that day of the library visit forward until the children entered secondary school, on each of my visits, we all went to the shopping mall to visit the bookstore and to select with each of the children two books. We tried to keep up a ritual of reading together, with Zinnia Mae and the children taking equal parts when the children were younger. As Donna grew older, she sometimes picked books she could read to us on her own. Zinnia Mae always sat close by her during these performances and mouthed the words with Donna. Whenever I visited during the years when the children were in primary school, they insisted on hearing sampled portions of my recordings of their mother when she was a little girl back in Trackton and of themselves reading to me and their mother in my prior visits. By the time Donna reached middle school, the living room had two shelves of books. We found a second-hand bookcase at the church store. Zinnia Mae and the children brought home books from the library each week.

Of the twins, Marcello developed language more slowly than Melvin, and both toddlers had trouble staying focused on much of anything for more than a few minutes. In association with a local dance school run by one of the church members, Head Start had put in place a creative dance and movement program that followed up on aspects of Johnny Jump-ups that Zinnia Mae's twins had attended. Head Start children created shows for the parents, and for special performances, older children from a nearby modern dance academy joined them. Teachers encouraged the parents to have the children demonstrate patterns of movement, sequences of steps, and hand gestures at home. Parents could also take home cassette tapes of the children's favorite music from their dance classes at school. Marcello began what was to become a long interest in dance, and he later became a lead dancer with the modern dance academy. In 1999, when he was fourteen, the regional summer dance camp run jointly by the church and several dance and martial arts academies enlisted him as an apprentice teacher.

From all those who moved into the upper levels of their program, the troupe required that they go through professional development seminars to prepare to work with younger children. So fearful was Marcello of being teased because of his hesitancy with speech that he almost stopped dancing rather than be forced to stand and talk before younger dancers. But he loved to dance. He stuck with the program, knowing he could count on having a job at the summer dance camp.

The next summer when Marcello was an apprentice teacher, a visitor from Ohio came to the camp. The next day, he stopped by the church office and asked about how he might locate Marcello's parents. The youth minister helped him find Zinnia Mae at the church's second-hand sales shop where she now worked. The youth minister explained that the visitor, a friend of the pastor, had met Marcello at the camp and wanted to talk with Zinnia Mae about the boy's future. After complimenting Zinnia Mae on her son, the visitor explained that he represented a fine arts boarding school affiliated with a small university in

Columbus, Ohio. He asked if she would consider having Marcello come to their school for next summer's term. While there, he could audition for a spot in the boarding school for his final two years of secondary schooling. The university would provide a scholarship to support Marcello's education, if he continued to keep his grades up and to do well in auditions throughout secondary school. With her pastor, Zinnia Mae and Marcello flew to Ohio to visit the boarding school late that fall.

The next summer, Marcello went to Ohio for the summer term. He did well in the audition and stayed on for his final two years of secondary schooling. Though he had struggled in his academic classes in Atlanta, dance centered his life. His first year away from home, he was homesick and resentful of the tough academic challenges of the boarding school. Adjustment came slowly as he made more friends and settled in to the regimen of classes, workouts, dance lessons, practice, rehearsals, and performances. When he graduated in 2003, a delegation from the church, along with Zinnia Mae, Donna, and Melvin, came to celebrate not only Marcello's graduation but also his acceptance into a Chicago-based professional dance company. He had decided not to attend the university, but to continue in dance.

In Chicago Marcello met Francisco, a fellow dancer and also the director of a dance studio attached to a private secondary school in a wealthy suburb. Three years later, Marcello and Francisco bought a condo together on the south side of Chicago. When the three of us went out to dinner together after a performance in Chicago in late 2009, Marcello teased that Francisco could do the talking, and he would do the eating. They were thinking about starting a restaurant when the time came that they were too old to dance professionally. Marcello quipped: "Yeah, he can make the money to support the dance school I'm gonna start for kids, and they won't be RICH kids neither."

Francisco laughed. He turned to me as though he thought he owed me an explanation. "Rich families have troubles too, I've learned. I grew up pretty lucky; my grandparents came to New York from Puerto Rico and started a carpet business. When my brothers and me were growin' up, we worked there, when we were not out doin' graffiti. We had it easy in terms of money, but when my youngest brother was just three years old, they said he was autistic. No amount of money could make him normal. He never learned to talk, and just takin' care of him took most of my mom's life away. The rest of us did what we could, but you know, teenagers never really get into the sufferin' anybody else has. I look back now, and I remember that rich kids have needs; we just don't see 'em when we focus only on poor kids. Ten of the kids in our dance school's early program are either autistic or have some kind of attention deficit, or so their doctors tell the parents. We think somehow dance is helpin' these kids."

Marcello looked at me and responded to Francisco: "Yeah, but there's lots more poor kids who need help than rich kids. We both know that."

Melvin and Donna stayed in school in Atlanta, where Donna struggled through middle school, skirting on the edge of trouble with juvenile authorities for playing truant and shoplifting. She dropped out of school at sixteen and moved out of the house. Melvin, feeling excluded from Marcello's life of success far away from Atlanta and sensing Zinnia Mae's pain over losing Donna, stayed on, squeaked through high school, and went to work in an auto detailing shop that specialized in cleaning, waxing, and polishing vintage cars.

Though his mom had never owned a car, Melvin had grown up as a fan of old cars. One of the businessmen from the church had let Melvin hang out around his gas station and auto repair shop from the time he was fourteen on the condition that Melvin not drop out of school. When Melvin turned fifteen, the owner let him work three hours a week cleaning up around the shop. At sixteen, Melvin increased his work to twenty hours a week, and he helped more and more with the auto detailing. The business owner had taken Melvin and Zinnia Mae to the bank and opened a savings account into which he put half of Melvin's earnings each week. "You'll be wantin' your own car. Here's the down payment startin' up. Don't forget you're workin' toward something."

God talk

Zinnia Mae's early childhood surrounded her with the narrative scripting of events that her grandmother provided for her and her blind mother. The family and neighbors said that Zinnia Mae talked early and never stopped until she reached the upper grades of elementary school. By this time, she drew the taunts of the school children, who called attention to her obesity, large breasts, and way of walking they called "waddle." Through middle school and into her teens, Zinnia Mae grew silent and sullen, talking to no one in Trackton. She stayed indoors or in the backyard garden. When she became pregnant with Jerome and he was taken away to live with her sister Rosa, Zinnia Mae seemed to stop talking altogether. School became more of a disaster, socially and academically for her, and no one was surprised when she dropped out. When she left for Atlanta shortly thereafter, no one in Trackton seemed surprised.

When I found Zinnia Mae in Atlanta in 1985 and resumed regular contact with her, she still seemed hesitant to talk. Her children grew up hearing conversations primarily from television and during the occasional visits Zinnia Mae had from a friend or the social worker.

When she and the children moved to downtown Atlanta into their own home, Zinnia Mae confided in me that she was having a hard time adjusting to the talk that went on in the second-hand store at the church, before and after church, and on the street in her neighborhood. She listened, nodded, and only occasionally joined in, and only then when someone addressed her directly. She told me:

"Before where I lived, and when I was growin' up, I couldn't talk to people. Now I wanna learn how."

I responded: "You can talk, you know that. You'll get used to what's going on in this new environment."

She did. Zinnia Mae found for herself the right impetus and the best listener. Soon after she moved to her little house, the pastor asked her to join a prayer group that met several mornings a week before the second-hand shop opened. Though hesitant, she went along. The youth minister saw the prayer session as a time to learn to "talk to God, who's the best listener you'll ever find." The group prayed together, each member contributing in relay fashion, and as the weeks went by, Zinnia Mae said she realized she could "talk to God" at home too. She taught the children to pray, repeating much of what the minister had said to the prayer group, and each night, she did a "prayer talk" with the children about what they had to be thankful for in their day, what they had to be sorry about, what they wanted God to do to help someone else, and how they wanted God to help them be stronger.

Zinnia Mae proudly audiorecorded many of these nightly sessions. In the first six months, the length of her utterances averaged forty words, and the utterances were repetitive of the prayer sessions. By the end of the first year, as the children began to contribute narratives to insert into the prayers, these talks with God became longer and included more complex patterns of weaving together wishes, promises, and stories of why God should listen. Eight-year-old Donna used these bedtime prayers as the means to tell her mother tales from school.

DONNA: Ma, tell God what I did today.
ZINNIA MAE: You tell 'im. He be listenin'.
DONNA: Okay, God, Jamie, you know, he be at my school. He ain't listenin' to the teacher, and he be havin' to go the principal office all the time.
ZINNIA MAE: Ask God to help Jamie find a friend who could play kickball with him at school and do sleepovers.
DONNA: I tol' 'im I hated 'im.
ZINNIA MAE: You know God don't want us to hate nobody. Why you hate Jamie?
DONNA: He pulled my hair and threw sand on the playground.
ZINNIA MAE: Well, you better aks God to forgive you for sayin' you hate anybody. Hate don't do nobody no good, 'specially the person doin' the hatin'. Pastor Lou say we gotta turn hate into love; there be too much hatin' in this world and not enough lovin' and carin'.

On several of my visits, Zinnia Mae asked me to listen to the tapes of her prayers with the children. As Donna grew older and drew away from her mother and brothers, often not showing up at either school or home, Zinnia Mae told me she "prayed hard and talked, talked, talked to God."

"What do you ask him to do?" I asked.

She got up, went to the window, and stood silently staring out.

"You don't need to answer. I understand," I said.

"No, I'm thinkin' 'bout what Pastor Lou said in las' Sunday sermon. He say everything, EVERYTHING is in God's hands. But we gotta know prayer have, he called it, 'spotty results.' He say what matter is God wanna hear from me, and I gotta be listenin' for his whispers. I listen now for him to whisper to me 'bout Donna."

I had noticed how much Zinnia Mae's language had changed since she moved from the apartments, spent time at her job in the second-hand shop, and went to church activities, the library, and YMCA events for parents. She watched Mrs. Zimmer read with the children, lead them to recognize letters, and help them take ownership over books and reading. Zinnia Mae had learned when she first had the chance to move to the house what a long-term loan meant, and what the conditions of payment had to be. She had to accept at the outset that staff from the bank and the church came to the house on a regular basis to help with maintenance questions, to review paperwork related to insurance and payments, and to offer assistance with maintaining the front and back yards of the house.

She went to sessions at the church that explained more terms and ideas foreign to her: *payroll tax, supplemental insurance, deductibles on insurance plans, property taxes, health directives*. Around each election time, the church held informational sessions with local and state candidates, helped those who had never registered do so, and arranged transportation for those who needed it to get to the polls on election day. Within the work of the second-hand shop, clients and salespeople negotiated prices, arrangement of the goods, and timing of sales. She had seen what an airline ticket looked like only when she and Marcello went to Ohio the first time and when she flew to Chicago for Jerome's wedding. She had consulted her pastor at the church and friends about the decision to let Marcello leave home to go to school. She had gone to deacons in the church to ask them to help her understand bank rules on the joint savings account she and Melvin had set up.

When Zinnia Mae moved from the housing projects in 1990, she and her children left a world in which she had almost no decision-making power. She and they entered an expanding universe of opportunities for seeing how other people talked about how they made decisions and how sources of information were available to those who knew how to find them. Zinnia Mae learned to think of herself as being informed and in control. The church's unique arrangement with the city and local banks for inner-city neighborhood renewal and community development meant that she did not have to wait until she made costly mistakes before someone would help her. The church and bank staff complimented Zinnia Mae, as her social worker often had, on her organizational talents. She used empty laundry detergent boxes to store paperwork, inserting large pieces of cardboard to separate her papers in different categories: school, dance, bus tickets, Christmas lists, insurance, house, etc. Her first Christmas in the house, the social worker, now her friend, brought Zinnia Mae a small rolling metal file cabinet with a huge red bow on top. Zinnia Mae and the children spent Christmas Day sorting out how its dividers worked, where to store the key, and where they should keep the file cabinet in the house.

Poverty and physical isolation during her first years in Atlanta had intensified the habits of silence Zinnia Mae had developed since early puberty. Her diabetes, obesity, and continual health crises had furthered her sense of help-lessness. The move into a community of respect that nurtured her sense of responsibility had done much more than give her a new roof over her head, a job, and a renewed spiritual life.[2] Zinnia Mae had gained people to talk with and to listen to her. She had acquired models and means of aspiration, and, most importantly, a sense of control over her life that enabled her to manage her diabetes and weight.

Advisors, formal and informal, had immersed Zinnia Mae in the kind of questions and explanations that she needed to manage herself as a parent, homeowner, neighbor, resident, and citizen. She learned to ask questions for herself and to encourage clients at the second-hand shop and parents she met at Head Start and the library to ask questions. As her children grew older, she needed to ask more and tell less. When a member of the church offered to give her a computer to use at home, she worked side by side with Melvin after they agreed that he would give her lessons twice a week for six weeks. Thereafter, she took classes at the library to learn software programs friends at the second-hand shop said could be useful to her. Though her weak skills in reading and her failing eyesight limited her eventual success with the technology, she learned enough to engage in conversations with her co-workers at the church about things she saw on the internet.

"Giving access and incentive" turns up repeatedly as a dictum in policy discussions about ways to alleviate poverty and to "get these people on their feet." The story of Zinnia Mae and her children portrays a unique combination of factors that lie outside governmental policy initiatives. The central threads of her story are the good fortune of having a knowledgeable and caring social worker and of undertaking an integrative affiliation with a unique church community.

When Zinnia Mae looked back on these fortunate turns in her life, she issued a strong caveat: "You gotta remember I grew up listenin' to a granny who talked all the time about everything goin' on around us. I always knew how to use my mouth, I knew how to look around me and see what might happen. I just didn't know how to make decisions. I let things happen to me. When I came here [to this church], they got me started talkin'. I thought they was tellin' me to talk *to* God. Then I finally heard 'em saying we need to talk *with* God. I got it. And that the way I see life now. It be the *with* that matters, what you do *with* life, not what you let it do *to* you. What you talk *with* your kids about, not what you talk *to* 'em about."

5   Lines of vision

Storytellers "talk on against time." Their stories depend on the possibilities that emerge when characters free themselves from antecedent conditions and envision new beginnings. Listeners want storytellers to put off the certainty of closure, and they distrust "happily ever after" endings for the strangers they meet in stories. The flame that consumes the fate of these strangers yields the warmth they desire in their own "shivering" lives.[1]

The characters in the stories told here are themselves storytellers who work against time: the past they leave behind and the future they envision ahead.

I see it in my head

In 1985, I reconnected with Zinnia Mae after some years of not knowing where she was. She was living in a high-rise public housing apartment in Atlanta with her three babies. My fieldnotes from one of my visits that year bring back a typical scene.[2]

Zinnia Mae searched through the kitchen drawer looking for another wooden spoon she knew she had. Two-year-old Donna was playing in the living room with one wooden spoon, and now she wanted a second. The twins, Marcello and Melvin, barely two months old, lay nearby on a pallet of blankets on the living-room floor. Donna was wailing. Zinnia Mae found the spoon, placed some cracker chips in a plastic bowl, returned to the living room, and set the bowl down on the floor beside Donna.

Zinnia Mae's favorite soap opera was playing on television. She turned to me: "Mind if I just watch this? Only a minute more." Before I could answer, she turned her attention back to her soap opera. I watched Donna propel cracker bits across the floor with one of the wooden spoons.

In 2004, nearly two decades later, Zinnia Mae and I sat around the kitchen table in her little house in a downtown Atlanta renewal zone. We were listening to an audiorecording from back in her old apartment. We could hear two-year-old Donna talking to her doll baby as she played on the living-room floor. I had placed a microphone on her shirt, hoping to pick up some of her self-talk over the background television noise.

My fieldnotes accompanying the audiotape showed that Donna was using one of her mother's shoes as a bed for her doll. She had torn off parts of paper napkins to create covering for the doll.

DONNA: Sleep now [hums]. Tuck you in, Mamma will. Stop turnin'. Stay here. You want more cover? [She leaves her baby to run to the kitchen. She finds a plastic fork and breaks the prongs. Back on the living room floor, she set her imaginary table with the fork pieces on part of another napkin she has laid out near the doll's shoe bed. Donna looks up at me. Zinnia Mae is absorbed in the plot of her soap opera.]

DONNA: You watch her now, she don't fall out.

Zinnia Mae listened intently to the audiorecording of Donna talking to her doll. When she heard Donna caution me to watch the doll in her bed, Zinnia Mae chuckled: "Remember first time you come, I tol' you she didn't ever talk. Now I see I jus' couldn't hear her."

We both laughed as we recalled my first visit to her in the public housing apartments. That time now seemed so long ago.

As Zinnia Mae listened to the snippet again, she tilted her head, smiled, and said: "Yeah, I 'member now I tell her when I put the boys on the bed for naptime: 'Watch the boys. Don't let 'em fall off.'"

I showed Zinnia Mae some of the approximately 1,000 lines of notes she had made of Donna and the twins over the years while she lived in the apartment. I had visited her there about every six months during those years. She remained on welfare, unsuccessful in finding a job, getting the children into daycare, or securing a place in kindergarten for Donna.

When we finished going over the notes from those years, I packed them away. I was searching around for the case for the tapes and audiorecorder when Zinnia Mae put her hand on my arm: "You know, I know the past was really there. But when I hear it now – here in this house, my kids grown 'n everything, it sound like TV – not like me. I see where me and my kids are today, 'n all I can say is 'Thank you, God.'"

While we read through transcripts and fieldnotes, Zinnia Mae remembered details. She had sold the kitchen table a month before I first visited in 1985. We set my suitcase across two chairs for me to have a writing surface. My notes recorded her explanation to me at that time: "Never used it much anyway. Donna don't care where she eat, and I just sit in my chair, my plate on my lap."

She remembered how each night for the years they lived in the apartment, she had put the twins to bed on pallets on the floor. Donna slept with her.

Zinnia Mae asked if I had with me any audiorecordings of her grandmother back in the kitchen in Trackton. I had brought along two, hoping I could get Melvin to listen to his great-grandmother and his mom on the tapes, but he was at work at the auto detailing shop that day.

Zinnia Mae's grandmother, like most of her neighbors back in Trackton, had kept a little garden behind the house. Vegetables always seemed available to pick, clean, pare, and cook. Zinnia Mae's grandmother talked while she cooked, narrating and commenting on the shape of turnips, her dislike of ladybugs [ladybirds], the need for a new stew pot, and her desire for more onions next year. Even as a toddler, Zinnia Mae had had tasks in the kitchen and garden. Zinnia Mae and I both remembered that for years she had loved to try to capture ladybugs brought into the house on the vegetables.

For the recording I chose for us to listen to, my fieldnotes showed that as her grandmother washed the turnip greens and baby turnips from the garden, she handed the largest turnip to Zinnia Mae, then four years old. Her grandmother gave her a potato peeler.

"Hold it straight and move the peeler. Like this [Grandmother demonstrates with her peeler], and move it around in a circle. See the clock [points to the big kitchen clock on the wall] like that [making a circle with her hand in the air]. You cut yourself, don't be thinkin' I got those bandaids like Annie Mae [a neighbor] if'n you bleed. You do it right." [Zinnia Mae struggles to hold the turnip and move the peeler. Her grandmother goes to the front room, calling back to Zinnia Mae]. "I'm gonna dump this water on my fern, and you stay right there. [She shouts to some men from the neighborhood who are sitting on the front porch.] Come in here, one of you. Get this bucket of water; put it on that fern."

"Like this?" [Zinnia Mae runs after her grandmother to show her that she has stripped away one round of peel.]

"Good, baby, good. Jus' keep holdin' it straight, not with that point up stickin' in the turnip. Do like I show you. Watch yourself now, and let me get that water boilin' 'n clean dem greens."

In contrast to tapes I had made of Zinnia Mae as a child with her grandmother back in Trackton, the tapes that she made of her own children's talk while they were living in the apartment were barely audible. Through the television noise, we could make out only a few words from Donna. The apartment had few toys but lots of kitchen and household items from which Donna created fantasy scenes for her doll – recasting bits of drama she had seen on television and replaying what she saw her mother say and do with the twins.

While we listened to audiotapes of Zinnia Mae as a toddler, memories of her grandmother and others in Trackton came flooding back to both of us. Zinnia Mae recalled what a jokester her uncle had been and how he had always seemed to be around whenever an especially good meal was about to go on the table. He and her grandmother teased one another endlessly, especially when garden weeds were high, and her grandmother told her uncle, "Do a little work for all you eat." We remembered the antics of neighbors, children's games on the open plaza, and the constant buzz of cars, bicycles, tricycles, and pull toys.

One day in the midst of our reveries about the past, Zinnia Mae said abruptly: "Now I 'member how lonely I live back at that apartment. I just cover it up by eatin' – and watchin' TV, of course." She shot a quick grin my way, knowing how much I had wished that television had not been there to spoil the quality of her audiorecordings. She continued: "Days would go by. If'n one of my friends from when I worked in that restaurant when I first come to Atlanta didn't come by, I didn't talk to nobody but the kids. I couldn't get out, the elevator be workin' 'bout half the time. Too dangerous down in the park outside, so I don't see nobody."

I asked: "When do you think you did most of your talkin' to Donna and the boys when they were just babies and toddlers?" She shrugged her shoulders: "Not much anytime, now that I think back."

We both observed from her recordings, however, that during the relatively few times someone else was in the apartment and the television was turned off, Zinnia Mae did talk to and about her children. She narrated in some of the same ways her grandmother had done: giving directions and asking rhetorical questions in the midst of a running commentary on what her children were doing. Transcripts of these occasions showed that she seemed to turn away from her visitor to ask the children direct questions about what they were doing and to offer them new items, such as magazines and fast-food giveaway toys or utensils for their play.

One day when one of her girlfriends and I were both visiting, Zinnia Mae had given Donna a scarf to use for dress-up. As Donna pranced about with the scarf draped around her, Zinnia Mae asked: "You think you gonna be in a show or you goin' out when you dress like that. Huh? You like that woman on TV, ain't you?"

She continued to direct Donna as though she were one of the soap opera characters, describing future scenarios that Donna in her current dancing mode might join.

Similar narration came through whenever I read books with the children during my visits. When they looked at illustrations in the books, they asked, "What dat?" or they inserted the figure or item into a brief narrative: "She goin' in her car. She buyin' ice cream. Dat her dog?"

Zinnia Mae always watched with interest as we read, and some of her recordings indicated that she occasionally reread the books with the children when I was not there. Though she remembered learning to read in church, sitting by her grandmother, she did not seem to enjoy reading. It was years later that the doctor treating her diabetes set up an appointment for her to have her eyes tested. Even when she started wearing glasses, her vision was not good, and she relied on the children to read to her the small print on medicine bottles and to find the Bible Scripture lesson during Sunday services.

The infrequent part-time restaurant work Zinnia Mae had when she was living in the apartment had required little of her in terms of reading, writing, or calculating. She had, however, done as her grandmother had: she kept a big calendar pinned to the wall in her kitchen. There she recorded receipt dates and amounts of her welfare check and due dates for major monthly expenses – rent, utilities, and medical bills. The location of her apartment and her own physical limitations meant that she had to shop in nearby corner stores and overnight convenience shops. There she had to pay nearly twice as much for a carton of milk as she did at the supermarket where we went whenever I visited.

Once when we drove out to the shopping center, Zinnia Mae unexpectedly pointed to a modest bungalow along the way and announced: "Someday I'm gonna have a house for me and the kids like that. I see it in my head. And see that church? I'm goin' back to church and take my kids."

Seeing toward the next generation

In Trackton, Lillie Mae Clark and her children, three boys and a girl, had lived just up the hill from Zinnia Mae's family. Her daughter, Sissy, was born the same year as Zinnia Mae. The girls were best friends through their primary and middle school years. When boys entered their lives, they both began to skip school, and the community knew trouble was brewing. Tony, Sissy's older brother, had gone off to college in 1979, and whenever he was home, he tried to talk "some sense into those girls." His efforts were futile. Sissy was pregnant by the next spring, and her son, Denny, was born just before Christmas of 1980, the same year Zinnia Mae had given birth to a baby boy (Jerome). After Zinnia Mae moved away to Atlanta, the girls stayed in touch sporadically.

In 1983, Lillie Mae left Trackton. At the time, she had a boyfriend who had worked in the textile mill for only a few years. When he lost his job, he had stopped coming by to drop off money to help with food for the children. Lillie Mae moved her family to a small community much like Trackton but closer to Alberta. The husband of a girlfriend rented her a run-down house she could afford on her welfare check while she waited for placement in public housing. Along with Lillie Mae's three younger children, Sissy, Benjy, and Lem, Lillie Mae's household also included Denny and the baby of a cousin who had moved away to Philadelphia to "get some education." Her cousin sent money to Lillie Mae each month and returned in the summers to visit the child until he was nine years old. She took him back with her that summer. She had finished college and become a music teacher.

I visited Lillie Mae's family several times each year. Her children had grown up in the 1970s with my audiorecorder and field notebook as a normal part of their environment. When Denny began to babble and do singsong repetitions of the end of utterances he heard around him, his mother, Sissy, always eager to make some money, audiotaped his language from time to time.[3] Since Lillie Mae did not work, she took Denny with her whenever she went to visit friends or family nearby. Much as Tony and Sissy had done as they were growing up in Trackton, Denny spent his early childhood hearing multi-party talk. Sissy sometimes played school, giving him crayons and paper bags and writing letters for him to trace. Lillie Mae sat Denny in her lap whenever she read the newspaper and any advertisements that came in the mail. She did not have a television until she moved into public housing when Denny was five years old.

Denny's ways of learning language during his preschool years differed relatively little from the ways in which Tony, Sissy, and the other children of Trackton had learned to talk and to become familiar with printed materials. Denny moved through three stages. His first stage was a period of repetition that began a few months after his first birthday. He picked up and repeated chunks from the end of utterances he heard in the multi-party talk around him. He followed this stage with a period in which he varied slightly these phrasal and clausal bits. Soon after his second birthday, he inserted himself into the conversations he heard going on around him, showing off his toys and striving to say things that would make adults stop their talk and pay attention to him. His biological father, who lived in Alberta, sometimes came and took the toddler to stay for a few days at a time with him. There Denny went to church with his grandparents and visited an Alberta shopping center and a large grocery store where he delighted in riding in the seat of the grocery trolley. Denny also had his first experience there with television.

Sissy went back to school after Denny was born. The next Christmas, just after Denny had his first birthday, Sissy left Denny with Lillie Mae and went to Atlanta to visit Zinnia Mae. At the local Burger King, she met Red, a twenty-two-year-old whose grandparents had come to the United States from the Dominican Republic. Red's dad had an engineering degree and ran an electronics firm in Atlanta. Red was following in his father's footsteps. He was in his final year toward a Bachelor's degree in engineering from Georgia Tech. He had stopped for a quick lunch on his way to class when he met Sissy at Burger King.

When Sissy came back from her visit to Atlanta, she announced to Lillie Mae that she was going to work harder in school. Over the next few years, she returned to Atlanta several times each year to visit Zinnia Mae. Each time Sissy and Red met at the Burger King. When she graduated from school, Sissy moved to Atlanta to find work. She left Denny behind with Lillie Mae. Sissy got a job at Burger King, quickly working her way up to manager on the evening shift. She rented a studio apartment and enrolled in a technical school. She wanted to become a medical technician, a career she had taken interest in during her pregnancy with Denny.

Sissy and Red became engaged and planned a wedding to take place early in the summer of 1990. Red insisted they both had to finish school and work long enough to pay in full for the wedding and to bring Sissy's family to Atlanta from South Carolina. Red had gone with Sissy to visit Denny at Lillie Mae's several times. He insisted now that they would take Denny to live with them after they were married. Denny called Red "Papa" and talked to him often on the phone.

After the wedding in June of 1990, Red and Sissy moved to a small town in New Jersey, where Red's uncle, a computer science engineer, had a job waiting for him. Red and Sissy drove to South Carolina in August that year on their way from Atlanta to New Jersey. Promising Lillie Mae they would bring her to see them for the Christmas holidays, they loaded Denny into the car and drove north. Red would start adoption procedures as soon as they settled in New Jersey.

By the end of the next year, Sissy came home from a doctor's visit with the news that she was pregnant. The happy news came, however, with some worrisome news. The doctors wanted her to come in the following week for some tests of her kidneys. Within a month, the couple had the grim news of renal failure.

After their healthy baby girl, Tameka, was born in early 1992, Sissy had a few months of improved health, but just before they celebrated Tameka's first birthday, Sissy's health deteriorated. The doctors determined she needed a kidney transplant, and she was put on dialysis several times each week. When they got the news that a kidney was available, Lillie Mae came to be with Sissy. Complications developed during the surgery, and Sissy never regained consciousness. She died within a week after she entered the hospital.

Red, Denny, and Lillie Mae drove together back to South Carolina for the funeral while Tameka stayed with Red's aunt. When Red and Denny returned to New Jersey, Red arranged daycare for Tameka and after-school programs with a soccer team and at the YMCA for Denny. His aunt helped out whenever Red had to stay late at work. Lillie Mae came often to visit for weeks at a time.

By the time of Lillie Mae's death in 2008, Denny had finished his Master's degree in civil engineering at the University of San Diego and was working in Seattle, Washington. Denny flew home to New Jersey when Red called with news of Denny's beloved grandmother's death. Red once again drove south for a funeral. This time both Tameka and Denny were with him for what they knew would be the family's last trip back to what had been Sissy's childhood home.

Comparative means and ends

Exasperated and angry, Denny threw down the baton, put his hands on his hips, and was about to yell at Tim, a twelve-year-old with Down syndrome, when Denny spotted the coach barreling down on him. "Denny, I suppose you're demonstrating what a bad sport does and how to get penalties in the Special Olympics? Good job. Tim, aren't you glad you have such a dramatic coach?" The coach patted Tim on the back and shot Denny an unmistakable look of caution. Chastened, Denny picked up the baton and kneeled down beside Tim and carefully demonstrated how to pass the baton in a relay.

The YMCA Leadership Club was helping to host the Special Olympics event taking place the next weekend. Denny and his sister Tameka belonged to a YMCA program that served special-needs youth from the surrounding area. Tameka was by far the more athletic of the two, but Denny had a real gift for teaching. He also had a gift for graphic design and helped Tameka learn to use several software programs. She followed her big brother whenever possible, and when he decided to defer his admission to a university in California for several years while he worked and saved money, Tameka could barely contain her delight. They watched movies together, shopped for electronics gear, and planned weekend camping trips with Red. Denny went to all of Tameka's track meets. He introduced her to algebra, graphic novels, and Harry Potter books.

When Denny went off to his first year at a university in California, Tameka and Red communicated with him by phone or email nearly every day of his first year. They told one another what they thought of articles in *Wired* and gossip they had seen on blogs about the latest software programs and rumored new products from Apple and Microsoft. Tameka was a loyal fan of Apple, her dad and brother of PCs.

When Denny came home after his first year away at the university, his old coach at the YMCA hired him to manage marketing for that summer's Special Olympics. Tameka had been given the job of helping the secretary at the YMCA order, check, and set up equipment, as well as preparing the list of judges and special guests. The administrator showed Tameka how to set up a spreadsheet and keep track of expenses. Denny helped Tameka and several older girls design posters and brochures for the Special Olympics. Denny and some of his friends trained forty young people with a variety of special needs to participate in the Special Olympics. Tameka helped out with track events whenever she finished her work at the YMCA office.

Tameka breezed through middle and secondary school and decided to attend Spellman University in Atlanta. She and her dad went back every year to see his parents and the cousins living in Georgia. Whenever they returned to Atlanta while Tameka and Denny were growing up, they had also visited Zinnia Mae, Melvin, and Donna, sometimes staying with them. They welcomed news of Marcello and how his dance career in Chicago was going, and Denny liked to spend time at the auto detailing shop with Melvin.

When Tameka went to Atlanta for her college interview, she and Donna met at a coffee shop near Spellman. Though nine years younger, Tameka had never backed down before the sometimes gruff persona Donna had adopted from early adolescence. Over coffee, Tameka teased Donna, reminding her about what a "loser" she had been as she was growing up. Donna ran with friends in a rough crowd that made fun of Tameka and Denny for the "fancy" way they talked. Donna had played truant, been held back [repeated the school year] twice, and had trouble getting through middle school.

Donna had landed in juvenile detention before she was fifteen and had painful experiences there that she never talked about. After her release, she had to meet conditions set by her probation officer, a tough woman feared by anyone who came in contact with her. Donna moved back in with Zinnia Mae and attended a secondary school designed for "troubled" youth. Donna joined the choir at Zinnia Mae's church, where she met a friend who offered to help with her homework in mathematics. Zinnia Mae stayed out of all arrangements Donna made, having resolved that now was the time when her daughter "might finally grow up."

Though not without setbacks, Donna graduated from secondary school, enrolled in a community college, and began working back at the YMCA where her little brothers had gone when they were growing up. While taking coursework to become a nursing assistant, she met a professor who told her he thought she showed good promise and should try to go on for a degree in nursing. After working for two years as a nursing assistant, Donna felt ready for university work.

When Tameka came back to Atlanta to begin her university studies at Spellman University at age seventeen, she had a scholarship and a job working ten hours each week on a research project in the chemistry department. Donna, now twenty-six, was working as a nurse, had her own apartment, and was taking extra coursework to become qualified for assignment in the neonatal unit of the city hospital.

When seeing ahead is not enough

Children who started out in Trackton and Roadville suffered the same range of setbacks as those widely reported in the media for other teenagers during the 1980s. Some, like Zinnia Mae and Sissy, chose the disruptions of teen pregnancy, school dropout, and separation from their families. Those who stayed in school had to adapt to life in desegregated and increasingly depersonalized classrooms. Children from Trackton or Roadville whose families moved into urban public housing projects had to learn to work their way through experiences with drugs, including crack cocaine, and violent unpredictable events in their neighborhoods and schools. Inequities and injustices the young could easily see, on the one hand, fed hostilities between black and white, and, on the other, created resentment toward brown newcomers from outside the United States.

In the larger towns and metropolitan areas where some Roadville and Trackton families relocated, their children met on the streets and in their classrooms peers whose families had come from Puerto Rico, the Dominican Republic, Mexico, El Salvador, and Guatemala. Gang battles, muggings, competition over girlfriends and boyfriends, and the easy draw of turf battles and drug organizations accelerated in the second half of the 1980s. Youth organizations previously dedicated to sports, arts, and community development realigned their priorities toward prevention of drugs, violence, and warfare between gangs who claimed allegiance to different racial and ethnic groups and particular blocks of neighborhoods.[4] National and state organizations seeking to reduce juvenile crime, drug addiction, and the rapid spread of AIDS committed funding to youth organizations that targeted "problem" youth and communities over which parents, neighbors, and the police had seemingly lost control. The decade between 1985 and 1995 ended futures for many young people from families who had migrated from home or homeland to find a new life. With the decade came death, prison, addiction, AIDS, and major breaks in the authority that migrant and immigrant parents could claim over their children, who came to disrespect them for their "old ways" and inability to find new ways. Dominant in the public mind was the image of teenagers as full players in the serious games of chance in the drug, gun-trafficking, and prostitution trades. Several states initiated tough laws and rulings that gave adolescents long sentences if they came before the courts three times. In some states, juveniles charged with major crimes were tried as adults.

As the new millennium opened, the intense negativity surrounding youth in the prior two decades eased. The young who had survived those years relatively unscathed as individuals often had siblings and parents who had not. However, friendships, partnerships, further education opportunities, and career choices were expanding for the children whose parents had migrated or immigrated to urban areas in the prior two decades. Civil Rights legislation, affirmative action, and diversity programs had helped push back against racist policies in housing, medical care, education, career entry, and promotion. Young leaders of color were increasingly evident at both state and local levels.

Unlike the parents who had lived in the *group* cohesion of the small worlds of Trackton and Roadville, their children moved through adolescence knowing they had choices as *individuals*. Group alliance now meant much more than claims of identity, turf control, or gang membership that had so often set powerful institutions *against* the young during the 1980s and 1990s. The new millennium had individuals of will, intelligence, and vision *within* institutions of power. Higher degrees opened doors into medicine, law, research, journalism, education, and politics. Black and white men and women gained professional positions of visibility in which they proved their ability to deliberate, argue, bring together sources of evidence, and offer opinions taking into account multiple perspectives. They reported the evening news on national and local television stations, argued in federal and state courts, and won public offices. They had taken every possible advantage of their education to gain a firm hold on the information and skills needed to collaborate with, as well as to debate, those who held positions different from their own.

For these successful young adults, however, there was still more to learn about negotiating the unrelenting public promotion of what they should own, wear, and do to be fully mainstream. They had to acquire property and surround themselves with material goods. The financial and regulatory worlds of their parents and grandparents had opened few options for owning property. The children who became adults in the late 1990s and first decade of the twenty-first century could not turn to their parents for advice on financial matters in the new world of sub-prime mortgages, McMansion houses of four bedrooms, and yearly cruises and ski trips.

In the 1960s and 1970s, their parents had paid rent, and federal and state taxes had been deducted automatically from their paychecks. The few loans available to them had been first with the local payday lending store for relatively small amounts with high interest rates and short due dates and later with local banks who gave thirty-year mortgages only to those who had good credit records, solid incomes, and reasonable choices in the prices of the home they bought. Necessary medical care was either covered by insurance from their employer or cost so little they were able to pay the bills themselves. For those medical tragedies that exceeded any amount they could ever hope to be able to pay, the debt simply stayed there or went away.

The children of Trackton who were in a position to own property by the late 1990s and in the next decade faced choices never before available. To fund their further education, some had taken out loans that did not need to be paid off while they were studying and working. Once they left advanced education, they faced impediments that would continue to be there for generations to come: increasingly complex bureaucratic processes that required financial literacy and scrupulous attention to details written in fine print. The first generation who encountered such documents along with the opportunity to own houses and new cars found the learning curve steep and the risks immense.

Central to making their way around this curve was an ability to read and understand details of documents, ask tough questions of others and of them-selves, and to consider the consequences of their current actions. They had to stay alert to changes on every side. Their banks changed names and became increasingly depersonalized, while offering new "opportunities," such as equity loans and no-questions-asked automobile and college loans for their children. No amount of hard work and successful schooling could ensure their full comprehension of the detailed documents related to these offers. Those who took out equity loans had no idea that they handed over title of their home to the bank as part of the agreement.

Some had earned a college or technical degree, now had successful small businesses, owned property, and took vacations. In the span of the two decades since the opening of the 1970s, children whose grandparents had lived their entire lives as domestics, menial laborers, and millworkers in the South found it possible to chart a course that brought them higher education degrees, home ownership, financial investment, and employment with a retirement plan and health insurance for their families. They had all they had ever dreamed of and far more than their ancestors could have imagined. They did not see all there was to blind them and their children in the coming years.

Trackton's children and their children

Trackton's children met hazards and heartaches, revelations and rewards. Some did not survive the perilous navigation of drugs, AIDS, and poor housing, on the one hand, and the pitfalls that came with new opportunities for which they had little preparation, on the other. The children of Trackton's children faced fewer obvious direct threats to their futures than their parents had. Whereas their parents had marked their progress by specific goals of achievement, their children saw their futures as expanding beyond measure. However, cavernous openings swallow those who enter ill-equipped and filled with naïve expectations.

In adulthood, Zinnia Mae avoided both enticements and entrapment. The interracial church's partnership with developers and Atlanta's inner-city urban renewal program shielded and guided her. The church provided friends, employment, parenting skills, and a social calendar. The library and YMCA supplemented the support she received from her church and neighbors.

Sissy benefited from good fortune in the accidents of friendships she made after she left Trackton for Atlanta. In her job at Burger King, an older woman guided her to night courses that cost very little, meaning Sissy incurred no long-term debt. As her friendship with Red grew, she heard and saw his caution about buying anything for which he could not pay immediately. She learned how to manage both a checking and savings account, and she came to accept as given that all young people had to have advanced training and a career goal.

Both Zinnia Mae and Sissy had the good fortune of growing up imbued with the idea that hard work was normal. Wise strong women had surrounded them in their childhoods. They had learned early how to look, listen, and talk, and they had witnessed their grandmother and mother taking care to pay bills on time. Stories that adults told on the front porches and in Trackton's lively world of teasing talk, jokes, songs, gossip, and church life meant that Zinnia Mae and Sissy knew a lot about how language mattered in educational and economic development. Yet neither of them successfully completed secondary school in the usual time frame.

Zinnia Mae's children had started their childhoods with relatively spare input from her and almost no interactive talk or experience in a world beyond their public housing apartment. Zinnia Mae could not act on these deprivations until she could see something else in her head. For her, action became possible in the purchase of her house and the return to church she envisioned for herself and her children.

In spite of all Zinnia Mae's hopes for her children, teenage Donna neither shared nor understood her mother's vision for her. With no clear trajectory and little planning on her part, Donna lived her adolescence as Zinnia Mae had: making one bad decision after another. For both mother and daughter, finding themselves locked in places they did not want to be moved them to make the changes necessary to turn their lives around. Zinnia Mae and her social worker found the little dream house and trustworthy mediators who made escape possible for her. For Donna, a stint behind bars proved to be a transformative experience.

The twins fared better than Donna, benefiting from the library, church, and YMCA experiences that brought them opportunities and supportive mentors. Marcello and Melvin also had the benefit of apprenticeships under the financial and educational guidance of outsiders willing to invest in their talents. In the case of all three children, intimate strangers, including Donna's probation officer, enabled them to avoid debts for their education and to find careers with promise.

Sissy made mistakes during her teenage years, but she picked herself up and accomplished much during her young adulthood. Her first son, Denny, had been fortunate to spend his early childhood in the firm embrace of Lillie Mae's love and the modeling of Sissy's older brother, Tony, who was the first Trackton child to complete secondary school and move on immediately to start college in another part of the state. Whenever he was home from college, Tony read to Denny, played games with him, and taught him to read and write letters and numbers. When Red first met Denny, he brought storybook puzzles and a train set. Denny and Lillie Mae spent hours around the kitchen table putting the puzzles together and reading the books that told the stories depicted in the puzzles. Narrative scripting of characters' actions, emotions, features, and settings went along with the stories and puzzles. By the time Red and Sissy took Denny to New Jersey to enter the fourth grade, he was already reading science fiction and doing mathematical puzzles on his own.

Though Tameka grew up without her mother, Red and his aunt made certain that she would be immersed in everything possible to prepare for the openings in education and career choices ahead of her. Her best guide was her big brother. Denny was her critic, mentor, and source of news on the latest happenings in the IT world.

In their adolescence, Zinnia Mae, Sissy, and Donna acted without regard for consequences. Their recoveries in young adulthood illustrate some familiar lessons about life's pathways. All three of these women had supportive patient caregivers in their childhoods. A social worker noticed something special in Zinnia Mae, whose relocation resulted in her genuine embrace by an inner-city church community. Sissy's firm advice from Red reflected habits and values passed on to him from immigrant ancestors who raised hard-working children and built successful businesses. Coincidence had brought Red, Sissy, and Denny together. Sissy's marriage enriched Lillie Mae's life and gave her a granddaughter whose promise she nurtured with joy. But all these good turns could not protect Lillie Mae's children from the vicissitudes of health, accident, and despair that would bring them down.

Tony, Sissy's older brother, was the star of Trackton throughout the 1970s. He excelled academically, played for the racially integrated soccer team for the city league, and won a soccer scholarship to support his education at a small hitherto all-white college in the South. He was helped to gain admission and financial aid by his good athletic and academic records, as well as by pressure from a consortium of black pastors who threatened suits against what had long been the college's decidedly "whites-preferred" policy. Everyone Tony knew was elated. Everywhere he went, he heard: "You won the jackpot! You set for life now. You got it made."

I knew Tony well; he was the oldest of the children in Trackton when I started being a regular in the community in 1969. I also knew the finances of the family: their monthly rent, costs for food and heating bills, and the amount of principal they owed and interest they were paying on layaways for Christmas gifts. The only sources of income were the occasional cash Tony's mother, Lillie Mae, made cleaning houses for white families in Alberta and the cash her boyfriend left a couple of times a month when he was in Trackton. Though the amount of funding the small college offered Tony seemed huge to his mother and everyone in Trackton, I knew what it would take to support Tony living away from home in college.

Tony and I worked out a budget through which we talked about the shortfall. We went to visit the college financial aid office and managed to secure several hundred dollars of additional funding for his first year. Tony had a savings account in which he had faithfully deposited each week most of the money I paid him as research assistant through his years of secondary school. He drew that account down to a balance of $100. I agreed to keep adding to his savings account for every successful completion of a college course. The summer before he left for school, we worked together reviewing algebra – the highest level of mathematics available to him in his local secondary school – writing skills, and reading comprehension. We talked about every aspect of college life from drinking to sports team membership to girls to clothes and shoes. We went shopping for the first piece of luggage Tony had ever seen.

In the second week of November of his first year away, Tony phoned me. Thinking he might be calling to arrange the time when I was picking him up to bring him home for Thanksgiving, my tone was humorous, my mood happy. Tony cut me short: "Things aren't goin' so good." His coursework was not going well, he was confused about what he was supposed to do to get extra help, and he was missing soccer practices. His coach had already warned him that if things did not get better, Tony would be losing his scholarship.

Tony was the first in a long line of Roadville and Trackton children and grandchildren who found that college was a poor match for their habits, values, and world views. The message that they were no match for university life was what they usually heard. In the first generation of Trackton and Roadville children, young people like Tony who completed secondary school and had modest grades plus excellent athletic abilities often received offers from universities for admission with some financial support. However, most of those who took up these offers left school before completing their first year of study.

Higher education – peril and promise

How does this happen? This question continues to plague administrators and professors in universities, private and public, across the United States. Reasons lie in both the minutiae of habits of time, space, and language usage, as well as in family relations and expectations. Of critical importance are complexities of finance that range from checking and savings accounts to property ownership and living from payday to payday. Foremost among the difficulties that students from Roadville and Trackton families faced when they entered universities were responsibilities that family members expected them to continue to carry while away at school. Neither parents nor children from working-class families knew the time demands students faced for studying, meeting assignment deadlines, and planning collaborative projects with fellow classmates.

Children from these families could go away from home for university study only if they received scholarships, financial aid, or in a majority of cases, both forms of support. Though these funds almost never adequately met the financial needs of students, their parents, nevertheless, viewed their children as having "come into money." Hence, Lillie Mae called Tony when he was away at college and asked him to come home to help Benjy, his younger brother, who had been jailed. Families who fell behind on car payments looked to the college student for help. "Emergencies at home" ranged from death of a family member to threat of eviction if next month's rent was not paid. Families expected college students to come home on these occasions, regardless of study demands and pending examinations. Students like Tony did not find it easy to share details of these matters with professors or other students in order to account for a missed class or to explain the reason for not being around to help with a collaborative laboratory experiment.

More incredible to professors, counselors, and friends who tried to help Tony was their realization of what was missing in his daily life. He had little of what professors thought "normal" college students packed when they went off to university. Among the first group of students from Roadville and Trackton who went away to school, none had either an alarm clock or slide rule. Among those younger than Tony who headed to university a decade or so after him, few had ever seen a computer, and they had no adequate means of maintaining credit cards. These needs came on top of the realization that the clothes and shoes they had with them when they left home had to be updated as styles, fads, and occasions demanded.

Even when astute and resourceful college personnel did detect and try to overcome some of these material shortages, more difficult shortcomings remained. First-generation university students came from families with few financial resources and even less experience with what higher education required in general knowledge and academic language. None of the first generation of children from Roadville or Trackton had ever visited a museum, zoo, botanical park, or art gallery before 1983. None owned an atlas, thesaurus, or hard-back dictionary.

Once away at college, some students might quickly accumulate these experiences and reference books. Far less easily achieved was ease in conversations related to distant places and people, unfamiliar places and people, and strange ways of referencing knowledge. Aside from Biblical texts and related information, Roadville and Trackton families did not introduce into their conversations places, people, and experiences unfamiliar to their neighbors. To do so was to risk ridicule or the charge of "thinking too big for us."

Advanced study beyond secondary school required fluency in "big" conversations drawing on sources of knowledge that could be referenced and were unlikely to be within the everyday experience of Roadville and Trackton children. Moreover, the academic literacy they met in both professional training schools and universities cross-referenced information from an array of sources. When they had to write, they were supposed to know the conventions for supporting arguments and verifying sources. They were supposed to put "original" ideas into their compositions. When professors asked them to write research papers giving "critical perspectives," "comparative analysis," and "persuasive arguments," they had no idea where to start. Professors and their teaching assistants rarely knew how to offer helpful explanations of these terms; they presumed that students were asking only for amplification and not basic definition, guidelines, and accessible exemplars.

Aside from their unfamiliarity with the terms of academic discourse, students from Roadville and Trackton lacked the oral-language fluency in ways of talking they needed to support reading and writing in higher education. Neither at home nor in their secondary schools had they encountered sustained practice in comprehending, interpreting, extending, and adding a creative slant to assigned reading materials. They had not been drawn into conversations that freely included references to information unknown to interlocutors. Their parents had not talked through books with them, questioning, comparing, and commenting on characters, events, motivations, and alternative outcomes or consequences. Such talk needed reference to books they read together as well as to their own interests and experiences. Books had to arouse curiosity about their content and stay in memory. Sharing knowledge, building ideas, generating experiences and the need to know: these academic and language practices had to be habituated long before entering higher education, where demands accelerated for written information as well as lived experience.

A heritage of learning ahead for work

By 1990, 84 percent of the children who were twelve years old or younger when their parents left the mills had completed some form of further education. Noteworthy were those within the 12 percent who did so within the first six years after achieving a diploma from a secondary school or a GED [Graduate Equivalency Degree]. Of the 84 percent, 6 percent had earned both a Bachelor's and Master's degree within a decade after completing secondary school.

These Roadville and Trackton children had the benefit of watching their parents, many of whom had never completed secondary school, undertake coursework and licensing programs at different points in their first decade of working outside the textile mills. While struggling to establish their families in new places, many parents found ways to take courses they needed for their work. Women tended to seek short-term programs in accounting in order to keep the books for small businesses. Some took courses to meet licensing requirements needed to work as nursing assistants in health care facilities for the elderly. Men in the construction industry completed specialized programs when new state and federal codes set strict regulations for hazardous waste collection and disposal as well as installation and maintenance of sprinkler systems for industrial buildings and large residential sites. Some of those who worked on these construction sites took courses in vocational schools and community college and applied for apprenticeships, which could require four to five years and a series of tests leading to approval for licensing and certification. Their jobs increasingly required not only that they bring specialized skills to their work, but that they also solve problems, read architectural blueprints, and collaborate with workers, inspectors, and managers on construction sites. Those who set up restaurants or worked in drycleaning establishments needed to be licensed and to know enough about health codes to pass state and local inspections. In the 1980s, Roadville and Trackton workers found it difficult to find employment that did not call on skills and language fluencies new to them. They needed to be competent in oral negotiations and to have substantial facility with extended written texts. In many cases, they had to translate into practice the complex language of manuals and regulatory codes.

Coursework, apprenticeships, on-the-job experience in different types of sites, and long-term service brought advancement. The take-home income of job foremen rivaled that of positions available to university graduates without hands-on experience or multi-year apprenticeships. Women who started vocational training in medical professions, such as occupational therapy, pulmonary therapy, and radiology technology, found that on-the-job experience brought advancement and higher pay. Flexible hours, offering clustered work days with several days off-duty, helped them have more time at home and to enroll in additional courses or training programs. Incomes for those with two working parents rose from approximately $28,000–$32,000 for each worker's starting salary in the early 1980s to $45,000–$80,000 opening-position salaries in the first years of the twenty-first century. With these jobs came health benefits plus advancement opportunities, possible transfers to higher-paying locations in other parts of the state or country, and occasional travel offers for specialized professional development courses in locations as far away as Hawaii.

What did not come with these jobs was training in financial literacy – reading mortgage contracts, service contracts for automobiles, and health policies. The kind of income these workers made was often unmanageable for them as parents and recent residents of suburban subdivisions where keeping up with the newest and latest became the norm. During the decades after the 1990s, many of these families believed their salaries could extend to meet not only their needs but their dreams. Houses, furniture, automobiles, recreation vehicles, toys and electronics for their children, and new fashions in clothing, décor, and holidays came easy with credit cards.

Earning a life

Tony struggled at college, suffering isolation and the realization that he was not prepared for higher-level education. The college let him graduate with a "general education" degree after five years and $40,000 of accumulated debt for college loans. Each year he had been there, the amount of his scholarship decreased, while his fees and costs for books, food, and housing increased.

In 1983, in what Tony thought would be his final year of college, he met Katisha, who attended an historically black college in the lower part of South Carolina. They became engaged and planned for a wedding within a few months of their graduations the next June. When Tony's graduation was delayed a year, Katisha went to work and waited. The wedding took place in July of 1985 after Tony graduated from college. Katisha's father, a pastor, officiated at the ceremony in her home town. Katisha's family, however, expected Tony to host a reception back in his home town. Tony borrowed the money to rent a small hotel near Alberta and to host a sit-down dinner for forty guests, complete with an engraved napkin ring for each member of the wedding party.

Tony landed a job at a rehabilitation facility attached to a hospital near Alberta and rented a small bungalow for the two of them. Katisha was hired by the regional organization linked with her father's church. By the end of their first year of marriage, the couple had accumulated debts totaling nearly $20,000. They had bought a new car but having had no experience with maintaining an automobile, Tony never changed the oil or took the car in for a checkup. Repairs in the first year cost over $600. When Tony could not pay the bill, the dealership had him sign the papers for a short-term loan at 21 percent interest. Tony still owed $40,000 in student loans, Katisha just over $22,000. Within a year, Katisha was pregnant. The baby, Timothy, was born two months premature in 1986 and remained in Alberta's neonatal intensive care unit six weeks. Tony's health insurance paid a small portion of the medical bills. Katisha had to quit work to stay home with the baby who had what seemed like an endless number of health issues.

Tony was overwhelmed. He borrowed money from a friend to keep the household appliances from being repossessed. A financial counselor at the hospital suggested he declare bankruptcy. Just after Christmas of 1988, shortly after he learned that his youngest brother Lem, the poet and dreamer of the family, had died of pneumonia, Tony committed suicide. Katisha and the baby moved back to her home town to live with her parents. I lost contact with her shortly thereafter. Lillie Mae's remaining son, Benjy, was in jail facing murder charges from a bungled robbery early in 1988. He maintained that he had done what he had to do to get money to help his two brothers.

Envisioning a future and keeping in mind the consequences of actions is not enough. Drawing cognitive maps of a desired future must be accompanied by specific kinds of insight. This insight is gained through practice with hypothetical reasoning articulated in narratives of cause and effect. Individuals must learn to see, identify, and consider details. Within the narratives they hear, whether from the bank loan officer or the furniture salesman, they must see themselves in terms of who they really are and the extent of their resources. They must see fine points in small actions and take note of whether the apparent objectives of those with power differ from their actual goals. Tony had little sense of his own self-image after he went to college and married Katisha. He did not know how to say "no." He had little preparation for understanding the implications of the lifestyle the couple was trying to live.

Tony's life in secondary school and on the soccer field had given him a false picture of his abilities. He did not envision scenarios that contradicted his view that athletic abilities and the backing of black ministers would carry him through four years of college. No one in his family or neighborhood had either a checking account or long-term loan. Tony had no idea how to reckon the literal or figurative costs of signing any piece of paper put before him. He had a dream, and he saw himself moving into that dream.

Human language binds events in time and space. For visions to be realized, individuals have to know how to narrate and question internally their course and to factor into what they envision the possibility of accidents, ill health, and unscrupulous actions by those in power. Visions have to have within them multiple stories of "what if?" and "what about?" The habit of extrapolating from such questions comes most easily when socialization during early child-hood has provided games, stories, conversations, and sociodramatic play. Practice is essential with models who say in response to a move that is not thought out in a board game or backyard building project: "Have you thought about what could happen if you did that?" The lessons of unintended conse-quences come along with an insistent voice: "Look ahead. Think about what could happen if you make that move or take that action." Children see that their actions can give others openings to defeat them when the opponent in a board game says: "Watch what that move you just made allows me to do. You should have seen that coming."

The promise of a fun-loving two-year-old tells less than we would hope about who he or she might become as a twenty-year-old. Similarly, we can never predict what children take from the habits and outlooks on life their parents and grandparents model. Donna's attentiveness to her doll's bedding and notice of her mother's concern for the safety of her baby brothers when they napped on the bed may have contributed somewhat to later success in her chosen medical career. Zinnia Mae never would have predicted that Donna might retain some of Zinnia Mae's meticulous practices in the management of household finances. When Donna bought her first computer, the software program she mastered in the first month was one that would help her keep track of her bills, receipts, and paychecks. Once released from juvenile detention, she was a model of frugality and cautious approaches to what others called "opportunities" and what she saw as potential pitfalls that could land her behind bars again.

Denny's early fascination with puzzles and train tracks may have contributed somewhat to his talent for a computer science career. Jerome's persistence and early experience with looking out for himself may have led him to music and theatre and a career in which he played to his strengths. The worlds of Denny and Tameka, even in the face of the great loss of their mother, expanded into special interests, essential community roles, and unremitting expectations of success in their university lives and careers.

All these children grew up in loving families. Yet they needed more than what parents and grandparents alone gave them. Essential for their development were social networks of face-to-face interactions with experts in play and work. In their churches, the YMCA, and community organizations, they found these networks. They needed more than sports. They had to be drawn into creative projects that required their sustained commitment, dedicated imitation and practice, and a curiosity that pushed them to know and do more. These out-of-school and beyond-family interactions allowed them to have hours of practice within adult roles in different places and with different audiences.

For all the children of the children of Trackton and Roadville, the mere specter of what they might be in their future was not enough. They needed a sense of consequences from current actions, whether in running internal "what if" scenarios or calculating interest on loans. Charts, diagrams, receipts, calendars, storage boxes, questions, and a healthy skepticism of easy answers had to be there as checks against hasty decisions. Talking with people in financially neutral environments, such as the church, meant listening to narratives of the triumphs and tragedies of others and inferring critical cautionary advice: do not be afraid to ask questions; do not sign anything until you review a copy at home away from the pressure of the moment.

The truth is that some children in families make it and some do not. Neither early language socialization nor earnest envisionment of bright futures can determine those who will and those who will not.

6   The hand of play

Six-year-old Martha clutches a paper bag filled with leaves, pinecones, and pine needles she and her mother, Catherine, have collected on their Saturday morning visit to the neighborhood park. When they arrive home, Martha lays her trophies out on the kitchen table while Catherine prepares lunch. Martha's colored pencils are scattered in front of her as she traces the largest leaf from her collection. Her mom leans over her work, asking: "Do we have two of those leaves? Is there another one here that's smaller? Let's look." Martha runs to find her magnifying glass. She and her mother study the two leaves.

Martha notes: "See, that part [pointing alternately to the veins in the two leaves] does look alike, but not the stem." Her mother agrees and suggests that the difference in the age of the two trees from which the leaves came might have made that difference. Pushing her lunch aside, Martha hums to herself and continues her tracing. Later that afternoon, she tears the two leaves she has traced into the "stew" she is preparing for her collection of stuffed animals.

Young children's play is quirky, repetitive, and flexible. Inherent in play is the combination of science and art that brings young children to fascination with caterpillars, dramatic re-enactment, scribbles and sketches, and reflections in mud puddles. They are scientists and artists from the crib.[1] Within their play, children take note of bits and pieces in the world around them that adults sometimes find difficult to see. Children offer theories about similarities and differences and conjectures about what other people think and do.[2] The details in imaginative play help children learn what they may become. Roles, tasks, and talents for creative adaptations vary according to individual abilities and special interests. Children's early play hints at particular gifts that may evolve into their work and leisure choices in later life. Early interests in play often reappear in choices adults make in their hobbies and favorite pastimes. Places, people, and objects encountered in early play stay in memory.

Throughout this book, the children of both Roadville and Trackton descendant families illustrate ways in which places, people, and objects in their early years of play influenced patterns of their adult lives. Martha was the granddaughter of Alice and Jay Turner, old-time residents of Roadville, whose ancestors had come down from the mountains to work in textile mills in the

1920s. When the mills folded, Alice and Jay grudgingly moved to Indiana. Their younger daughter, Catherine, left Roadville before them to attend a university in the Washington, DC area. Play had motivated and vitalized her childhood as it had for other children, like Martin and Danny Brown, with whom she had grown up back in Roadville.

Playing ahead

In Roadville as a child, Martin had been king of play with his younger brother Danny serving as knave or servant, depending on Martin's mood. After the boys saw a poster in Alberta advertising the coming attraction of a magic show featuring Houdini's most famous tricks, Martin and Danny decided to try their most complex feat yet. They created a box partitioned to accommodate a small child in one end. Then the boys could saw the box in half. Costumed in a long black shirt taken from his dad's closet, a tall black hat created of cardboard, and a wand made of a dried lily stalk, Martin held shows for which he charged either a nickel or cupcake. Their plans ended when they sought in vain for a neighborhood child gullible enough to try their experiment and sufficiently small to occupy only one-half of the box.

Both boys took their fondness for big imaginative projects with them into adulthood. During college, Martin had been head of seasonal festivals for his fraternity. For Halloween, Valentine's Day, and St. Patrick's Day, he rallied fellow students to plan parties, decorate the exterior of the fraternity house, and draw up rules for costumes required of party-goers. When he went to dental school, he joked with fellow students that the tools he used reminded him of ones he had as a child when he put together his Erector sets.

When Martin and Danny left home for college, they had insisted that their mother keep the toolboxes that each had treasured since they were children. Martin had helped the men and older boys in Roadville with small building projects, creating dollhouses for neighborhood girls, and finding inventive ways to use scrap lumber. When Danny was just a toddler, Martin began teaching him to name, identify, and use tools. The boys made birdhouses and a tree house with a ladder. For their next-door neighbors, they built a two-level sandbox. When they were not gardening, they worked with tools, and as soon as they both had bicycles, they put to use their hours of watching older boys work on motorcycles and bicycles.

By the time the boys were old enough, the family reserved Saturday nights for card games and board games. They moved from Candyland (a board game popular with children and parents alike) and other simple games that required knowledge of numbers and colors, as well as simple strategies, to Monopoly and Yahtzee. The children relished catching their mother between chores for a quick game of tic-tac-toe (noughts and crosses), and any car rides the family took together were times for rhyming games in which one family member threw out a word, and someone else offered a rhyming word. On the rare occasions when they drove more than fifty miles from home, the boys loved to count states indicated on license plates or to make up words from the letters on the plates.

Lisa and Sally, who lived just up the road from Martin and Danny, grew up making clothes for their dolls. They had toy-sized sets of dishes, pots and pans, and utensils that were miniatures of those in their mother's kitchen. The girls collected scraps of cloth from their mother's sewing basket to adapt as table-cloths for their dolls' tea parties. Whenever their mother had piecrust dough left over, she let the girls use their miniature wooden rolling pins. They created strips to which they added a mixture of cinnamon and brown sugar they baked for warm treats. In their room, the girls had a corner dedicated to their dolls. Their father sometimes helped them glue small pieces of scrap wood together to make furniture for their dollhouse. They had a wooden toy box that had once been used to store kindling on the back porch. The girls had cleaned and painted the box and decorated it with decals (stickers) depicting figures from Mother Goose rhymes. Both girls grew up knowing how to make and adapt things, but Lisa was the tomboy of the two who came to prefer outdoor play to dressing dolls or doing chores in the kitchen. Sally led young children of the neighbor-hood in playing school.

In the neighborhood fields around Roadville, impromptu softball and dodgeball games happened for boys and girls often during the summer and on Saturdays. Some of the Roadville boys tried T-ball, a version of baseball designed for young children. Some of the older boys joined Little League baseball, but none of them stuck with the teams because lawns had to be mowed, a dad could suddenly decide on a fishing trip, and an excursion to the shopping center was always a possibility. Any dad or neighbor might take eager boys along on an expedition to find a truck part at the junkyard or to get dry ice, a cooling agent for hand-crank ice cream makers. At least twice each summer, ice cream socials brought neighborhoods together. Dads organized children as volunteers to turn the cranks on the ice cream makers assembled in one family's driveway. Moms made "box cakes" from commercial cake mixes, and children helped create swirls in the chocolate frosting and added multi-colored sprinkles.

Television entered Roadville households only when families had enough cash to pay "outright" for what most women of the neighborhood thought were needless gadgets. Quickly alert to the pull that television exerted on children and husbands, women tried to make watching television a family affair, limited to those occasions when everyone was together on the sofa or sprawled on the floor of the living room. No one watched television while anyone else had work to do.

When televisions became near-universal household items, toddlers quickly learned that the remote control could give them instant access to cartoons laden with advertisements that often had more appeal than the cartoons. As the prices of televisions and computers dropped, both appeared as separate entertainment centers in children's bedrooms, as well as family rooms, dens, and kitchens. Young people had more available time for exploratory practice and "playing around" on their computers than their parents did. As a result, they knew more about a wider range of programs, sites, and innovations than their parents. Erector sets, board games, and the challenges of Monopoly faded in popularity.

By the late 1990s, media reports of kidnapped children and "stranger danger" led parents to be afraid to let their children play alone outdoors or in nearby parks and wooded areas. Exploring natural surroundings took place only with supervision. Media exposure of the danger of children playing on their own and the explosion of computer videogames pushed children indoors. By the late primary school and middle school years, peers gathered in one another's bedrooms, dens, and family rooms to search the internet for sites related to their interests. They debated their preferred brands of athletic shoes and sports fashions modeled by favorite players on sports teams. They assessed different types of cellphones marketed with logos based on entertainment figures. Videogames were a frequent topic of writing assignments and re-enactments. The tide had turned from play as spontaneous free-ranging performance planned by children. Now the young were in command of their means of entertainment, connection with their friends, and videofilms of their antics. Instant and constant gratification offered them little incentive to ask: "How does it work? What is it made out of? Where did what it's made of come from?"

After 2000, the differential of knowledge and skills between adults and adolescents already established with computers and home entertainment centers was rapidly repeated with cellphones. Adolescents learned more readily than their parents how to make these phones do a widening array of tasks and to function in an expanding number of roles. By the end of the decade, early primary-school children asked Santa Claus to bring them $300 cellphones. They had been taking pictures and playing games with their parents' cellphones since they were toddlers. Now their friends and older siblings demonstrated, researched, and debated the relative merits of different models. Their counterparts a decade ago had been given toy cellphones and miniature tape players. Now toy stores no longer carried such items. An entire segment of the toy business had become obsolete because of young children's insistence on the "real thing": iPads, laptops, and the latest fashionable cellphones.

As the young moved into middle and secondary school, they requested as holiday and birthday presents the latest in videogame consoles and computers of certain types and colors. Computers stayed around longer than cellphones or portable devices for storing and playing music, because of their high initial costs, plus their need for updated software and professional maintenance. Parents became mediators between their children and customer service lines when products proved faulty or to have been packed without a vital connector or plug. Packing up electronic gear for return to the manufacturer often became "too much of a hassle." Rejected goods added to the growing pile of discarded electronic gear in the corner of garages.

Talk by hand and mouth

Between 2005 and 2010, in the households of descendant families of both Roadville and Trackton, it was difficult to find a time of day when either a parent or child was not in front of a computer screen or checking cellphones, often with either a radio or television on somewhere in the household. Exceptions to this pattern came in those households where parents ruled that specific topics, times, or circumstances (e.g., when guests were present) were to be off-limits for technology use by either parents or children. When these rules were broken, parents were the most frequent offenders, saying to the child: "Oh, this is [so-and-so]. I need to take this call. I'll only be a minute." By the time the parent was off the phone, the child had often returned to a preferred activity or become engaged elsewhere in front of a screen or on a phone. Teenagers' travel with either parent almost never occurred unless every member of the family had agreed to go to the same place for a special celebration or vacation destination. Nevertheless, children over fourteen often wriggled out of these occasions or asked to bring a friend along.

Between 2001 and 2003 and again between 2008 and 2010, as the US economy experienced rising unemployment rates and changes in availability of credit, the frequency of family vacations by air travel to faraway places dropped precipitously. Automobile travel to visit relatives or to go camping increased, but these trips did not mean more time for family conversation. By 2000, technologies of entertainment had worked their way into family cars and vans. Sometimes those in the family car could agree on the same audiobook. But within a few years, the more familiar pattern for long road trips placed adults in the front seat while each child in the back seat enjoyed his or her chosen entertainment on individual DVD players. Cellphones, videogames, iPods, and iPads also provided individually selected entertainment for members of families thrust together in one vehicle. Traveling with one or both parents, younger children invariably carried along an electronic device that provided their entertainment and precluded talking or reading with adults.

By 2005, home videogame consoles from Nintendo, Sony, and Microsoft were holiday gift favorites purported to bring young and old together in their play. Late in 2006, however, Nintendo promised that any prior efforts to create such family-together home play would now be superseded by the Wii. Advertisements claimed, "Wii would like to play" and offered a "new way to play." The double *ii* in the unusual name was said to have been chosen to indicate two people playing together. In 2009, when the economic recession led many families to give up air travel for summer and winter holidays, the Wii broke all previous records for home videogame console sales. Children picked up from the advertisements the selling point that the Wii was for the "entire family" and begged for the $300 outlay accordingly. Teenagers and young adults disliked the Wii wristband designed to hold the remote securely during play. Microsoft's Xbox 360, requiring no remote and responding to body motions, became the new favorite in 2010.

Creativity at the fingertips

Play lives in relation to five critical features of context: time, space, tools, models, and partners. Roadville and Trackton children in the 1970s and early 1980s had considerable decision-making power over their play. They played outdoors and indoors turning chores into play. Afternoons and weekends, they gathered neighborhood friends to create their imaginative projects or to play ball. They put together available materials in their play. They borrowed old pots and pans and utensils from their mothers and tools from neighborhood dads. They improvised at every turn. They enlisted adult partners as needed to build tree houses, umpire softball games, or play peacekeeper during dodgeball games. Adults in real and storybook worlds provided models for some of their play, whether during times when older girls could coerce young children onto porch steps to "play school" or when older boys could make younger siblings walk the gang plank to the brandishing of swords by fearless pirates.

Figures 6.1 and 6.2 give an overview of patterns in the play of children through adolescence. These figures also give a sense of the sequencing of types of play and preparatory activities leading through the teenage years toward jobs and careers. Figure 6.1 reflects features of play between 1980 and 1994. During the earliest of these years, the provisions of play for infants and young children had malleable features. Ideas about safety, as well as the tendency for such items to be handmade, dictated soft pliable materials. Simple crib mobiles made of paper moved at the slightest touch of a breeze from an open window or the stretched leg or hand of an infant. Stuffed animals were made from scraps of fabric or worn towels and stuffed with old tee shirts. Teddy bears were among the first "bought" toys for children. What followed soon for toddler girls was a doll baby with a cloth body and soft plastic hands, feet, and head. The only sound these doll babies made was a soft cry or whimper when little girls squeezed or shook the dolls gently. The set of clothing that came with the doll baby was soon supplemented by homemade doll clothing and miniature wooden table and stools. Little girls had baby carriages outfitted with homemade blankets and pillows, accessories to their sociodramatic play as "mommy."

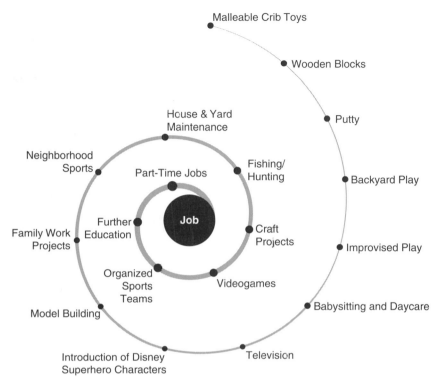

Figure 6.1 Patterns of play and work, crib-to-job, 1980–1994

Toddler boys had wooden pull toys in the shape of animals. They played with rubber balls, sets of wooden blocks, and wooden puzzles. Some Roadville mothers made or bought play dough for supervised use on wax paper laid out on the kitchen table with beans and peas as decoration. On car trips and during Sunday services at church, children carried along a basket of crayons and big pencils and coloring books featuring animals, boys and girls at play, and characters from fairytales, Mother Goose, and Bible stories.

These items of play responded to the hand, changing shape, function, and relationship to other artifacts through manipulation by little fingers. Pull toys in the shape of big dogs menaced entire miniature towns set up along railroad tracks. Doll babies entertained teddy bears at tea and rode in baby carriages. Paper dolls and their clothing required blunt-nosed scissors used with care to cut around the tabs used to hold the dolls' clothing in place. Such play prepared girls for their first sewing kit, outfitted with real scissors, fabric scraps, large-eyed needles, and

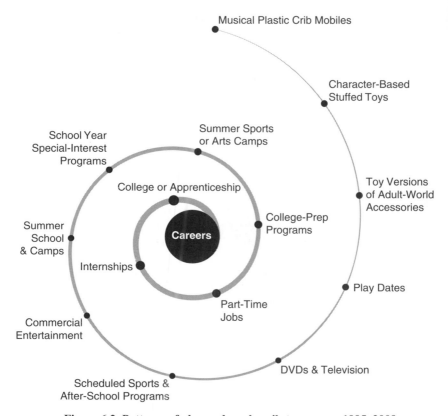

Figure 6.2 Patterns of play and work, crib-to-careers, 1995–2009

wooden spools of thread. In their sociodramatic play, children ventriloquized characters around them, unintentionally entertaining nearby adults who could readily identify the person being mimicked as mamma, boss, or whining toddler.

As both girls and boys entered primary school, they continued practice with scissors and added printing with over-sized pencils without erasers. They played with clay in corners of the classroom dedicated to art projects. The rug where children gathered for reading lessons was often adjacent to the alcove of the room where they could build with wooden blocks when bad weather kept them indoors during recess. Lunches came to school in brown paper bags or miniature metal lunchboxes with thermos bottles tucked inside.

As families from Trackton and Roadville scattered in the early years of the 1980s to find work in larger towns and metropolitan areas, their children saw peers at school carrying lunchboxes dedicated to Walt Disney characters and superheroes. Soon they too wanted such lunchboxes as well as clothing and shoes, plastic purses, and backpacks that were miniature billboards for movies, television programs, professional sports teams, and shoe and clothing companies.

Baby cribs no longer had soft pliable homemade mobiles or stuffed animals and rag dolls. Instead they were adorned with brightly colored plastic mobiles and store-bought stuffed animals with plastic eyes and mouth. Toys for children as young as three years of age needed batteries of specific sizes for their lights and moving parts. Little boys learned to make G.I. Joe and other action figures crouch, shoot, and assume fighting stances. When the boys played war, they wielded life-sized plastic weapons in colors and shapes too realistic for the comfort of some Vietnam veterans.

Toddlers and primary-school students wanted look-alike toys from the adult world around them: telephones with cradled receivers, typewriters with covers, and metal toolboxes with tools. Metal wagons and miniature cars powered by little legs pumping pedals replaced red wooden wagons with removable sides. Plastic tricycles that chipped and broke overtook metal versions that rusted. Children's vehicles for play came in greater varieties – vans, campers, and vacation trailers – to match their counterparts in the adult world.

As late as the mid-1980s, some families, especially those living in mid-sized towns where commercial entertainment was limited, worked together to build model airplanes of balsa wood and worked on weekends to clean the backyard or create joint projects. Mothers still kept their sewing machines up in the spare room or corner of the family room, and mending baskets sat beside mom's chair. Men spent their leisure time with neighborhood sports, visits during hunting and fishing seasons to relatives living in rural areas, and craft projects, such as refinishing a piece of furniture or upholstering a chair.

By the end of the 1990s, cracks in these patterns of play widened. The thriving economy enlisted mothers and fathers for full-time employment in jobs. Plastic figures attached to crib mobiles portrayed characters that toddlers came to know as they sat in front of DVDs or television cartoon programs while waiting for dinner. Their plastic pull toys, block sets, train sets, dolls, trucks, and cars carried advertising logos linked to spectator entertainment.

The majority of Roadville and Trackton descendant children now lived in households with single parents or two parents, both of whom had jobs. Infants and preschoolers were dropped off at daycare by parents on their way to and from work. Children took to daycare lunch and snack boxes and food packages featuring their favorite television or DVD characters. They ate with plastic utensils off of plastic saucers, and they played, for the most part, with plastic toys. They raced one another around the play yards of their daycare center with tricycles, scooters, and other vehicles chosen to meet safety standards and to hold up to heavy use. On days of rain or snow, they played inside in kitchen areas with plastic kitchenware, block areas with both wooden and plastic blocks and puzzles, and dress-up corners with commercially purchased Disney-character and superhero costumes and accessories.

For their children's birthdays, parents bought toys and vehicles that often went unused on weekends, because parents and children alike favored commercial entertainment, such as movies or special holiday exhibitions. As children grew older, their toys and vehicles were displaced by bicycles and streamlined metal scooters, as well as electronic gear. Use of the garage's storage area for outgrown toys and vehicles now made it even more difficult to get the car and the van into the garage.

Neighborhood sports events that had taken place in backyards and vacant lots became the province of organized sport teams with coaches, uniforms, team names, and tournaments. Items that were homemade or handcrafted, wooden or metal, did not bear the fashion labels and similarities with their adult versions that children and young people now valued. Automobiles, campers, and boats were made of fiberglass, and their junior versions had to have the same look and texture as the real thing. Young people wanted more and more electronic gear and looked for part-time jobs to help pay for what they wanted.

Figure 6.2 shows the change in pace and sources of play between 1995 and 2009. During this period, parents increasingly reported that they wanted to give their children "every possible opportunity." Childhoods were "cultivated" to "expose" the young to experiences that parents understood as prerequisites to enter university study and to prepare for multiple careers and not just jobs.[3] In their families and with friends, young children relied on adults to schedule play dates and sleepovers and to plan parties for birthdays and graduations from kindergarten and primary school. These latter events became more and more elaborate, especially in the lush years at the end of the 1990s. Paid entertainers and gifts for every child, catered menus, or travel to commercial entertainment marked competitions among parents for the most original, the coolest, ideas for birthday parties. Birthdays for girls in late primary school and middle school introduced them to pedicures and manicures. Boys invited their friends and their dads to go along on birthday celebrations to huge sports facilities to see professional sports teams play.

Parents encouraged their children to try various after-school programs in arts and sports for which fees, uniforms, special equipment, and frequent travel were necessary. As noted in Chapter 3, each week children in middle and secondary school had overlapping activities, some with compulsory practices during their season. Summer camps, internships, and apprenticeships supplemented special interests that children developed during academic-year activities. Parents rarely made their children stick with an activity if they did not enjoy it or were critical of the coach or director. Parents intervened in these activities often, asking for explanations of why their children spent time on the bench or did not make the cut for the next level of choir, theatre cast, or team. Parental involvement became especially intense when community organizations could not accommodate all students on special fieldtrips, such as travel to the regional marine biology program. Through college-preparatory summer programs to internships and part-time jobs, parents pushed their teenagers to seek experiences that would give them topics for their college application essays.

Changes in uses of language became increasingly noticeable as craftwork and creative uses of the hand and fingertips in play diminished and then disappeared. As Tables 6.1 and 6.2 illustrate, parents saw their time with their children shrink for playing, building, and creating with crayons, clay, blocks or sand. "I hope they're getting this kind of thing at daycare" was often the comment when

Table 6.1 *Adult–child (age 8) interactional time (in minutes), Saturday afternoons, 1–6 p.m., 1979–2009*

	1979	1984	1989	1994	1999	2004	2009
Engaged in joint projects*	148	137	72	29	24	10	20
Watching same event as spectators	36	42	41	51	32	49.5	38
Talk within extended genres**	80	63.5	61	31	21.5	10	9
Adult watching child perform	40	40	58	57	70	55	69

Numbers of minutes are based on means of samples taken during fall, spring, and summer months for families living in urban, suburban, or rural communities. Note that these interactions often overlapped with one another.
* Joint projects, indoor or outdoor, are defined as any collaborative activity requiring planning, materials and equipment, manual creativity, and assessment.
** Extended genres refer to any contiguous string of utterances, collaborative or monologic, recognizable as narrative or explanation.

Table 6.2 *Adult–child (age 14) interactional time (in minutes), Saturday afternoons, 1–6 p.m., 1979–2009*

	1979	1984	1989	1994	1999	2004	2009
Engaged in joint projects*	180	141	55.5	62	90	36	48
Watching same event as spectators	32	46	90	85.5	90	98	56
Talk within extended genres**	88	100	71	58	24	16	9
Adult watching child perform	33	37	75	104	109	110.5	61.5

Numbers of minutes are based on means of samples taken during fall, spring, and summer months for families living in urban, suburban, or rural communities. Note that these interactions often overlapped with one another.
* Joint projects, indoor or outdoor, are defined as any collaborative activity requiring planning, materials and equipment, manual creativity, and assessment.
** Extended genres refer to any contiguous string of utterances, collaborative or monologic, recognizable as narrative or explanation.

Table 6.3 *Types of language support for children's self-monitoring*

Type	Critical feature	Example
If–then propositions	Content unrelated to child's direct self-interest	If Maris's granddaddy hadn't been old, would he have died?
Cause and effect statement or questions	Content refers to depersonalized concrete actions or abstract ideas	Does the moon looks closer some times of the year because of how clouds are? Do the pipes freeze because the water inside turns to ice?
Time-related statement or question	Content refers to depersonalized concrete actions or abstract ideas	Did the person who painted this picture ever know that king before he painted him? Did he have to get famous before he could paint a famous person like that?
How or why questions	Content unrelated to child's direct self-interest or here-and-now events or scenes	How can people decide when a picture gets to go in a museum? Why do people dig up bones of animals and then put them together in a museum?
Comparative or analogic thinking expressed in statement or question	Compares one situation taking place at any point in time with another with an indication of awareness of certain features or actions that warrant the comparison	Is changing into a butterfly like shedding your skin, like snakes do (asked while watching a caterpillar crawl on her arm)?

I asked about time at home for little fingers to work creatively. Tables 6.1 and 6.2 indicate for eight- and fourteen-year-olds the changing patterns of adult–child interactional time in the thirty-year span from 1979 until 2009. What happened across these years was a significant drop-off in the time that adults and children joined together in projects of either work or play.

As a consequence, the nature of language use changed, making extended talk less frequent as were opportunities to plan, look ahead, and weigh consequences of current actions. Table 6.3 indicates the supportive language that joint project work models for children. Since collaborative work and play rely on the hypothetical and conditional, individuals taking part in such activities learn to talk about topics other than themselves. Children have to focus on an object, person, or state that does not relate directly to their own immediate self-interest. They are involved, but their language does not refer to their own needs, emotions, or feelings. The attention goes elsewhere: the veins in a leaf, details of doll's furniture, and the fashion of paper dolls. Language moves action and information along. Critical here is the need for practice in talking about content that is depersonalized. Extensive interactive practice with depersonalized talk helps children internalize such talk. Doing so is important, because an assessment of consequences of one's current actions relies on an ability to distance the self from emotional involvement and perceived self-interest. Children who grow up in households where adults read children's literature to them learn early how to infer the mental states and intentions of others. If these children mature into adolescents who find their way to young adult novels, they continue to take in words that convey how characters consider consequences of their actions and intuit the feelings and motivations of others. As language arts and English classes in school decrease their reliance on literature, children lose an important context for seeing and thinking about how language conveys much more than self-interest and immediate concerns.

Over the years indicated in Tables 6.1 and 6.2 and Figures 6.1 and 6.2, adults increased the amount of time they spent watching live or televised events with their children. They also spent increasing amounts of time watching their children perform on sports teams, as well as with community organizational and school events. Joint spectatorship on these occasions sometimes involved an older sibling and a parent watching a younger sibling perform. These times tended to generate talk about past events and how they happened or came about, but only rarely did joint spectatorship spur adults and children to talk about depersonalized content related to what they had seen.

The pattern of being joint spectators extended to the commercial entertainment forms (e.g., concerts, circuses, etc.) parents chose to appeal to both older and younger children in the family. Some parents also sought out special exhibitions at children's museums, science and natural history museums, and zoos. Only rarely, however, did any of these spectator events generate depersonalized talk or follow-up activities within families through subsequent weeks or months.

Plastic crib mobiles and toys left little room for creative maneuvering by infants and children. Unyielding bodies of plastic dolls and foam-filled stuffed animals would not remain seated in their carriages or lie across a toddler's knee to be burped. Toddlers could make screens come alive in their play with remote controls, and as they grew older, they could flip from one form of entertainment to the next on their videogame devices, cellphones, and computers. But children could not make these devices converse with them and adapt what they did in response to give-and-take negotiating talk. Faces on screens of electronic toys could not chat with toddlers, narrate their fantasy play, or join them in block-building projects. Children did not take in the talk of screen figures as the basis for their own creative uses of language; they needed human interlocutors narrating and negotiating with them in their joint social activities.

If toddlers could engage in metacognitive analysis to express what they wanted and needed most, they would echo the findings of neuroscientists throughout the opening decade of the new millennium: young children are social creatures who need direct face-to-face interaction that enlists eye gaze, mutual tuning-in to the world around them, and collaborative projects that enlist fingers, hands, and arms.[4] When toddlers see new objects and actions, they first learn to distinguish their specific attributes through touch and manipulation as well as trial and error with their hands (and in their mouths). Vision and touch are highly efficient ways of knowing. As children mature, they expand their means of exploring through visuomotor capacities that enable them to engage in kinesthetic exploration and to develop haptic representations of the world as they mature. Tactile and visual input stimulates mental modeling of objects in space and promotes a sense that consequences generally follow from actions. Brain circuits that link perception and action of self, other, and object support learning by looking and touching.[5]

During the period reflected in Figure 6.1, little girls and boys were likely to hear instructions for cutting out paper dolls, sewing on buttons, building tree houses, and repairing bicycles. This kind of talk along with demonstration and follow-up requests of "you try it now" ingrained sequential processes and cause and effect operations in several ways. As adults manipulated little fingers into the correct way to cut out clothes for paper dolls, their instructions were filled with hypotheticals: "Careful! Without those tabs, the clothes won't stay on your paper doll. You don't wanna cut those off." The message was that being creative works in some places in some ways, but in others, it is best to follow the rules.

Young Mark watched his dad, Martin, make the fine adjustments necessary around the bicycle gears. His dad let Mark handle a C wrench (spanner), while Martin explained all the ways it could be used for nuts and bolts of different shapes and sizes. When he brought out his childhood electric train set, Martin demonstrated the merits of needle-nose pliers for repairing the wiring of the tiny street lights at the station on one section of the track. When Mark found a small specialized nut on one of his toy metal trucks, Martin watched him run to the toolbox to look for the appropriate C wrench. Mark's Erector set, parts of which had been his father's when he was a boy, gave practice in following diagrams and encouraged him to envision his own creations, for some pages of the booklet of directions had been lost.

The movement of the fingers and the hand that make imitative and creative play possible do more than help children develop their fine motor control skills. Movements dependent on finding ways and means to maneuver small bits and pieces gave Mark practice in attending to the details of sketches, distinguishing nuts and bolts used for different purposes, and assessing the precision and function of the range of tools in his father's various toolkits. Hard lessons about the consequences of impatience and haste came along with attempts he and his sister, Rebecca, made to put things together and to plan building projects that exceeded their skills.

In the period reflected in Figure 6.2, young children and adolescents in families of Roadville and Trackton descendants became adept in handling remote controls and figuring out how to play new videogames and to set up new cellphones and computers. They moved quickly from point-and-shoot cameras with film to digital cameras. They created Facebook pages and updated them almost daily with photographs of themselves and their friends. Adolescents used the family video camera to document sports events and to create pieces with their friends to put up on YouTube. Some developed a keen interest in programming and in building computers, though most preferred to stay attuned via the internet to schedules of new products, software, and videogames. After 1995, teenagers who learned to manage electronic gear used a relatively narrow range of fine motor skills and few larger hand motions.

When adolescents and older children received new pieces of electronic gear, they rarely turned to written directions, preferring instead trial and error based on intuitive learning from their experience with prior versions. When intuition failed to work, they read sketches and diagrams on the abbreviated "getting started" instruction sheet, leaving aside the plump book that provided incomprehensible or useless directions in several languages. When reading diagrams on the "getting started" sheet failed, they turned to the internet for help.[6]

Far less evident among those growing up during the period of Figure 6.2 was any creation of representational images in their exploratory play and development of expertise with electronic gear. Few children during this period spent their leisure time using their hands to draw, sketch, design, or model. For those young children like Martha who did choose to do so, they took a work-is-play approach, taking care to choose "just the right" drawing pencil, crayon, paper, fabric, or clay. Their places and times to create art were those they selected, often creating long-term projects in a series of pictures or clay figures. They wanted their drawings displayed, reviewed, and appreciated by adults around them.

As these children grew older, they often honed in on specific aspects of one or more art forms they could create and study by themselves. Older children consulted the internet in search of information, models, and new developments in the art form of their choice, whether it be graphic novels, young adult literature, or animated films. In person or on the internet, they shared their work less often with adults than with peers who had similar interests. For preteens and teens, these projects sometimes extended over several years. They talked of "my book, cartoon series, portfolio . . ." In general, young artists who played happily in their creation of such works rejected their parents' ideas about taking writing classes or art lessons, preferring their own ways of teaching themselves and seeking out their personal choice of models, peer mentors, and arts professionals in their schools or community youth organizations.[7]

Once children who had done a lot of creative work in their leisure time at home entered school, many found themselves disoriented and later disgruntled that they could not represent what they knew through their visual art. Girls adapted to school requirements for writing assignments and worksheets somewhat more easily than boys, but both resented the imposition of rules that set aside or dismissed their drawings, sketches, and diagrams. As these children reached secondary school, where they rarely found sufficient opportunities to take art classes, they sometimes turned their distaste for the ways of school into behaviors that led to their academic downfall.

Making and understanding images

Catherine and Tom, Martha's parents, knew well the perils a curious artistic child faced in school. Catherine, the elder daughter of the Turner family from Roadville, had a degree in public health. While studying for her Master's degree, she met and married Tom Armstrong, a biochemist at the National Institute of Health. They settled into an older home for renovation in Silver Spring, Maryland. Their only child, Martha, was born in 1993. She was a sickly child who started drawing when she was barely two years old. She grew up going to the art museums in the nation's capital, and by the time she was twelve, she was begging her parents to take her to New York for special exhibitions there.

When Martha started elementary school, Catherine and Tom worried. From the time she was a toddler, Martha had pushed her "I'll-show-you" attitude in her parents' face. When frustrated with the plastic toys that required matching sizes and shapes in constructing towers and inserting figures of the correct shape into the seats of toy trucks, Martha threw a temper tantrum. It did not improve her disposition when she discovered that the Barbie dolls she begged her mother to buy came with clothes that required patient alignment for dressing Barbie and buttoning her coat or slipping on her high-heel shoes.

In the first two years of school, Martha spent most of her time drawing, resisting her teachers' efforts to persuade her to write more than a few words at a time. She drew in response to assignments to read or write; she read books by looking at their illustrations. She was quiet, rarely talked, and her teachers feared she was language delayed. By the fifth grade, she had made a friend who liked to draw comic figures based on Manga comics. The two girls started a comic book of their own that featured female characters based on their school-mates. The idea fizzled out when they realized that coming up with ideas for plots was much harder than they had thought. When social studies teachers asked them to write accounts and analyses of past events or when their science teachers asked them to collaborate to write out plans for an experiment in biology and to provide a summation afterwards, Martha and her friend com-plained: "I don't know what you want." When teachers provided templates for them to follow, they resisted step-by-step directions or plans for what they should be doing. Their analyses often fell into narrative summaries of events in which one or more named characters did something or made something happen.

Concepts such as interdependent circumstances that bring about events over time did not fit with the penchant of Martha and her friends for thinking that some person always had to be behind something that happened. Depersonalized forces or a web of causes and consequences did not fit into their life narratives. So far as they were concerned, people made things happen, and most things happen now, in the present.

Martha's grades were a source of constant concern for her parents. However, they wanted her to remain in public school, believing strongly in the benefits she would have learning and studying in the midst of the increasingly diversified population of Silver Spring. Catherine and Tom felt they could compensate for any shortcomings in the school's academic challenges by spending time with Martha at home and in cultural and artistic events around Washington, DC. The family spent very little time watching commercial entertainment at home, and when they went for family outings, they preferred museums, cultural events, and hiking.

When she successfully finished the sixth grade, Martha got her own computer, complete with the latest software in the arts, including graphic design. Martha was too shy and self-conscious about her small stature to take part in after-school programs or to go on her own to any community organization programs. When Martha entered middle school, her parents noticed a change in her attitude. She became belligerent and withdrawn. She stayed in her room with the door closed, spending most of her time on her computer. In the ninth grade, Martha spent sixteen hours a week social networking on her laptop. In April, the month in which ninth graders in her school took the third set of examinations that were required during the year, she dedicated twenty-three hours to sending messages, photographs, and forwarding YouTube videos to her closest friends in her online network. She had left MySpace behind and moved on to Facebook. Her grades were falling lower.

Teachers called Catherine in for a conference. Martha would need special tutoring in algebra and English if she hoped to move forward into the next grade. Catherine and Tom devised a plan. That weekend, they took Martha to visit the space in which the Discovery Museum would soon be opening in downtown Silver Spring. Tours of the space were led by a woman who looked young enough to have entered university study only recently. She explained that the Museum would be developing arts programs for primary-school children, and they hoped to recruit talented teenagers as mentors. Martha listened, and shortly thereafter Catherine and Tom saw her talking to the tour leader.

The next weekend Martha told her parents she was going to meet "Ximenia" at the Discovery Museum. "Who's that?" Catherine shouted after Martha as she ran up the street to the bus stop. Later that evening, Martha went to the kitchen where her parents were preparing dinner and announced: "I've got something to tell you." Catherine and Tom exchanged a worried look. Martha explained that

Ximenia had been their tour guide at the Discovery Museum and when Martha told her that she was an artist, Ximenia had asked to see Martha's portfolio. Ximenia suggested that Martha think about interviewing to become a mentor in the youth arts outreach program at the Museum. Martha asked her parents: "Do you think I can do it? You know I don't like doing what anybody else tells me to do. And I'm not sure I'm good enough."

Martha's portfolio passed review by the board which was selecting mentors, and she thought her interview had been "fair." Within a few weeks, Martha met with the group of mentors chosen for the trial period. All the other mentors were older than Martha, and they all went to private schools. A few were beginning their studies in graphic design at a local commercial art school. Martha felt that everyone was thinking someone so young and petite as she could never handle the challenge of managing younger children. She came home and told her parents: "They're thinking, I know, that I can't do the job."

Martha had a stubborn streak, and it had gotten her into trouble in her classes at school. The difference now was that she really wanted to do what the situation called for. With her "I'll-show-you" attitude, she went online to learn all she could about the history of the idea behind the Discovery Museum. She asked Ximenia where she could get to know the inside of a museum arts program designed for children.

On weekends, Martha took public transportation into downtown Washington, where she had arranged interviews with junior staff members of the education outreach programs of several museums. She wrote notes and collected ideas and materials. In the weeks ahead, Martha worked out a scheme called "Picturing Words," which set out stricter guidelines than she herself would ever have adhered to at school. She planned to ask the primary children to write short biographies for each entry within the portfolios they were to develop. Within the format requirements, children would create portfolios of their sketches and drawings of materials in Discovery Museum exhibitions. They would follow each entry with a description of the space, idea, or person that had inspired pieces in the exhibition. In this way Martha could connect what the children drew and wrote with the goals of the Museum itself: get young children interested in inventions and innovations as well as the artists and scientists who created them. Martha asked members of the Discovery Museum education outreach program what they thought of her ideas and if some of them would be critics of the children's portfolios. The members were intrigued to see if the youngsters would take to the proposal that they compose, edit, and submit their work, along with their drawings and sketches, to outside critics. Martha was making some good impressions during her trial period for the mentorship.

Martha's blending and blurring of media forms had come from her involvement with MySpace, Facebook, and also her study of online networks of young artists. There she saw and evaluated the postings of others and spent hours each week working on her own site. In school, she met with her teachers and worked out a way to do extra work to bring up her grades. She still preferred projects that did not depend on writing. Whenever possible, if an assignment gave room for her creativity, she worked in music, video, cartoons, and photographs to complement her written work. Her English teacher was always saying, "Show, don't tell," and she hated it when other teachers did not seem to "get it" – that showing came easiest when students could use several means of showing what they wanted to tell. Martha thought the same ideas could apply in mathematics, and she intended to test this idea in her work at the Discovery Museum. She was accepted to be a mentor, and she moved on to the tenth grade.

Ximenia was at the Discovery Museum on Tuesday afternoons and Saturday mornings when the young artists took their sketchbooks and moved through the Museum with their mentors. They learned the behind-the-scenes work of curators, scientists, and artists. One day, Ximenia asked Martha if she wanted to visit Ximenia's art school. Martha showed up at the appointed time on Thursday afternoon in a grumpy mood. Ximenia walked Martha over and introduced her to Carol Anne, a senior art student who was working on a large clay pot near the sink at the other end of the studio. The girl ignored Martha and continued wetting her fingers and shaping the clay around the lip of the pot. Martha watched for a few minutes before she headed for the door. Carol Anne called after her: "Bring your portfolio tomorrow; I'll be here. Do you know what a real portfolio is? Mine's over there in the stand-up file. Look for the one with 'Carol Anne' spelled with an 'e' at the end of 'Anne.'" Ximenia looked on and smiled when she saw Martha bristle before she walked back in silence to the stand-up file.

The next day, Martha brought her portfolio and set it down beside Carol Anne, who said nothing. Martha walked around the studio looking at students' work, and made no effort to engage any of the artists in conversation or to ask them questions about their work or earlier experiences in art. Later that day, Ximenia asked Martha if she could come on Thursday afternoons to a drawing class at the art school for which Ximenia was a teaching assistant. Martha barely nodded, but she showed up every week with her sketch pad. On these occasions, Martha was sullen and showed no signs of appreciation. Ximenia continued to welcome her each week, but she did not push for conversation.

A year or so later, I caught up with Carol Anne at a coffee shop near the art school.

She pushed a thin portfolio over to my place at the table: "Martha's not bad, you think?"

Gone were the Manga figures I had come to expect in Martha's work in elementary and middle school. Her portfolio included portraits, shadow studies, and a few starts at botanical illustration.

"What's next for Martha?" I asked, studying the fern frond complete with spores that was the last piece in the portfolio.

"We're goin' to the botanical gardens tomorrow." Carol Anne explained that she had started ten months of Saturday classes in botanical illustration at the garden. She stayed on at the art school during the week and showed Martha her latest work whenever the teenager came to the studio.

Carol Anne took Martha to the botanical gardens where they both sketched. That pattern continued every week until Martha graduated from secondary school. She continued to live with her parents and enrolled in the art school for night classes. Her Saturday visits with Carol Anne kept going. When Martha was sixteen, she applied to the illustration program at the botanical gardens. She was the youngest student ever allowed to enroll. The instructor, whose "day job" was professor in botany at Johns Hopkins University, treated Martha as though she planned to be a botanical illustrator. Martha heard her instructor talk each week about her passion – the evolutionary developmental biology of palm trees. Each summer she took a group of students to places around the world where they could study palm trees. After class one day, Martha asked her instructor: "How did you figure out this was what you wanted to do?"

he next fall, Martha was accepted in the first group of students admitted to Johns Hopkins for the following year. She entered with a four-year fellowship from the university's botany department.

When I met up with Ximenia for coffee the following spring, our conversation turned naturally to Martha. I asked: "What made you take her on as your mentee? You must have guessed she would not make it easy for you."

"Someone had done it for me," Ximenia replied.

"Will you tell me about it?" I asked.

"Like Martha, I was a shy kid who kept my head in my art. My only friends were on the internet. I loved my art in elementary school, but when I got to middle school, we had no art. I got into trouble with my grades, and I tried to cut school and stay home, but my grandmother caught me. When I got to secondary school, there was one art teacher, Mr. Lane, but classes were only for juniors and seniors. One day, when I had enough money to take the city bus home instead of the school bus, I marched into his studio. I announced that I wanted to be in his class. Mr. Lane looked surprised, then told me to show up the next day after school with my portfolio. I did, and he looked through my work. I waited; he made no comment. He handed it back to me and told me to show up in the studio after school every Friday. He asked if I needed bus fare, and before I could answer, he handed me a twenty dollar bill and told me to show up for six months. That guy ended up being my mentor. He had a couple of other kids who came the first week, but they didn't keep coming. Why he kept on being there for me when I showed up in the studio is more than I know. Every time I went, he just kept on doing whatever he was doing. But he always nodded to some tool, print, open book, or newspaper article soon after I came in. Then he'd talk and point to the sink where the clay was or to the counter where there was a new set of paints. He never talked about what we were doing. He just talked about art and artists, techniques he liked and didn't like, and the art exhibitions at the museums. At the time, not much of this talk made any sense to me, but I would always start to work, and I'd listen.

Mr. Lane changed my life. I know that sounds trite, but it's true. That's why I wanted to work with the Discovery Museum in a program for older students who wanted to do art and little else and were failing or falling behind in school. Martha seemed like that kind of kid."

At the time she informally took on mentoring Martha, Ximenia did not think her interest in the teenager would particularly matter. Martha had resources, unlike Ximenia, who had grown up poor with parents who worked all the time and knew nothing about the arts. But Martha's resources had not been enough for her until external incentives and new opportunities came her way.

Ximenia did not imagine that Martha would go to art school or end up on the honor roll in her secondary school or graduate early with honors in three subjects. Ximenia did know that she and the Discovery Museum program had thrown down the gauntlet to a young woman who had the fighting spirit to take up a challenge. Until Ximenia came along, Martha did not connect what her school classes asked her to do with what she wanted to do. Martha had to see for herself how art worked in the wider world before she understood the value of writing, researching, sketching plans, and talking them over with others.

Martha never wanted to be without a way to use her art to express herself, and she knew that she loved exploring the out-of-doors. At Johns Hopkins she brought her art and science together and saw parallels in the ways the two had worked in her life. Though this was not without troublesome consequences in her teenage years, Martha had rearranged givens, created systems of rules, and laid out explanations of what she observed and what she understood. Her teachers had difficulties with Martha's need to rework what others thought of as fixed. She constructed theories based on what she saw; unable or unwilling to express her ideas verbally, she remembered these images and ideas as visual representations.[8] Like a scientist, she was keenly perceptive, filling her head and ordering her own world through her drawings. She explored points of view and symbolism, created metaphors, and worked out denotational and figurative values in her early cartoon work and later in her effort to create a graphic novel.

As a child and adolescent, Martha differed little from other teenagers in both Roadville and Trackton descendant families who wanted to create art in some form – videofilms, comic books, or graphic novels. They often started projects they did not finish, if they found they needed research, study, or planning they had not anticipated. Only occasionally would they jot down notes about plans and sketch out crude storyboards and sketches. Rarely did they refine them or refer to them while shooting or editing.

The children maturing in the period reflected in Figure 6.1 created with their hands and enacted sociodramatic play in backyard games. In doing so, they habituated rule-making that seemed to help them in their academic work. On the whole, they had lower rates of academic difficulty than their counterparts in the period portrayed in Figure 6.2. As videogames and television became normal parts of children's lives in the late 1990s, creative play decreased. Many children who grew up in front of television and DVDs expected to be entertained and to have on demand immediate responses from adults and electronic devices. Computers too slow to handle the newest videogame had to have new hard drives or be replaced entirely with the latest computer. Animation entertainment switched scenes with dizzying speed. Children rarely spent time visually settling in on detailed pictures in books or pictures and diagrams that remained stable. In spite of increasing cautions from physicians and child developmentalists, many parents availed themselves of the babysitting benefits of television, DVDs, and electronic videogames. Catherine and Tom differed from these parents, because of their own pleasure in music, art and science museums, as well as the outdoor life available in Washington, DC most of the year.

Proportionally more of the children represented in Figure 6.2 than in Figure 6.1 had trouble in academic subjects that required the understanding of concepts of change, such as osmosis or revolution, that inevitably appeared in academic texts. They reported that they could not "see" what the teacher or the text meant. Almost none of these students had spent time sketching, drawing, or sculpting by hand, and they did not sketch out their ideas for essays when they ran into difficulty with texts heavy with concepts they could not readily reduce to labels or short phrases. Their childhoods of entertainment, organized group activities, and interaction with digital means of communication had given them less direct use of their hands than their peers had experienced in prior decades. Instead they were multi-tasking and attending in short spurts to whatever they were doing without thinking consciously about how to remember conceptual materials. Those whose lives are represented in Figure 6.2 did not have extensive experience with the haptic feedback of fingers and hands that enhances the act of mentally visualizing.[9]

Playing for sport

Play is universal and goes on throughout the life span. Though its artifacts, sources, and motivations differ, it lives on as a major attraction for the human mind. As individuals grow older, play gets grafted onto work or the other way around. People play to their interests and not to impress others. In human development, play's key function has been to provide movement practice for the hand, body, and mind and to ready children for adulthood through imitative enactment of adult roles.

When the children of Roadville and Trackton left their neighborhood fields to join organized sports teams, they came to view play as dictating winners and losers. As adolescents joined more sports teams and arts-centered youth organizations, such as those in which Rebecca and Mark, and Robert and Richard spent so much time, they developed an ability to look ahead, anticipate consequences, and assess current performance against prior games or events. They played adult roles with the responsibilities that went along with these roles. They spoke in voices that carried the authority of their organization. They were creative, but within limits and in accordance with rules of the group.

Their involvement with sports meant that they were likely to listen to broadcasts of their favorite professional sport. These broadcasts modeled scripted talk that paralleled action on the field, court, or rink. Such broadcasts also included sports narrators whose job it was to fill in spaces of time-outs, half-times, or delays in the game because of injuries. These narrators gave background information, told stories, and offered comparative analyses of this game's events with those of recent games, rival teams, or seasons of the past. These narratives usually centered on a particular protagonist that could be a team, individual player, or the game itself, facing situations, teams, or individual demons as antagonists in the drama.[10] For widely popular and often nationally broadcast team sports, the coach and the players thought to have the best information about the game at half-time or after the game talked with sports broadcasters about specific plays and their view of how the game had gone. These narratives were told and retold as young sports fans re-played in dialogue and gesture what they had heard.[11]

Whether in a tennis game or multi-party role-playing computer game, children gain practice in visually predicting possible moves. Games force players to envision consequences around the question: "If I make this move, what positions will open for me, and how will my move determine the actions of the other party?" The central nature of play carries at least a double focus. It is about what happens now in surface actions, but it also has an inner aboutness. There is the text at hand as well as the inner or long-term text. Board games such as chess, as well as videogames, reflect this feature of play with every move. Only the most naïve players state the objective of a current move. It is the job of every player to figure out that the move of the moment has its lasting effects and therefore warrants looking ahead for possible consequences.

As they grow in experience, players become comfortable talking about something more than individual plays or moves. They indicate their understanding of the real work of their play, its inner aboutness. The experienced player from the losing team in a championship game can surely sum up key plays of the game. He is also likely to hint at good or ill turns of fortune, the brutal finality of time, and the need to respect the winning side. Though these appraisals begin with the immediate, they lead to some notice of lasting moral truths.

Fifteen minutes behind schedule, Dana and I raced off in the van to pick up Cordelia and Lily from school. Dana looked at her watch again: "Oh God, Cordelia'll be in a foul mood, I know. She hates for me to be late." Children's Broadway Theatre was having its first meeting of the season and the director was introducing the year's new play.

Dana was the younger of the two daughters of the Turner family from Roadville. She had followed her older sister Catherine to the Washington, DC area where they both had lived since they finished college. Dana had high aspirations and energy to match. We were rushing to collect her sixth-grade daughter Cordelia from school.

As Dana and I drove into the school parking lot, Cordelia and her friend Lily were deep into conversation just outside the school door. When they saw the van, they ran and jumped in the back seat with a quick "Hi" before they resumed their talk.

CORDELIA: I just hope we don't do one of those plays where you have to kiss and get all gooey with a guy. I'm not tryin' out if it's that kind of play.
LILY: You won't have to. Sheila'll take that role, especially if she gets to kiss an eighth-grade guy.

Dana tried to break into the girls' conversation: "You think they're gonna give the older kids the lead parts this year? They won't be around next year when they go off to McLauren [the secondary school]." The girls ignored the question and continued their talk. Dana asked her question again.

CORDELIA: Mom, you know that. Of course, and they're auditions, tryouts, like, you know, they do at community theatre, and the director=
LILY: =picks, but we've got a committee of any of us in the theatre more than two years. We have a say, and the lead ones have to have stand-ins.
CORDELIA: They're called understudies, stupid. Don't you know that?
DANA [firmly]:   Cordelia, it's not nice to call your friend names.

Two hours later, we picked the girls up from Children's Theatre, and they reported that the new play would be *Annie Get Your Gun*. Both girls had speaking and singing parts, and they seemed satisfied. They announced that they would *not* be doing any kissing.

128

Dana started singing the opening lines of "There's no business like show business." Cordelia asked: "How do you know that song?" Dana looked at me: "Didn't that hit Broadway in the 1940s?" I asked: "Didn't Ethel Merman play in the original cast?" Dana replied: "But there was a revival with Bernadette Peters in the '90s. That song is one of those that sticks in your head once you hear it. Peters was really good. I remember crying at the end of that show when Todd [Dana's husband] and I saw it on Broadway. I loved that show."

Both girls leaned over from the back seat and asked: "Was she pretty? The girl our director chose to play Annie has red hair!" Dana and I said: "So did Bernadette Peters!"

On the short ride home, Dana and I tried to interest the girls in the history behind the show, how the 1999 version had adapted by omitting the stereo-typical renderings of Native Americans that had been in the 1946 version, and how in the 1999 version, a white woman married her part-Native-American boyfriend. Detecting a glimmer of interest from the girls in this history, we rushed to tell them more. We wanted them to know how the 1999 version had changed the final shooting match between Annie and her boyfriend, out of a fear that feminists would object to the old ending in which Annie let her male opponent win. The girls lost interest.

As they jumped out of the van once at home, Cordelia shouted: "Don't go there, Mom. That stuff's history!"

Dana and I laughed in resignation and gathered groceries from the back of the van.

History has nowhere for us to go

As we made dinner, the girls watched a DVD in Cordelia's room. Dana and I stayed with the topic of history. Thinking of Cordelia's last comment of "That stuff's history," I asked Dana how much history Cordelia knew about Roadville and her grandparents, Alice and Jay Turner.

Dana had drifted off into her own thoughts, but after a bit, she responded: "Kids today don't care about history. You heard the girls in the van. They don't see that it gets them anything they want, and they don't care about knowin' any stuff about family identity. Today grandparents of most of the families I know live so far away and in another world, and they can't really relate to what the kids are up to these days. Cordelia never seems to take any interest in things my mom or I did. As soon as Cordelia was old enough, she stayed here in town rather than visit Todd's parents or my mom." She continued: "Last summer when we insisted she go visit my mom, Cordelia escaped behind her ear buds whenever she could. She listened to her iPod and bounced back and forth in time to her rap music. My mom thought it was funny, but I didn't. Sometimes I just want to yank those ear buds out of her ears. I used to hide them from her when she was younger. Now I think, what's the point?"

Dana's parents had left Roadville for Fort Wayne, Indiana in 1983, and they went back to the Carolinas only in the first few years after the move. For more than twenty years, they had not gone back, since all their friends there had died or moved away.

"When Dad died in 1998, we kids decided not to bury him in the graveyard of their old church back home. We buried him in the cemetery of the big Baptist church they belonged to in Ft. Wayne. Mom wants the same, of course. But she says she's not goin' there soon. Can you imagine that my mom is still workin'? She doesn't need to, I know. Dad had a good retirement from his job as manager at the big plant in Ft. Wayne. But she likes to keep busy, so I say, 'Go to it, girl!'"

Dana paused: "She's promised to come here for Christmas, you know, to visit me and to see Catherine and Tom's latest renovations on their house in Silver Spring. And she wants to see Cordelia and Martha, Catherine's daughter, too, of course."

Dana hesitated before she went on: "I have to say, though, I almost hate havin' her here. She's got a nose for any trouble that's brewin'. She'll for sure smell that Todd and I are in financial trouble, and we're havin' problems between us too. We haven't paid the mortgage in four months, we're $9,000 in debt on our credit cards, and the bills keep comin' in. He yells at me for not cuttin' back on expenses. I blame him for how the mortgage for this great big house the three of us don't really need has drained us for the last eight years."

Just over a year after this conversation, in November of 2009, the bank foreclosed on their house in suburban Virginia, and they sold the car. Todd kept the van. Before the foreclosure, Dana and Todd had decided to start the one-year separation necessary in Washington, DC before final divorce proceedings could move forward. Dana moved into an apartment in downtown Washington, where she could go by public transportation to her government job as a budget officer. Todd took a one-bedroom apartment in Arlington, Virginia close to his job in a government lobbying firm. Cordelia lived with Todd during the week and went to school there. The public schools in downtown Washington could not match the surburban schools in quality, and Dana and Todd could not afford private school. Dana picked Cordelia up from the subway early on Friday evenings and took her back out to Arlington on Sunday afternoons. Dana and Todd agreed on little except the need to keep Cordelia involved in "healthy" after-school activities. They both still wanted to give her "every opportunity."

Breaks in time

Dana's assessment of the lack of interest that Cordelia and her friends had in looking backward in time with members of the older generation stood up well to my survey in 2005 of 200 individuals, ranging in age from twelve to twenty-six in descendant households of Roadville and Trackton families. I asked three questions: Where did your grandparents grow up? What kind of jobs did they have? For either your mom or your dad, can you tell me something about their early life? To the first question, 38 percent identified the Carolinas correctly as the location of their grandparents' early lives. Others said they did not know or thought it was "somewhere in the South." To the second question, 12 percent said they thought their grandparents worked in factories. The remaining percentage had no idea, but among the respondents in their twenties, some commented that they knew their grandparents had not gone to a university, so they must have done some kind of "other work." When I asked what this description meant, they said: "You know, like farmers, plumbers, electricians, mechanics, telephone repairmen. I'm thinkin' if they didn't work in factories, they would've had those kinds of jobs."

Tabulation of answers to the third question was difficult because nearly three-quarters of the respondents initially gave me the names of the universities their parents attended or completed. They seemed to link their parents primarily with their educational identities. When I pushed the point that location of college was not what I had meant by "early life," most respondents brushed off the question. Many who tried to improve on their earlier answers did so by remembering photographs they had seen of their parents as children. They talked about specific physical features – long blonde hair, knock-knees, and pudginess – they remembered from those images. When parents had divorced, separated, or realigned with a partner other than the respondent's biological parent, children's answers tended to center on the parent of the same sex. Young adults among the respondents sometimes commented: "Now that you ask these questions, I'm thinkin' we just never talked about family history in our house. Now you've got me curious. Next time I'm home, I'll ask my mom [or dad] some questions of my own."

My survey showed that families talked little about family history. When references to the past came up, they related to relatively recent past events that one or more members of the household had experienced directly or heard about. Decontextualized events or people of the past rarely came up in conversations among family members. Events that had taken place at school or in after-school events, such as sports games, dance or theatre rehearsals, or exhibitions of visual arts or films were the most frequent topics among older children and their parents when they were engaged in a joint activity such as occasional dinners together and en route by car to events or activities.

After teenagers got their drivers license or had friends who could drive, parents had to work hard to find time for more than brief conversations with their teens. Within two-working-parent households or single-parent families with teenage children, parents tended to work longer hours, and teens had an increasing number of activities that kept them away from home for regular mealtimes. When the time came for secondary-school students to make university choices and to decide on those to which they would apply, some parents and their children came together for road trips or flights to other parts of the country to visit colleges of that region. Applications brought parents and their children together to deliberate essay topics and answers to such questions as: What is your greatest weakness?

Conversations at home or in the car among family members lacked the critical contextual feature of connection to either long-term personal interests or current projects needing both a backward and forward look. These conversations increasingly showed a narrowing range of temporal markers as well as a widening range of ways to omit any tense or subject markers. Shortened questions among children in the car asked, "There?" (in reference to shared knowledge of subject and action in a question such as "Were they there?" or "Had they been there?"). Questions about the success of a shopping trip for a specific item or after searching for an overdue library book were likely to be expressed as "Get it?" or "Find it?" (meaning "Did you get it?" or "Did you find it?").

Most of the university-educated parents of the first generation out of Roadville and Trackton wanted to help their children with their academic work. These attempts, particularly when writing essays was involved, were rarely successful. To a tenth grader composing an essay for history class, parents made exasperated comments such as: "That happened before the event you're talking about. You've gotta know what came *before* the time you're trying to talk about. When you write, you've got to show that one thing came before another thing. You can't just put everything down as though it all happened at the same time." When students in middle school were still bringing home worksheets with blanks for filling in responses to a novel or series of short stories they had read, parents urged: "Just write a complete sentence. And try to say something *original*![1] Do you think you could do that?" Frustrated parents often ended homework sessions abruptly with sarcastic rhetorical questions, such as: "Don't they teach you *any* grammar in school?"

Roadville and Trackton descendant parents had been the first in their families to complete secondary school and the first generation of university graduates. They were proud of their education as a mark of status they had worked hard for in the spirit of their own parents' work ethic. Now they wanted their children to follow in their valuation of being educated and "cultured" enough to use "good grammar" and to know something about history, museums, art, music, and theatre. Having an occupation and a professional identity was not enough for parents who saw themselves as high achievers and wanted their children to be the same.

Questioning parents

Table 7.1 compares the frequency of different types of questions parents addressed to their school-age children at home and in the car in the two periods

Table 7.1 *Parents' questions to their school-age children (8–14)*

Question type	1980–1992	1993–2005
Clarification	1166	988
Information-seeking	1265	4056
Confirmation	2008	906
Appraisal- or opinion-seeking	1492	893
Desire, want, or need solicitation	643	5237
Situational assessment solicitation	126	947

Data are based on 120 hours of randomly sampled audiorecordings of parent–child
times together after school and on weekends with selected times divided
between homes and car travel of both Roadville and Trackton descendant families.

of 1980–1992 and 1993–2005. In the first period, parents were likely to be part
of their children's activities both at home and in the neighborhood. In the second
period, children grew more independent of their parents and reliant on the
company of friends, sports teams, and community organizations. In the first
period, children were as likely to ask questions of their parents as parents were
to ask the young for information, opinion, clarification, and confirmation. In the
second period, parents had to ask questions to keep up with their children's
lives. Parents needed specific points of information: "Which weekends this fall
are scheduled for the school play?" As background for this information, they
sought from their children narrative accounts: "So what happened behind stage
in the second act? What was all that noise?" Acknowledging the greater knowledge on the part of the child, parents asked their opinions: "I heard the judges at
the art exhibition were tougher than anyone expected. What'd you think?"
Parents also wanted from their children overall assessments of situations in
which the young had been involved. The most ubiquitous questions of both
decades were "How'd it go?" and "You okay?" Quantification of questions
means little in terms of the range of number of morphemes in each. Some were,
of course, long and complex, stringing together requests for information,
opinion, and situation assessment. The major portion of the questions in both
periods ranged from one to six morphemes ("Okay?" "Over by 6, you think?").

  In the second period, Dana and other parents had to ask their children
management questions regarding schedules, homework, tests, and events in
school or after-school activities. In dual-working-parent or single-parent households, parents' schedules for work and leisure, including time for physical
exercise, often conflicted with those of their children. Balancing time in weekly
schedules was often a delicate matter, especially when parents separated or
divorced. The number and frequency of questions multiplied with two parents

in two locations and with different allotments of childcare responsibilities week by week and at various times of the year. Children easily grew defensive and cautious about transmitting information from one parent to the other. Parents often prefaced their questions with the statement: "I need to ask a simple question: 'When's soccer practice this week? Did coach say you'd need new cleats [studded shoes]?'" The information sought was needed to fill the other parent in on where and when children had to be for practices or events, homework assignments and up-coming tests, and where missing garments, sports equipment, or school books might be.

The marked increase in the second period of information-seeking questions from parents to children correlated with a decrease in length of sustained conversations and exchange of extended narratives between parents and children. These aspects of language interaction in turn correlated with the increase in children's levels of activity outside school hours. The compression of time between parent and children also related to a reduction in the number of utterances within narratives that children provided in response to questions from their parents. As interactions between Dana and the girls in the car indicate, the length of responses from the girls was no match for the narrative history Dana and I wanted them to hear. This pattern of brevity in narratives extended to conversations on the same topic. There were, of course, exceptions to these patterns. They tended to be from households such as that of Lisa and her sons Robert and Richard, who had to think, talk, and work together to maintain the ranch, an investment of all three members of the family. While their talk sometimes included narratives and other extended conversations on the same topic, most of their talk took place during their long car rides between the ranch and town. Lisa called these rides "down time," during which they talked, had "quiet time," or listened to audiobooks.

Table 7.1 also reflects the marked shift between the two periods in frequency of adult-generated questions that solicited the desires, preferences, and needs of their children. During the later period, the frequency of these questions, especially directed to younger children, soared. When I asked parents about this increase, they showed no surprise. Most just shrugged and seemed to think nothing of the matter. Those who tried to explain the change pointed out that asking their children to say what they needed, wanted, or thought saved valuable time. Arguments and debates took too much time. Parents explained: "There's no point in arguing or trying to change my kid's mind. It's just simpler to find out what she [or he] wants." Parents asked: "What do you want to eat tonight?" "What time do you want me to pick you up?" "Do you want to take the birthday present with you to school, so you can go to Alicia's party directly from school?"

Parents who held managerial or executive positions told me that they wanted their children to learn to take part in decision-making. These parents also spoke in terms of the rights of children and the need for parents to respect these rights.

Parents whose occupations did not involve management positions seemed more inclined to point to the need to save time, energy, and effort for both themselves and their children. They did not want to spend time or money buying clothes the children would not wear or preparing food their children would not eat.

To this end, parents asked their children to write their desires out for birthday parties and to include guest lists, options of entertainment and food, and preferences for any adult attendees. I have a collection of such lists made by children over the years, with those of recent years showing more elaboration of detail than those of earlier years. Most of these recent wish lists went out as email attachments, prefaced by a brief note from the child saying that since the recipient of this message was probably going to buy a gift for this occasion anyway, the wish list might be helpful. The emails with attachments went out to relatives and parents' friends. A different list went to the friends of teenagers likely to be invited to the birthday party.

Writing such lists was an effective prompt that parents gave to reluctant writers and readers who generally resisted receiving or transmitting any information in written form. Younger children wrote their lists by hand and decorated them with drawings and stickers. Older children did their decorating simply by using different fonts and colors to signify most desired brands, items, and colors. Teen girls ranked clothing, accessories, and perfume first, technologies second, and renovation and redecoration of their bedrooms as a final category. Gift cards from specific stores floated among categories. Emoticons punctuated the direness of need: "My iTouch is almost out of gigabites!" was followed by a sad face, while a request for an iPhone was followed by a smiley face.

In 2000, four primary classifications of activities emerged from data that I gleaned from parents' diaries of time with their children aged six to sixteen. Time spent in transport was included in all four categories. The first category was time dedicated to *entertainment* such as movies and specialty shows or events such as holiday parades, car shows, and state fairs. The second category included times given over to *instrumental activities*, such as shopping for groceries, school supplies, or sports clothing. The third category involved *family play*, times in which the family played games together or went for bike rides or camping trips. The final category included time devoted to *communal obligations*, such as practices, meetings, and events related to school, religious institution, or community organization. My talks with adult family members during my visits subsequent to reading their dairies added details surrounding their activities: initiator, frequency, cost in time and money, and parental reflections on the extent to which the family later brought up in their conversations the activities they had undertaken in these four categories. Ritual or special events like birthday outings, graduations, tournament games, and dramatic performances in the *family play* and *communal obligations* categories were occasionally recorded and sometimes downloaded in family photo albums or videos. Such archiving was done by parents and occasionally by staff or a volunteer parent for a sports team or drama or music organization. Conversations recounting these recorded events usually took place within the week following but were rarely referenced thereafter.

As children grew older, they spent more time with their friends than with their family members. In the summer of 2009, Rebecca, Mark, and I developed a survey to help settle a debate we were having about how teenagers managed their time. I asked some of the teenagers in other Roadville and Trackton descendant families to take the survey and to pass it around to their friends. Rebecca and Mark asked their friends to complete the survey. At the end of that summer, Rebecca, Mark, and I had 184 surveys that had been completed by young people who were between sixteen and eighteen years of age. My debate with Rebecca and Mark had centered on my hypothesis that technology would be the dominant draw for the time of teenagers. Rebecca and Mark disagreed, arguing, "Kids our age don't let technology dictate everything we do. It's mostly about doin' stuff *with friends*." Survey responses in Tables 7.2 and 7.3 proved Rebecca and Mark correct for both summer school breaks and during the school year. Respondents *did* spend many hours each week during both the school year and their summers surfing the net, blogging, checking out YouTube and their

Table 7.2 *Self-reported estimations of time distribution on school days*

What's time to you? (Data collected summer of 2009; 184 respondents, ages 16–18)

On school days, I . . .	Females	Males
Wake up to the alarm on my cellphone	74%	62%
Wake up when a friend calls me	10%	12%
Am late to the bus or to school	2%	8%
Have to finish my homework	18%	38%
Wake up someone else in my house	7%	4%
Phone to wake up a friend	13%	7%
Have a fixed schedule of after-school activities	63%	68%
Have a special time to do homework	15%	12%
Have a paid job outside the house for four or more hours	2%	2%
Spend two or more hours on homework	28%	20%
Spend an hour or more cleaning or doing laundry	32%	12%
Spend an hour or more preparing food	37%	10%
Spend one–two hours calling, texting, and emailing my friends	42%	29%
Do stuff like Facebook and Twitter for at least two hours	39%	38%
Over-estimate what I can do that day	94%	96%
Feel stressed that I don't have enough time	91%	84%
Read or write texts more than a page in length	29%	27%

Table 7.3 *Self-reported estimations of time distribution during the summers*

What's time to you? (Data collected summer of 2009; 184 respondents, ages 16–18)

On most days in the summer, I . . .	Females	Males
Sleep as late as I want to	26%	38%
Figure out each day as it comes	38%	47%
Spend four or more hours calling, texting, and emailing my friends	48%	52%
Do stuff like Facebook and Twitter for four or more hours	33%	29%
Do sports with friends two or more hours	16%	38%
Work out at the gym an hour or more	9%	16%
Go shopping with friends an hour or more	43%	4%
Have a paid job outside my house for four or more hours	13%	11%
Clean or fix things around the house an hour or more	47%	19%
Shop for food for the family an hour or more	8%	3%
Over-estimate what I can do that day	87%	92%
Feel stressed that I don't have enough time	72%	63%
Read or write texts more than a page in length	9%	2%

favorite websites. But Rebecca and Mark pointed out firmly that they were spending time *with* their friends when they were communicating with them by texting, emailing, or social networking through chats and Facebook, Twitter, or Foursquare. When friends moved away, they stayed in touch, at least for a few months, by the same means plus video calls.

Keeping it "totally"

Knowing the span of years of my audiorecordings, parents of the third generation of Roadville and Trackton descendants often asked me how their children's language differed from the language they or their parents had used. Among the most memorable features of their grandparents' language were vocabulary items referring to objects and events no longer familiar to the current generation. These included terms such as tobacco *slide*, meaning the wooden slide pulled by mules from fields of tobacco at harvest time. Grandparents also had euphemisms such as *darn* or *danged* for curse words such as *damn* or *damned*.

In addition to vocabulary items, an obvious difference between the language of grandparents and grandchildren was the early generation's use of Southern colloquial expressions. Many of these related to behavioral norms linked to inexplicable outcomes. For example, at least a dozen centered on the use of salt to ward off bad luck or to bring good luck.[2]

In earlier chapters, differences in the range and frequency of uses of past tense have been mentioned. Though Roadville and Trackton grandparents had, in many cases, not completed secondary school, they used past perfect ("she had asked") and future perfect ("she will have asked") tenses within their informal speech. They also frequently scattered Biblical phrases and lexical items into their talk.

The speech of their children, particularly those with advanced education degrees, even during informal conversations, was not as "colorful" as their parents' talk. Most notable among the children was the absence of narratives that featured characters or historical references that came to be judged as "politically incorrect" during the 1980s. Black and white grandparents told racist stories that stereotyped segments of the other race ("po' white trash") as lazy, "no-good," "dropouts," or "welfare moms." As young children, the first generation of Roadville and Trackton recited rhymes and sang songs that included lexical items that were ethnic slurs. They passed these on to their young children. Grandparents used expressions and sayings without apparent recognition of their historical reference and embedded stereotypes. For example, the phrase "a long row to hoe" refers to the work of slaves in cotton fields, and the expression "He's free, white, and twenty-one" refers to privileges exclusive to whites through much of the history of the United States. Grandparents sprinkled these and similar references to work and judgment through their conversations.

Though parents politely tolerated my overly detailed answer to their question about their grandparents' talk, what they really wanted to know was: "And what about the way kids talk today?" They feared that popular culture, popular music, particularly rap music, and electronic media were corrupting their children's language. They expected me to confirm and explain trends in "teen talk."

Instead I gave them the information included in Table 7.4 with several caveats. Primary among these was the point that oral language differs from written language, and that both vary in relation to audience, function, stylistic choices, and genre. Most notably, their children's oral language relied heavily on the intimate knowledge they had of images, sounds, and performances that supported and complemented oral language. This knowledge and experience meant that their speech tended toward being multimedia in style and presentation. I reminded parents that language neither corrupts nor becomes corrupt. It simply remains in dynamic interdependence with the social and material environment in which it is spoken and in relation to the increase in images assumed in many of the language uses of the young. Parents could identify with the close ties between image and word when they reflected on the rapid growth of the requisite use of PowerPoint presentations they experienced in the business

Table 7.4 *Characteristics of adolescent peer talk (1998–2010) in contrast with style features of written academic discourse*

Style features of peer talk	Conventions of academic written discourse
Layering of symbol systems including gestural, musical, and body decorative	*Required:* Extended written texts; images (e.g., charts, tables, figures, and photographs), if included, must be labeled and their contents referenced within the written text
Repetition of layered collaborative narratives based on shared experiences	*Proscribed:* Repetition of content, other than in limited uses (such as transitions or summations)
Repetitive commentary on the same range of topics	*Required:* Attribution to original retrievable reference of any content repeated (cited) from a source other than current author
Strong preference for narrative genre over explanation or description	*Required:* Expository, reportative, and persuasive texts including an argument of key points with limited use of narratives to illustrate points
Sequencing of events within narratives marked by coordinating conjunctions	*Required:* Clauses linked primarily through causal and temporal conjunctions; introduction of additive points permitted with the use of *furthermore, in addition* (etc.) and summative points with the use of *thus, therefore, as a consequence* (etc.)
Frequent use of judgment in absolute terms	*Proscribed:* Author's value judgments and adverbs leading the reader to assess judgments of content (e.g., *unfortunately, even, obviously*)
Redundant use of "shallow" syntactic constructions and familiar vocabulary	*Required:* Technical or specialized lexical items and dependent and independent clauses
Dominance of present tense with narrow range of past or future tenses	*Required:* Fluency with range of tenses needed to indicate relationships among ideas and events
Frequent use of *if–then* propositions as threats or challenges	*Proscribed:* Use of second-person pronoun (implied or stated), thereby precluding use of hypotheticals as threats or challenges
Preference for use of hypotheticals for recast events rather than future projections	*Required: If–then* propositions ranging across past, present, and future
Preference for unbalanced *if–then* propositions with one variable on one side of the proposition and several on the other side	*Preferred:* Balanced hypotheticals with variables on either side of the *if–then* proposition relatively equal in number and semantic weight

meetings and conferences of their own work lives. The websites of their businesses carried more images than text and offered links to more images.

Table 7.4 contrasts conversational language of adolescent peers (1998–2010) with style features of written academic discourse. During these years, adolescent peer interactions increasingly integrated visual images (e.g., cell-phone photos), gestures, and voice modulation. Language socialization by peers both in face-to-face interactions and in chats on the internet intensified over these years in frequency and expectation of entertainment, for either comedic or shock value. Internet conversational exchanges through social media such as Facebook and blogs encouraged the layering and referencing of images, moving and still. YouTube encouraged amateur videos that invited critique and commentary in social media. Tweets developed regional dialectal differences and stylistic features that had no corresponding forms in spoken or written language elsewhere.[3] The online photo management and sharing application Flickr allowed the young to tell any story they wished through photographs and to compare their photographs with those of others.

In their conversations with one another, teenagers layered their collaborative narratives. They could do so because of shared time in one another's homes, fast food restaurants, sports events, musical gigs, and popular music concerts. They had an overwhelming amount of shared knowledge from the same experiences whether in their schools or during their recreational time. In addition, the shared experiences of those active in community organizations provided extensive material for retellings of known events in which they had all participated.[4] Junctures were much more common than interruptions with disruptive semantic content or syntactic contributions incongruent with smooth completion of an utterance another speaker had initiated. Young people judged retellings of known experiences embellished with repetition of phrasing and exaggerated elongation of key words as highly entertaining, especially when these retellings included dramatic re-enactment of the gestures and body language of individuals who had participated in the event being recounted. Retellings were filled with repetition of adverbs, such as *totally* and *absolutely*, as well as summative exclamations, such as *awesome, far out, you're kiddin' me*.

In their informal talk with one another, older children and adolescents rarely used complex syntax or unfamiliar lexical items that might mark the speaker as being outside the norms of the current group (for example, too coarse, serious, academic, nerdy, sexist, or moralistic). Verb tenses stayed in the simple present, past, and future, with occasional use of the present perfect and past perfect, but with rare use of future perfect ("she will have asked") or past perfect progressive ("she had been asking") or future perfect progressive ("she will have been asking"). Preference for simple tenses fit the desire of young storytellers for the sense of an on-going and continuing action, giving listeners the feeling of being directly within the scene of the action. Since the perfect progressive forms express actions that continue up to a point in the present, past, or future, these forms do not function stylistically to create the effect of simultaneous inclusion desired in retellings. Nuances of timing and causal links slowed rapid-fire overlapping and layered retellings and re-enactments.

Consequently, many educated parents who wrote extended texts in their professional work viewed the syntax or "grammar" of young people's talk as "shallow," without complex constructions, multiple prepositional phrases, or conjunctions, such as *because, since, when, until*. When a young person held the floor in talk among friends, the use of coordinating conjunctions, such as *and, or, yet,* and *so* pushed the story along with a sense of immediacy that subordinating conjunctions did not convey to peer listeners in the same way.[5]

In their academic classes at school, adolescent speakers met requirements for written genres such as essays and research reports that differed significantly from their habits of peer talk. Table 7.4 indicates for each feature of casual talk the corresponding requirement in academic writing. Academic writing called for uses of narratives and pronouns, choice of tenses and vocabulary, and fluency in arrangement of ideas within complex sentence structures rarely expressed in young people's talk. Ease in composing genres called for in academic writing was difficult to achieve for young people who spent little time deliberating decontextualized ideas or planning collaborative projects with adult models.

In the casual talk of young people, introduction of topics or situations not already "on the table" could mark a speaker as an outsider unaware of the unspoken preference among adolescents that, once they got going on a topic, they wanted to say more and more about the same events, people, concerns, and shared experiences or feelings. They did not want to jump to an entirely different topic until a social leader of the group took leadership in doing so. The norms that held friends together might be described as "close-up," having to do with clothing, manner, likes and dislikes, family similarities, school identity, etc. Within friendship groups, young people wanted to be unmarked so as to remain with the group's patterns of interactions. Social leaders sometimes introduced new marks from commercial sources. Certain brands of clothing figured centrally in marking individuals for group membership and sustained acceptance. Within any particular group of teen girls, Old Navy garments might be favored over those from Abercrombie and Fitch. A few weeks later, a casual comment or joke by a social leader rearranged the order of preferred retailers, suddenly elevating Forever 21 or Wet Seal to the top. Other groups spurned name brands and new clothing, priding themselves on shopping "vintage" and knowing the best used-clothing stores around town.

Marks of being "with it" carried different meanings, depending on spatial location and composition of groups. For example, individuals marked themselves in dress, language, and demeanor for a particular ethnic or racial identity only in certain contexts where they met with friends who might not have shared or joined their other friendship circles. In those friendship circles where such marking might signal out-group status, the goal was to fit within this context and not to be marked by overt signs of ethnic or racial membership. Adolescents like

Jerome, Tameka, and Bernardo, whose mixed-race heritage and linguistic facility enabled them to take identities according to social need, monitored themselves in accordance with contextual and performative shifts. They remained especially alert to who and what was "in" and who and what was not.

Multimedia writing

By the opening of the new millennium, teachers and parents saw the influence of numerous media other than the printed word on the written language of young people. They wanted to rely on images to convey intensity, immediacy, humor, personal connection, and representation of authorship. They thought of writing as collaborative, drawing freely from sites they accessed through the internet and from their friends. Texts might be "singular," but authorship was "plural."[6]

When Wikipedia came onto the scene in 2001, adolescents jumped on the model, often justifying their slight attention to citation, editing, and length of written texts by referring to the "encyclopedia" of Wikipedia. Teachers, sometimes aided by parents, needed to explain to students concepts such as *intellectual property*, *authorship*, *original*, and *jointly authored*. They needed to distinguish Wikipedia from earlier encyclopedias through concepts such as *refereed*, *fact-checked*, and *confirmed source attribution*. Teachers had to explain to students that simply listing a bibliography of references consulted was not enough; the sources themselves had to be of certain types in order to qualify for admission into the genres of writing preferred in academic contexts. Students had to learn what the prepositions that teachers attached to "writing" meant in terms of specific required types of citation. "Writing out" their ideas for research papers, reports, or essays was the preferred kind of academic text in secondary-school classrooms. For this kind of writing, students had to keep track of the sources they consulted and their use of ideas and quoted material from these sources. As they "wrote up" their ideas, they were generally closer to the final product and had to attend to organization, argument, supporting ideas, and style. Through both types of writing, writers were expected to draw upon sources in order to elaborate and confirm their "original" idea.[7]

Writing in extended texts on depersonalized topics was generally unpopular and often troublesome for nearly all the third-generation children of Roadville and Trackton. Exceptions like Robert Avery, whose work within youth organizations involved speaking extended and deliberative texts, had an easier time than did those young people who had little such practice. Robert's oral work in his youth organization transferred for him easily into the required norms of composition in academic life. Cordelia and Martha both struggled in their academic writing, though for what appeared to be different reasons. Cordelia viewed her refusal to write as a way of resisting her parents. Martha simply preferred to find ways around the production of extended texts by illustrating and demonstrating through images and with the fewest possible words. Denny and Tameka, adept and quick to communicate orally, preferred cross-referencing internet sources when they were asked for information. They both knew how to program. Both of them sketched and created models in their work with computers. Both made impressive oral presentations that smoothly incorporated audio and video materials. Both regarded extended stand-alone written texts as outmoded, inefficient, and generally unnecessary in their work, study, and social lives.

All their views regarding the merits of multimedia and use of several modes of presentation simultaneously did not, however, mean that young people did not write. In fact, between 2000 and 2010, pre-teens and teenagers in descendant families of Roadville and Trackton composed a wider variety of genres than their counterparts in the prior decade. To fuel their imaginative work, they read and consulted a variety of sources on the internet and in magazine sections of bookstores. They created 'zines and graphic novels, wrote scripts and advertisements for their friends' videos, and annotated photographs of their bike rides, hikes, soccer games, theatre events, and parties. The genres they composed ranged from advertisements and guarantees to reviews of movies and novels; all included images as well as written texts.

In 2009, on several occasions, I worked with a dozen or so teenagers to review their recent writing on the internet, in school, and in any other contexts they were willing to share with me. The group included honors students as well as some who admitted they were barely hanging on even in their easiest school subjects. All were involved in several different after-school activities, and most attended some kind of summer program or camp or had summer jobs. Of their views on writing, the most apt remark came from a twelve-year-old who joined the teenage group. As we listed and categorized types of writing and the kinds of images they used, he said: "For me, if I can't see it, I can't get it." Though the others laughed, one senior honors student jumped in to agree, pointing out the extensive use of drawings, sketches, models, and diagrams both in his science textbooks and in project directions for the upcoming Intel Science Competition. Young people know what they mean when they talk about their need to envision and embody knowledge. They sense that cognition is designed for action. Representational models of information they create and visually embrace stay with them, and they can move from their visuospatial knowledge to verbal explanations more easily than they can from verbal expression to visual or enacted representations.[8]

The language behind seeing and doing

In subsequent group meetings with teenagers, I brought up the idea of "If I can't see it, I can't get it" to explore how they might respond. No one disagreed with the idea once they understood its meaning, and they began to collect examples from their own school subjects and, most especially, their own interests.

However, they also argued that when they wanted to use or to be able to return to ideas they had seen in books or magazines, on the internet, or in models, they had to have words, in their head, in notes, or in conversations with others about the ideas and images. Visual learning drew upon and needed support from language to bring these into comparison, collaborative negotiation, and instantiation within creative work (films, exhibitions, school projects, etc.). Some young people, especially those who traveled in pursuit of their interests or pastimes such as cycling, also pointed out that having a paper map in a backpack and some kind of itinerary came in handy when they were outside zones where their cellphones worked or they were unable to get to an internet café. In other words, they were not inclined to dismiss entirely the value of hard copy as memory supports, critical sources of information when electronic technologies failed them, and sources of new ideas or confirmation of their own opinions and sources of information.

Since many of the young people with whom I met were in several different collaborative projects at the same time, I asked them to record digitally for me their talk during these times of work and play. In their deliberations, they did not intend to reach consensus, but to share ideas and to respond to the sketches, scripts, models, or drawings before them.[9] Their language had much in common with the talk of educated adults in the joint work of informal learning environments, such as studios or laboratories, family vacation planning, and youth organization discussions.

Several of the young people supplied videorecordings of their group at work, and these indicated the extent of gestural attention-pointing, use of visual representations, and sustained attentiveness of participants. These recordings showed the ways in which group members listened to one another, often changing a course of action under way in order to incorporate suggestions from someone in the group.

Though the deliberative conversations the young people recorded for me meandered and often took off in unexpected directions, my analysis of their recordings confirmed three primary functional features in extended stretches or chunks of their talk. These are *relational*, *referential*, and *extensional*. All three kinds of language chunks help speakers "see together" and achieve joint long-term planning, consider consequences, and gain a sense of agency for individuals and the group as a whole. Oral and written language work together, along with visual representations in a variety of forms, such as graphs, maps, charts, photographs, sketches, and models.

Relational language brings members of the group together and relies on joint oral recall of information known to everyone. Relational language becomes readily identifiable through the prevalence of *vocative call-ups* that members use to identify specific participants and to ask questions of clarification. Here, one speaker uses the name of another within the group and simultaneously gestures toward the individual and/or looks in his or her direction.

Vocative call-ups (e.g., *Raoul* in (1) below) come as direct vocatives or within attributions of source for an idea or experience in need of clarification (e.g., *Susan* in (2) below).

1. Raoul, you weren't here then. What do you need to know to get up to speed?
2. Susan, that time you tried to film while you were on your bike, you used the strap off your backpack?
3. Let's see, Kurt, when you went to drag that into this file, Riley said we weren't ready. What made him say that?

In these instances, the attention of the addressed individual is called for, and the group is reminded that this individual has made a prior contribution to the conversation at hand or to past shared experiences familiar to group members.

A second means of bringing about relational interaction comes through the use of the *attributional call-in*. In (3), Kurt is being asked to respond in a confirming or expanding way to an idea that Riley has previously contributed. If Riley is physically present, he is implicitly given the conversational floor to explain, deny, or expand on the idea attributed to him. At this point, attention of the group is directed toward a common object for viewing (the computer screen) as well as an idea under consideration.

Hence, the focus in relational language is not merely on a specific person; it is also on individual sources of ideas or actions being reviewed by the group. Other examples given below include clarification as well as confirmation of attribution.

4. And when Roger worked on this design, you [nodding the head toward Roger] used this [pointing to a set of calculations on the computer screen]. Okay with that?
5. Heather's idea is that we get the filming going again and deal with details later. Everybody okay with that?

In both (4) and (5), the speaker calls on the collective attention or recall of an idea being noted. Therefore, a common experience is being attributed to any and all members of the group who might see the conversational floor as cleared for any member of the group to contribute further or to expand on the point being referenced.

An additional role of relational language is to call on the self as speaker in the present moment and to note the need for an accounting of prior mental states or internal dialogues and also to note a possible need for correction and clarification. In (6) the speaker asks for both specific information and explication of the mental processes that might have gone on to bring about the current action (often a visual representation of some sort).

6. What did I do here [looking at detail of drawing]? Hmmm, I'm not sure, now that I think of it. Let me see if I can remember.

This request for verbal contributions from other members in response to the articulated mental processes of the speaker is an *accountability call-in*. Such a call-in need not be centered on the individual speaker; it may also invoke all members of the current deliberations as in (7).

7. We've not made this step clear [pointing to a particular feature of the diagram on the computer screen]. If we're gonna do that part, I'm thinkin' we've got trouble with that part bein' able to move in the model. Anyone else see what I'm talkin' about?

Here the pronoun *we* and the use of *anyone else* make clear the need for members of the group to relate to one another and simultaneously to the visual image before them.

Relational language sometimes includes members who are outside the immediate scene. In (3) above, it was not clear whether or not Riley was physically present, though the group obviously included him at some prior point in time. Relational language indicates that a speaker is "inside" the head of another member of the group and anticipating the need to account for actions and representational forms currently under review (6) and (7). Relational language avoids the first-person singular pronoun and instead depends heavily on first-person plural and second- and third-person pronouns to sustain a sense of the shared identity and responsibility of the group. Deictics, such as *here*, *there*, call on the visual attention of all those in immediate physical contact or jointly attending through video calls. Gestural narratives in relation to schematics, models, or other visual materials lay out progress from a current state toward a future or intended set of moves.

Referential language is the kind of talk that members of collaborative projects use to cite verifiable retrievable evidence from sources all members know or can access. Primary within such language is reference to a source that will be retrievable for all beyond the present moment and that can be referenced and accessed by individuals not part of the current conversation. Such language often includes specialized vocabulary used by those who share the interests of the current group. The most easily recognized type of referential language is the naming of a shared known authority as in (8), (9), and (10). The authority can be a generic form of sourcing, such as a list of reference sources everyone uses or a newly discovered source introduced to the group by a current member. Young people tend to cite as authorities specific individuals, websites, television programs, events, and concerts rather than generic references, such as "reality TV shows."

8. With that kind of entry list [pointing to a map and listing of all the European cyclists expecting to take part in a northern California bike race], they've got to be pullin' some folks from the east coast too.

9. Those directions aren't worth shit. Look at 'em. Does anyone ever read this shit [referring to a set of directions all the members know and have previously talked about]?

10. Did you [addressed to the group as a whole] check out Drake's website?
    Cool, huh? He's totally awesome [referring to a site that the speaker does
    not know is familiar to all the members].

As (10) illustrates, it is common in any chunk of referential language to include
several names and kinds of authorities. Material supports, gestural directions,
and on-the-spot visual representations (drawn in the air, sketched on paper, or
called up on a computer or cellphone) guide and reinforce forward movement of
the group's work.[10] The primary function of referential language beyond giving
the group a shared retrievable source for cross-referencing and return-checking
is establishment of an information platform from which the work under way can
move forward.

Extensional language, the third kind of talk used in collaborative projects,
provides a way to move the group away from past expressed ideas, which may
have been based only in the relations known to group members or in the
common reference base of all. To move forward into a future beyond the current
group, such language intentionally calls attention to the future thrust of the
group's work and extends current deliberation toward future achievements.

Extensional language includes the naming of a range of variables that may
affect the project's path of action and likelihood of success, as in (11) and (12).

11. And if we could just find someone who could put us up, we could get there
    for this race. Then would we be able to get the shots to post on our website?
    When's the race starting?

12. What about pulling in my dad? He could drive us there, and he might know
    somebody who could put us up for the night. Would that work? You think?

By implication, as well as by highly specific mandating language, the chunks of
extensional language within deliberative discourse make clear what must or
should be done. Therefore, the language generally includes modals, such as
will, *would*, *can*, *could*, *should*, and *must*, and verbs with imperative intent, such
as *ought to* and *have to*.

Critical within extensional language is the laying out of variables or conditions related to temporal and causal considerations. Thus extensional language chunks include conjunctions and prepositions that mark time as well as
act and sequence (*when, then, because, since*), set out hypothetical propositions,
and raise questions of *what if?* or *what then?* Such language indicates the
interdependence and complexity of variables that may affect outcomes or the
future projections of tasks.

Relational language provides the social and mental glue of group focus and
interactional history, while referential language ensures a common informational base for all members of the group. Relational and referential chunks
enable the work of extensional talk. Extensional language enacts a long-
standing axiom of collaborative work: moving projects forward means hypothe-
sizing possible events or outcomes in relation to given conditions.

Through extensional language, the group prepares not only to commit to the future, but also to do the comparative and contrastive case analyses on which future work depends. The point of such analyses often rests in specific cases, but emotive and opinionated responses personalize the work at hand. Prior instances need not be within the knowledge base of all group members; however, if known to current members, these instances are often introduced, described, and explained by individuals in relation to the focal task of the group. This tactic allows the group to consider not only how to place itself in relation to other teams, projects, or tasks, but also how to evaluate its own situational planning.

Extensional chunks may also include individual emotional responses to the project. These can affirm, contradict, deny, or supplement issues within the discussion frame, as in (13).

13. I'm just not seeing where this is going. I'm thinkin' we're not gonna be able to pull this thing off. I just don't see the point of takin' all the stuff we're talkin' about.

Implicit in such a statement is the contrast between what currently seems to be "where this is going" and what others in the group had thought would happen. In many instances, speakers who set forward such a comparison single out their own experiences or specific knowledge of other cases, as in (14).

14. I remember one other time when I felt like this. We were plannin', you remember, to go to Boise, Idaho for a race. I'm feelin' that way now, like all this might not be worth it.

Emotive responses and value judgments, offered by a single speaker and stated as generalizations or opinions, often open the floor for other speakers. Thus one speaker can lead the full group to amend the direction of deliberations in order to think and work more effectively toward the future.

Relational, referential, and extensional language chunks may appear chaotic and disjointed. However, the strength behind the ethos of collaborative work in situations of collective endeavour, be it voluntary or with-profit, youth or adult, comes from the mix of types of talk. Interweaving personal experience with retrieval references and with hypothetical projections creates the common purpose of project work.

This book has been about the talk, work, and play of families descended from two working-class neighborhoods of the Piedmont Carolinas and first described for the decade 1969–1981. The goal has been to lay bare for the descendant families of these two neighborhoods some of the intricate ways that broad economic, social, and geographic forces press on parents' ways of talking and interacting with their children and adolescents. The stories here should be treated as a source of insight and information on the social history of families and communities adapting to radical economic, social, and technological changes at the end of the twentieth century and the opening of the next. I make no claim that their stories are a point of reference for "typical" families and individuals, though in the communities where they live and in their places of work and play, those around them see them as ordinary and normal "just like the rest of us."

Their stories will be read and evoked for a thousand purposes that neither they nor I would have dreamed of nor wished for. No coherent narrative can ever convey all that lies behind the collection of words and ways, numbers and names. Beyond certain cultural conventions of social history and ethnography, preferences and avoidances have shaped this work. Certain theories and themes enabled comparative analysis of the lives of individuals whose stories fill these pages.

As author, I have selected and ordered this collection of narratives in line with my inclination not to recount lives destroyed by lost opportunities. Instead I try to make visible the motives, habits, faith, and responses to turns of fortune that enable individuals and families to pursue the actions they choose. Many of their adaptive ways speak to health, education, transportation, and environmental policies, and yet few leaders in these fields will ever learn about these ways. In 2010, 15 million children lived in poverty in the United States. Of these, 1.35 million children were homeless, most of them black or Latino. Children, though only one-quarter of the nation's population, accounted for 36 percent of all people living in poverty.[1] Such figures encourage the prevailing dichotomy that divides those who make it from those who do not. Most Americans do not see the poor as individuals and families or take into account the fragility and fluidity of their situations. Policymakers and the public media rarely portray the healthy adaptive skills of those who live below the poverty line. Thus Americans find it hard to have confidence in the resilience and determination of those who go about making and remaking their daily lives the best they can.

Humanity is experienced on a spectrum. Any particular day selected at any point in an individual life will be neither all good nor all bad, neither entirely full nor completely empty. I have chosen not to dwell on the bad and the empty. Though I have included cruelties of neglect and unimpeded ambition, I have not dwelt on the turns of fortune and mindlessness that propelled them.[2] I have followed characters around these turns.

Racism, race, and identity

Of the social history of those whose parents left Roadville and Trackton between 1981 and 1985, it is logical to ask about differences in the trajectories of families from the two neighborhoods – one white, the other black. In the *long* view across the three decades since the early 1980s, I found few significant differences in how children of the children of the two communities made their way through each day. Across the years, families of both groups experienced tragedies that resulted from bad luck and bad decisions, from being in the wrong place at the wrong time, and from over-reaching for themselves and their children.

If, however, we extract specific time blocks out of the full run of the three decades, the years between 1981 and 1992 did show some differences between the lives of blacks and whites. By 1981, over a decade after the legislative achievements of the Civil Rights Era, racism had by no means been significantly reduced, but it played out differently in various parts of the nation. Black working-poor families that left Trackton met discrimination in housing, school-ing, and employment opportunities regardless of where they went after the textile mills closed and agrarian life could no longer adequately support their families. The few families that made their way to cities such as Washington, DC or New York City had to live in crowded housing projects and compete for low-skilled jobs. However, Southerners, including those from Trackton, generally out-paced northern native blacks in educational achievement, earnings, and resilience.[3]

Most of the black families that left the textile mills and farms in the 1981 recession stayed in the Southeast, which in the decade of the 1980s had only a few major metropolitan areas. These did not have decaying inner cities as did northern urban centers that had been home to waves of immigrants. Aside from Atlanta, Georgia, most southern cities built inner-city housing projects more slowly than northeastern cities or not at all. Families from Trackton who scattered through the South could, more often than not, find duplexes and small bungalows managed by local landlords, some of whom exploited poor families and others who simply wanted the rent and "no trouble."

Those black families who did go north to urban centers tended to head for cities, such as Philadelphia and Boston, where relatives had previously gone, and middle-class black communities dated back before the Civil War. The achievements of these ancestors, however, did not protect poor blacks clustered in miserable housing and living in dire poverty from the insult of schools in horrific condition or the ravages of alcohol, random violence, and drugs, especially crack-cocaine. The decade of the 1980s took a toll that can never be adequately recounted by me or anyone else.[4]

The economic recession in the first half of the decade of the 1980s, along with high unemployment of young blacks, fed an underground economy in drug-trafficking marked by hierarchical sophistication. By the end of the decade, young adults who had come through levels of this economy as "kids" were fighting for a position in international drug cartels, and the stakes were getting higher and the reach of drugs wider.[5] Some mid-sized towns that clustered the poor in run-down apartments on one side of town with no public transportation or social resources felt the destruction of drugs, gun violence, and gang culture in their children's lives. As the spread of drugs affected more locations in more states and as public media spread more information about the international drug business and the centers of its operations outside the United States, state legislatures cracked down with stringent laws. These new laws rarely touched the leaders of drug production and distribution, but they hit hard young dealers and users living in poor black communities. A trio of offenses, one or more of which could sometimes be minor, brought long, even life prison sentences. By 2000, nearly every American knew that black men in prison outnumbered those in higher education.

Far less widely acknowledged in the general US population were the achievements of black men and women who overcame childhoods of deprivation, family disruption, neighborhood violence, and racial discrimination to achieve political office and distinction in legal and academic fields. Their diverse trajectories of achievement came and went in the public media, confined more often to fictional and autobiographical accounts than to front-page headlines or feature sections of newspapers and television reportage.[6] Negative stories, particularly of blacks and especially of young black males, fit stereotyped story molds and were therefore easier to broadcast than complex nuanced accounts of individuals, groups, and places.

People organize themselves and their opinions, actions, and accusations along the lines of power and ideology. Words such as "savage," "ruthless," "crazed," "senseless," and "ignorant" cling easily to negative stories, whereas descriptors within plots and character lines of positive accounts require more thought. They also have to be told with reference to political and social contexts that bump against stereotypical views and ordinary expectations grounded in the racism of US society.

In the 1960s and 1970s, the Civil Rights Movement brought legislation and regulations proscribing "separate but equal" and reinforcing the need for "equal opportunity" as well as legal protection against discrimination. But not until economic advances of the 1990s did retention of blacks in higher education increase significantly. In that decade, role models as leaders of industry, entertainment, and politics grew in number and geographic distribution. Many, now powerful alumni of universities, insisted that higher education institutions engage the leadership of young black men and women within campus organizations dedicated to building professional identities for young black men and women entering fields such as engineering, mathematics, economics, political science, and medicine. Public evidence of the achievements of the young generation of black leaders escalated, with key figures in business, journalism, law, medicine, and politics. Their biographies gained visibility, and, more importantly, their leadership and diversity of perspective affirmed them as individuals, not tokens.

These leaders helped turn public attention to the shameful imbalance of justice in racial profiling, wrongful convictions, and recidivism rates for black males in state and federal prisons. Underclass blacks, Latinos, and immigrant laborers were disproportionately locked into unskilled jobs, limited housing choices and mortgage chances, as well as inadequate health care. Political leaders and investigative journalists dug into cases of wrongful imprisonment and urged the nation to address issues surrounding ethnicity, equity, and environmental hazards. Civil Rights leaders insistently pointed out the need for more educational, political, and legal resources to challenge the crisis in urban housing.

By the mid 1990s, rapid changes in housing, schooling, and employment that had taken place in the prior decade steadily nudged a growing portion of the United States to affirm the value of letting go of the idea that racial, ethnic, or gender labels were absolute determinants of identity. Individuals could choose to use or to ignore in their own self-identities old and new labels. Taking on multiple identities became part of the daily lives of individuals playing many roles and moving within several circles of professional and social connection. For a while, debates swirled over terms such as *black*, *of color*, *African American*, *European-derived*, *Caucasian*, *Latino*, *Chicano*, *Mexicano*, and *Hispanic*. A benefit of these debates came in public media presentations of the specific histories of colonization and slavery, emancipation and reconstruction, and movement and migration that stood behind each of these labels. Academic associations, such as the American Anthropological Association and the American Psychological Association, dedicated portions of their annual programs to debates surrounding the social construction of labels and the dubious scientific bases of significant biological differences between "the races." Books on the history of science, along with contemporary social science examinations of families and communities, kept the ambiguities of *racial*, *cultural*, and *ethnic* churning in the public mind.

By the opening of the new millennium, the idea of identity as an essentialist label was crumbling. The accelerating rate of socioeconomic and geographic mobility and access to social capital outpaced racial or ethnic membership as determining factors for some individuals in their choice of education, residential location, professional identity, and political power. Classes entering universities for undergraduate and graduate study included many more women, foreign students, and US citizens of color than had been the case a decade earlier. As many as a third of these would complete their university degrees and move on to advanced degrees. Celebrated works of fiction and nonfiction told the stories of individuals of mixed-race parentage. A decade earlier, young black attorneys, economists, physicians, and academics were regarded as "tokens," appointed and acknowledged because of affirmative action regulations. Now individuals reflecting a range of racial and ethnic, as well as linguistic, backgrounds increasingly appeared on corporate boards, the floor of the stock exchange, university faculties, and national news programs. Innovators in technology, finance, and niche-marketing came from far-flung parts of the world. They hired and advanced members of their companies not on the basis of ethnic classification but on evidence of expertise, original ideas, management skills, and collaborative ingenuity.

To be sure, rural areas and small towns, especially those reliant on migrant agricultural labor or low-skilled workers in food processing and packaging, lagged behind in diversifying their public face. Denied educational, medical, housing, and legal access, immigrant families remained cut off from resources because of their ethnicity, language, length of residence, and failure to own property. Rural areas rarely lay in easy reach of industries or higher education institutions dedicated to professional development of a diversified labor force.

Most evident in the social history of effects on whites and blacks of the economic recession that began in 2007, however, have been the effects on black households of their not having accumulated long-term assets. For most families, their homes, acquired in the 1990s, were their primary asset when the recession started; twenty-three households of Trackton descendants lost their homes to foreclosure between 2007 and 2011. By 2009, black household assets across the nation averaged less than $10,000, and the wealth of black households had fallen 53 percent between 2005 and 2009. Though relatively few Trackton descendant households had lost fully half of their worth in this short span of years, the national numbers tell a deeper story that began back in the decades before black workers (especially in the southern states of the United States) were admitted into the manufacturing labor force. Savings accounts were few, landholdings scarce, and residential property either rented or heavily mortgaged. Thus, in the first decade of the new millennium when the recession hit, even those households of Trackton descendant families supported by two working parents holding well-paying jobs had little or nothing by way of substantial long-held assets on which to draw. Nationally, approximately one-third of black households had zero or negative net worth in 2009; only about 20 percent of Trackton descendant households were in this situation.

While a few Roadville descendant families had some accumulated assets when the recession that began in 2007 hit, these disappeared quickly, and just over a third of these families lost their homes to foreclosure between 2008 and 2011. Across the nation, the median wealth of white households was twenty times that of black households, and white households lost only 16 percent of their median worth between 2005 and 2009. Roadville descendant households lost double the national figure in their wealth holdings. Thus the stories of both white and black descendants from the Piedmont Carolina manufacturing and agrarian life of the 1980s illustrate the vulnerabilities of a working-poor heritage and limited long-term financial holdings. In spite of these vulnerabilities, however, the majority of these families held strongly to their desire to give their children "every possible opportunity" and to pass on to the young a strong sense of themselves as mainstream individuals sure to overcome adversities and to get ahead.[7]

Proliferating choices

The policies, public perceptions, and local practices that resulted from the three decades of change summarized here cannot be forgotten as the backdrop against which descendant families from Roadville and Trackton lived. By 2010, the youngest generation thought about their social identity in terms of their choices of residential location, friends, fashion and technologies, leisure and health, universities, and careers. Many saw advantages through being bilingual and biracial. They were happy to live their lives by the mantra: "It's what you can do and who you are as a person that counts – not how some ignorant person puts a label on you."

The 2010 Census questionnaire indicated the extent to which this view affected behavior. The standard questionnaire provided a handful of racial and ethnic membership boxes for respondents to mark as their identity. Nearly 60 percent of the individuals under forty whose stories appear or are reflected in this book either refused to return their Census questionnaire or to check one of these boxes. Most of them shared the sentiment of Marcello, who explained when I asked how he had responded: "I didn't. Why should I? Me and Francisco don't fit in any of those little boxes."

Those who had celebrated their thirtieth birthday before the new millennium admitted that they had made mistakes and credited any success they had achieved to persistence and forward-thinking as well as support from family and community. They looked back saying that those who came out of Roadville and Trackton had shown determination in their attitude of getting out and starting over elsewhere. They seemed to sense that they might someday have to do the same kind of starting over. They rejected suggestions that either *culture* or *race* shaped their fundamental choices. They saw their ways of dressing, eating, celebrating holidays, and worshipping as options they could choose to represent any identity they wanted to assume for whatever reason, whenever and however they wished.

Any concerns they had about their choices centered on the kind of work they wanted in the several careers they felt they were sure to have over their lifetimes. Most wanted work with meaning, colleagues with similar interests, and locations that offered choice in lifestyles. They wanted work that valued their talents and interests and gave some room for their imagination, energy, and resolve. They desired most of all a secure salary with bonus for extra effort.

Masters of the mainstream life

Between 1981 and 1998, Roadville and Trackton parents with children under the age of fourteen moved households an average of four times. Children like Jerome who were placed with relatives or in foster families moved an average of seven times. During this period, parents moved either in search of employment or because of mandated military or employment transfers. During their first years of higher education and initial employment between 1990 and 2010, 87 percent of working-age Roadville and Trackton descendants lived either in major metropolitan urban areas or in towns of more than 100,000. By 2010, 88 percent viewed their workplaces as being influenced in some direct way by the global economy.

Between 1991 and 2003, just over a third of intact two-parent descendant families from Roadville and Trackton who moved within the same city relocated to a house larger than the previous one. During these same years, nearly 40 percent of these families set up one or more additional households as a vacation or second home or for an elderly parent or a child attending a distant university. These figures do not include families who separated or divorced during the 1990s or between 2000 and 2010. In these two decades, 52 percent of descendant families experienced divorce or separations. Most of these break-ups took place in the first decade of marriage. Of the children who were in their twenties between 1994 and 2010, 40 percent did not marry, though the majority have had live-in partners at some point. Of those who entered their thirties during this period, most married or entered a long-term partnership when they decided to have children.

By 2010, approximately 45 percent of the descendants of the original Roadville and Trackton families either were or had been in multiracial or multiethnic relationships. Over 30 percent were bilingual. Multiple types of households and combinations of residents existed. University students lived in houses in which they rented a room and shared the kitchen and living space with students of both sexes. Serial monogamy or sequenced partnerships increased the likelihood that children grew up with half-siblings and step-siblings and spoke more often of where they "stayed" than of where they "lived."

Separation, divorce, and new partnerships, sometimes in distant cities, brought recalibrations by children of norms that had previously been relatively consistent. New caretakers, especially when step-siblings and half-siblings were involved, invariably brought inconsistent rules. While half the week could be spent with a parent who allowed children to watch only specific television programs and then only after homework had been completed, the other days of the week could be spent in a household with no monitoring of either television viewing or homework completion. Diets differed, as did rules for scheduling showers, taking care of clothing, making beds and cleaning rooms, having friends over, and playing videogames.

The pain of some children in trying to adjust showed up frequently in language. Some expressed their distress in fits of anger liberally sprinkled with profanities. Some withdrew interest in reading or doing homework. Others used drawing, gaming, refusing to talk, or writing in diaries guarded with ferocity as weapons of control and ways of gaining private worlds. Young adult novels, many of which echoed young readers' own family situations, became favorites of some young readers.[8] More than a dozen descendants of Roadville and Trackton ran away from home in the decade of the 1990s; all but one returned. This was the first decade in which "disappeared" posters of children showed up in public places and their cases were featured on local evening news hours.

In 1994, in Roadville and Trackton descendant families, 60 percent of females between twenty-four and fifty-two years of age worked part-time or full-time beyond the family home. In 2004, this figure reached 84 percent, though approximately half of these either took leave or stopped working during the preschool years of their children. With these women in the workforce, the institutions of family, church, and school for which their mothers and grand-mothers had once volunteered now had to hire their administrative and support staff. While weekly church attendance had been the unquestioned pattern for their grandparents, by 2004, only 40 percent of households descended from Trackton families attended church weekly. More than half of those who attended church regularly were over sixty years of age. Only about a quarter of the Roadville descendants between the ages of twenty-four and forty-four participated regularly in church life, though they did attend church for family events linked with traditional religious holidays such as Easter and Christmas.

Scattered in fourteen states by 2010, 486 descendant Roadville and Trackton households included a child under the age of twelve. Of these 297 were two-parent

households and 189 single-parent families. In 42 percent of the two-parent households, the mother worked either full-time or part-time outside the home. In single-
parent households, only four of which were a father plus one child or more, 146
parents worked outside the home, either part-time or full-time. In 2010, twenty-
eight third-generation families had children.[9]

Two-working-parent households and single-parent households turned
Sundays into times for rest and recreation or "catching up" on grocery shopping,
laundry, housecleaning, and paying bills. Gendered division of labor defined
time distribution on weekends, with a focus in many families on "doing something with the children." These events took place primarily outside the home
and included the children's sports or other organized group events as well as
commercial entertainment, with boys usually going with the male in the household and girls with the female.

Almost entirely omitted from everyday life by the opening of the twenty-first
century were intergenerational activities, aside from visits or attendance at
family rituals, such as weddings or funerals. Vacations were increasingly
directed toward commercial spaces or family outdoor activities in which grandparents had no interest or experience. Children and adolescents often insisted
that family holiday travel include one of their friends, so that the social life of
the school year could continue during vacation times. The older generation who
had grown up in Roadville or Trackton sought out mid-sized towns where
assisted care facilities and home nurse visitations were available. Families
with children were not inclined to use their vacation for visits to areas where
opportunities for entertainment, sports, and consistent internet connection paled
in comparison to those available closer to metropolitan regions or in beachside
resorts or on family cruises. By 2010, video calls, not face-to-face visits
involving all family members, became the primary means of keeping in touch
across generations. However, older children rarely took part in these conversations unless parents directed them to transmit the requisite "thank you" for a
birthday or holiday gift.

Language in between time

Living with strong opportunity-centered ideologies of "too little time with too
much to do" carried implications for language. Constraints on time based on the
work hours of parents, along with the reduction of access to extended families,
placed intense pressure on weekdays from three o'clock to nine o'clock. Young
children were often tethered to televisions or computers in the family room
or their bedroom. They grew up multi-tasking in chats, web-surfing, instant
messaging, and emailing, often while trying to focus on two or three different
homework assignments at the same time. Earbuds and earphones cut children

off from conversations or shouts from the kitchen asking about dinner preferences.

Family dinner time competed with sports, organized activities, homework, and appointments for medical and dental care. Squeezed in with transport to these activities were errands to purchase groceries and other goods. Often such trips provoked negotiation between parent and child over a possible treat or favorite frozen items. Home-cooked meals with parents and children working together had disappeared. Much of the food of households that had a family car or van was brought in from take-outs or delicatessens or bought in bulk at wholesale clubs. Shopping became routinized as joint outings for one parent and usually the youngest child. Significant in such occasions was the resulting "freedom" for the other parent to do something else with another child.

Talk on such outings tended to focus on what *is* currently present in the environment of the wholesale club, grocery, or deli and not on what *is to come*. Conversations such as these were action-scripted, both drawing from artifacts in the immediate environment and centering on the pacing of whatever was currently under way. Explanatory talk that went into details or history generally came in spurts of short utterances centered on the immediate.[10] Arguments happened on the move to and from the car or on the way into and out of the shopping center. More often than setting up future worlds, conditionals came as directives or threats: "If you don't stop whining, you'll go sit in the car." Connections of *because*, *then*, and *since* either had to be followed through quickly or, often, picked up later. There was never enough time for parent–child talk about making plans, assessing past events in terms of their consequences, or giving extended accounts of what happened.

In the first decade of the new millennium, young parents and their children read and wrote in fewer *extended* texts than their parents and grandparents had. As technology became constant and increasingly diversified in play and work, individuals encountered and produced images and print in a widening array of combinations, often brief, and frequently with music. Though strong creators of social networks, sometimes solid, more often passing, the texts of tweeters and bloggers were quick and passionate. Readers and writers insisted on visual images, immediacy, and opinion. YouTube and Facebook accelerated sales of digital and video cameras and cellphones with cameras. Redundancy of content mattered little so long as it was entertaining, generally light-hearted, and suggestive of something beyond itself. These transmissions via cellphones and the internet made *text* synonymous with brevity: text messages, chats, and tweets.

Listeners and viewers did not feel compelled to comprehend, remember, apply, or attend to any information that did not carry connections to their current interests and needs. Ignoring and forgetting became primary means of surviving the constant advertisements within, through, and alongside texts that carried desired content.[11] Finding information or seeking services required that individuals learn to negotiate decision trees. While the logos of phone services and airlines appeared everywhere, efforts to locate a living human being by telephone or at an airline counter became almost impossible. Checkout lanes, malls, elevators, buses, freeways, and airports flashed visuals, played music, and beamed photographs, films, and television during the in-between times of being somewhere and getting somewhere else. Redundancy of news, narratives, and commerce showed up everywhere, encouraging children and adults to tune out by the sixth time an advertisement appeared during a Cable Network News (CNN) program. Niche market technology allowed consumers to pay for services eliminating intrusive or irrelevant advertising from their television, email, and internet searches. Digital media accelerated their ways of encouraging twenty-first-century youth to innovate, combine, archive, replace, discard, and forget. Negotiation of wants and needs relied less on oral argument than on having and using the right technology.

Memory of factual information mattered less than adeptness in finding information instantly through use of any one of several electronic devices. Young people pointed out to their parents that they did not need to use a telephone book to find the telephone number of a movie theatre. "Smart phones" meant they had at their fingertips flexible ways of finding the phone number, directions, scheduled films, recent reviews, and trailers of movies currently playing and coming up.

Ideologies of parenting

In the realm of social and personal responsibility, several key patterns in the life of school-age children stand out for Roadville and Trackton descendant families in which one parent or both parents had a relatively steady middle- or upper-income job between 2000 and 2010. Parent–child relationships around homework illuminate the extent to which children in these homes could avoid accumulating much experience with taking responsibility for their own lives. For children in elementary schools, especially those of high quality and consistent demands, parents became deeply involved in homework, and particularly in the creation of projects assigned as end-of-term homework. Parents reported to me often: "I feel I have to make this happen. I have to find out about it, get it rolling, keep it rolling, and see that it gets finished and transported to school on the correct day. This can become as cumbersome as my projects at work, and I feel as though I am the one who has to be in charge."

In studying parents and their primary-school children in relation to homework, I wanted to know: a) how much interactive talk between parents and children took place around the creation of assigned projects; and b) who took leadership in management and execution of the work. Increasingly, after 1998, adults in Roadville and Trackton descendant families who saw themselves as mainstream took more and more charge of homework projects for primary-school children not yet old enough to be engaged in projects sponsored by community organizations. In 2003, with the help of several adolescents who had younger siblings in primary school, I surveyed ninety-eight children who were between the ages of nine and twelve in thirty-five different homes in more than two dozen geographic locations. We recorded the children as they talked with us about school projects they had turned in as homework assignments in the past year or two. We wanted to know the history of the ideas that went into at least one of these projects and the work the children remembered doing in the process of preparing and delivering the final product.

Our first difficulty came in the fact that a quarter of the children could not remember any projects they had done during this time. The second difficulty came with the realization that the majority of those who did remember such a project targeted the one assignment of the year in which they had been able to choose their own topic within a broad field of choice. For example, children could choose to do a project on swans for a school unit on animals. In giving histories of these projects, few could remember where their ideas came from, but they could remember how they wanted to approach the creation of the project. Many made comments such as "I knew I wanted to do a fold-out book with photographs and drawings."

In those cases in which the children mentioned their parents' involvement with school projects, we followed up whenever possible. Most of the parents still had the project and teachers' evaluation of the work. Therefore, we had the advantage of being able to target features such as index, subheadings, glossary, reference list, etc. For each of such features likely to be found in extended texts, we asked the children to tell us the name and definition of each item, what its purposes were, and where they found the information they used in these items. In just over 80 percent of the cases, children recognized the feature. Only about a quarter of the children could, however, tell us what these features did or how they worked within the project as a whole. Only about 15 percent could retrace the process of either finding or re-creating the feature.

When asked questions that centered on responsibility for homework and attribution of credit for the work that went into the project, about one-third of the children said they did not feel full ownership of the project. Several children elaborated on why they could not tell us much about the project: "Mom did most of it, and one day, she had to call Dad at the office to tell her how to do something on the computer." Of these children, most indicated they had "lots" of help from parents. They made comments such as: "If I had to do all that stuff again, I wouldn't have a clue. I'd call a friend or get it off the internet"; "If I didn't have help, I probably couldn't do that again"; "I hope I'm never asked to do things like that again, or if I am, I hope my mom's around. What she did looked hard."

A preponderance of remarks from the children indicated that they had, in large part, "looked on" as spectators to the creation of these projects, which were often the capstone for their term grade. Most of them had high praise for the project, saying: "I thought it was pretty good, and the teacher did too." For 40 percent of the children in the survey, parents had accompanied their child to school on the due date in order to ensure that the project arrived without damage.

The mainstream teenagers who worked with me in collecting these data asked if I had collected histories of homework in other homes where parents were not so involved. A discussion of equity emerged. I explained that such parental help was not possible in many single-parent households and two-working-parent families who were not financially secure as mainstreamers. Moreover, numerous interventions could derail the best intentions of parents: sickness, a special-needs child in the household, or an aging parent needing placement in a care facility. The female teenagers took in the various stories I told with intent seriousness. The males shrugged and seemed to brush off these differences. The girls, however, neatly summarized the stories by comments that indicated they were already thinking about the multi-tasking that working mothers faced and that might await the girls in later life.

The next year these same teenagers helped me determine how much young children ages twelve to fourteen ($n = 42$) in their own families helped manage their time and knew about their own schedules. These data echo some patterns we found in homework projects of younger children. There was a similar displacement of responsibility to adults – both family members and the intimate strangers who run after-school programs in community organizations.

We asked young people in upper primary school and middle school from dual-earner families to fill in a schedule of their coming week in the after-school and weekend hours. We wanted them to describe three activities they had coming up in the next week. We also asked them to look ahead and tell us what they would be doing two months from this point. Over 80 percent of the young respondents replied that they did not know the specifics of their own schedules for the upcoming week; they knew in general terms that they had soccer, piano, karate, drama, etc., but they were uncertain about which came first in the week or on any given day. Someone else in the family knew that, and "My coach will remind me too when I go to practice the first time this week." In looking ahead to what they would be doing two months from the time of the questioning, answers were even less precise. Respondents would generally name only a block of time and its activity: "I know we're going skiing in spring break"; "We'll go to the beach this summer."

When I showed them transcripts of what their children said, parents did not seem surprised. They reported consistently that they felt a sense of obligation to maintain a schedule of activities for their children and to oversee activities, such as homework, that they saw as critical to their children's academic future. They confirmed that most of the talk that went on between parents and children in the car or van or at home in the evenings was about scheduling. Parents said they had to ensure that each child had in his or her backpack or sports bag the correct sports gear, sheet music, art supplies, snacks for after-school activities, and books, homework, glasses, lunch, and permission notes needed for school.

Many parents lamented that their children had no idea of the value of the items in their backpacks and sports bags or of the importance of keeping track of possessions. One mother echoed other parents when she said of her daughter: "When she comes home without her glasses, and I ask where they are, she seems not to register why I am so angry. She just says, 'Mom, really, I don't know; I lost 'em. Maybe I left 'em in Molly's mom's car. You could call her.'" Only a few parents said they forced their child to try to track down lost items or followed up with punishment if the children did not do so. "It's just easier to take care of it myself. She was probably ready for another pair of glasses anyway."

The long view

The integrative effects of how families live show up in the accelerating layered commercially driven pace of activities and demands on the time of young and old. Across the three generations of descendants from the original residents of Trackton and Roadville, three features of language and interactional change stand out as most critically challenged.

First, occasions of extended talk – deliberative give and take on a single topic – among novices and experts, adults and children, appear almost exclusively in connection with collaborative planning toward project and goal achievement in play or work. For working parents, it is difficult to find the time and incentive to initiate, sustain, and complete projects of work or play with their children. When homework projects or special events such as school plays come up, parents push to help their children make good appearances and fulfill expectations others may have of them. But these projects demand time and focus. Both are often in short supply in busy households.

Parents and children need to co-create project ideas and execution. Only with deliberation can parents prevail on children to think through ways to put their images of what they want to do into design, plan, and preparation. These discourse situations lay down patterns of communicating especially critical to fields of science and art, as well as family health care and financial planning. When the young are not socialized at home into these patterns, they must gain this experience elsewhere or move into young adulthood unaware of the consequences of their own and others' behaviors.

LIBRARY, UNIVERSITY OF CHESTER

Second, the kind of deliberative talk that instills habits of self-monitoring and planning depends on fluent use of certain syntactic structures such as conditionals or hypotheticals, as well as facility with specific kinds of questions and narratives regarding process, sequence, and evidence. Children can gain fluency with these forms primarily through feeling joint ownership and responsibility to either their own activities and projects or collaborative work and play with adults.

Third, in language socialization, patterns of interaction with talk, print, props, and media representations need to vary in accordance with the range of role embodiments possible for children. The accelerating pace at which fashions and fads of teenagers are being promoted to younger children is leading many parents to realize their children are not prepared to make good choices. Parents acknowledge that household scheduling provides too little time for playing, working, and talking *with* children rather than going to places and activities *for* them.

"How can we as a family do things together that will be meaningful for all of us?" "How can we all feel we own some part of the responsibility for this household?" Parents in the mainstream fret over these questions while they also worry about the need to provide their children with specific kinds of opportunities. Parents are ever mindful of the need for their children to gain the technological, academic, and social expertise they are most likely to need as they move through secondary school and into university study and career preparation.

Language is the major carrier of moral and ethical codes. Individuals need the language fluency to think and say, "If I do this, then do I know what is likely to follow?" To make ethical decisions, individuals must be able to draw on analogies, compare one situation with another, and consider responses or outcomes that result from similar conditions. Children must perceive the intentions and needs of others and examine these in relation to their consideration of alternative decisions.

In spite of pervasive and multiplying forms of representational media, face-to-face extended talk dominates and is likely to continue to do so. The most life-supporting projects, for individuals and the society at large, come about with direct human resourcing. We see this most clearly when our own life possibilities are altered by the achievements of others: development of new lines of medical treatment; design of toxin-free housing construction materials; engineering safe redistribution of river waters; and legislation in support of inspection and rebuilding of decaying transport infrastructure.

No endeavor, mundane or sublime, can happen without extended discourse among individuals with varying areas and levels of expertise who commit to common goals and tasks. Achievement depends on individuals who can think together, envision what must be as well as what may be, and take responsibility for plans and designs through to completion. Group practices in committed deliberative membership become guiding voices in the mind.

Jerome, Eduardo, and a group of their friends had gathered for dinner at Tia Maria's on a Sunday afternoon in 2009. Both Jerome and Eduardo were now teachers in local schools attended by children of families who had immigrated from all over the world. They asked me about "the book." "How's it comin'? What's it gonna say?"

"I'm writing about how easy you guys have it today, compared to the way your parents and grandparents lived," I said.

Guffaws and protests arose and Tia Maria turned to me and asked: "Why do you say that?"

The professorial side of my nature jumped on this question, and I responded with a long answer: "The two generations who came before you kids around this table had little choice in education, housing, or jobs. They lived through the violent struggles of race relations before and during the Civil Rights Era. Changes in the world economy took away their jobs in the mills, their hope of making a living as a small farmer, and, most important, their sense of possibility. They had to pick themselves up after the economic hard times of the early 1980s. When they moved to find work, they had to remake themselves."

Tia Maria looked down at her hands: "Sounds like immigrants to me." The young people looked at her and waited for her to go on. In a soft voice at odds with Tia Maria's usual commanding presence, she told what she remembered of the journey that had brought her as a child with her family to Miami.

"My papa had been a storekeeper in Puerto Rico. All of us kids worked around the store, cleaning, running errands, and helping out. When he got it in his head we were comin' to Miami, my mama went around her little flower garden and kissed every one of those flowers. Miami didn't treat us so good. Papa thought some relatives there would take us in, and they did for a little bit, but that didn't work out, so we lived in a shed in the back of a warehouse where he got a job cleanin' and watchin' the place at night.

"Next thing we knew, he wanted to go to New York, where somebody told him he could find work and a place for us to live. We took the bus. I was nine years old, and I'd never been to school. No English, no books, no money. In New York, things got a little better, but the Puerto Ricans there resented new-comers. We were scared of the blacks, and the crime, dirt, noise, and police. It wasn't easy, I'll tell you. I went to school, but never finished. Stayed home to take care of Papa after he had his stroke, so Mama could work."

Silence settled over all of us. We had thought we knew this woman who seemed so secure, successful, and solid. Tia Maria announced it was time for cake.

Jerome stared out the window.

The next time we got together, Jerome turned to Tia Maria in the middle of Sunday dinner: "Thank you for tellin' me what you did about you. It's helped me think about my students. They've come from Somalia, Bosnia, Turkey, all over. So much of what I think they oughta know, they have no clue. I feel like I have to start their lives all over again in my classroom."

"What is it they don't know that most surprises you?" I asked.

Jerome reeled off bits and pieces of operational know-how for getting along in everyday life: how to wake up in the morning, how to make change, where to get bus tickets, how to keep track of their school books, how to ask questions when they didn't understand what the teacher wanted, how to get assignments in on time, how to make friends, how to keep from insulting someone in the hallways.

"How did *you* learn these things?" I asked insistently.

Jerome looked puzzled. "I just did."

Eduardo added: "I never thought about these as things to *learn*. It's just what you *pick up* . . ."

Jerome broke in: "And figure out by watchin' what's goin' on around you."

Tia Maria reminded both boys: "You had somebody around you doin' that stuff. These kids don't. Someone has to be there to copy – a mama, granny, uncle, teacher. Another thing, you boys and you girls too, knew that if you didn't do what you needed to do, nobody else was gonna do it for you, and you might not get any dinner." She winked at them, and Jerome jumped up and gave her a playful hug.

Epilogue

For the fragment of a life, however typical, is not the sample of an even web: promises may not be kept, and an ardent outset may be followed by declension; latent powers may find their long-waited opportunity: a past error may urge a grand retrieval.

(Eliot 1871–1872/1963, p. 810)

Anthropologists have been accused of representing an essential linearity about generations across time. That is not the case for the individuals whose stories are told here. They follow few lines or paths that might have been predicted for them. Instead they have worked and played in spots of time and place; theirs are dotted rather than straight lines. All indications are that these dotted lines will continue to go in many directions and will have beginnings and endings along the way, spinning out into webs of differing proportion, strength, and connection.[1]

Where are the children of Trackton and Roadville and their children today and where do they see themselves headed?

Zinnia Mae has become a deaconess in her church and a part-time co-manager of the second-hand shop at the church. She volunteers at the library where she and her children first learned to love books. Once each year, she travels to Chicago to visit Jerome, Marcello, and Francisco.

Jerome and Lucia have two sons in preschool, the elder already eager to bang on his father's drums at every opportunity. Jerome continues his triple career as elementary teacher, director of after-school drama at his school, and occasional drummer with a jazz group. Lucia teaches art in an elementary school, takes part in a research project on arts learning, and designs sets for two community youth theatre groups. Tia Maria has moved from her old apartment into an assisted living residence near Jerome and Lucia, and she babysits the boys two evenings each week.

Donna lives in Atlanta. In 2009, she married a medical intern from Kenya who expects to remain in the United States and specialize in tropical medicine research. They visited Kenya in the summer of 2010, and their first child was born in the spring of 2011. After Donna's maternity leave, her husband changed work hours, so that he and Zinnia Mae could share childcare when Donna returned to her position in nursing administration at the hospital.

Marcello and Francisco have established a small catering service adjoining an arts center where Marcello still teaches dance and Francisco is a choreographer. They have not given up hope of establishing a school of dance and music for young children some time in the future.

Melvin moved out of his mother's house in 2009 into a condominium near the auto detailing shop he bought in 2008. He added to his busy life by becoming a part-time teacher in a technical school. He explains: "I want to pay ahead [repaying a favour from someone by investing in another person or cause that will benefit the future] by giving some young person the same kind of opportunity I had when I started out in my business." At the technical school, he has found a young person who will apprentice with him and learn the business. Melvin would like to be able to leave the shop for an annual vacation of more than a few days. He has decided he wants to travel: "I'm ready to see the world."

Red still lives in New Jersey. The 2008 recession took a toll on his company, but he is optimistic that "the worst is behind us now." He volunteers at the YMCA where his children were active, and he has remodeled the family home. He and his uncle have created two engineering scholarships at the state college for students whose families are from the Dominican Republic.

Denny lives in Seattle, Washington and works for a software company, for which he runs off-site training programs throughout the United States. He travels to New York City often, where he and his step-dad meet and head to New Hampshire for hiking or skiing.

Tameka is in her second year of study at Spellman University, where she is debating whether to major in mathematics or civil engineering. She slips away from the university at least once a term to visit Denny in Seattle, and she returns home to be with Red during the summers. She spends part of each summer working in the engineering firm Red now owns, and they both expect her to take over from him before she reaches forty. In the meantime, Red encourages her to keep her options open.

In 2010, Jay took six weeks off from his engineering job in Colorado to travel with Bernardo to organic farms and poultry farms in the East that label themselves "sustainable." The two ski as much as possible and hiked the Appalachian Trail before Bernardo started his first year of study at Cornell University in New York State. He has become a senior board member for the Catacombs, the youth organization he joined when he was thirteen. He is urging the board to plan the addition of a community garden on a vacant lot adjoining the building.

Martin and Cindy Brown still live outside Boston, Massachusetts. Etta comes once each week to have dinner with Rebecca and Mark, and she had a front-row seat when the two graduated from secondary school. Rebecca decided to apply to universities only in the Northeast to double-major in environmental sciences and art. Mark chose Brown University, where he remains very much the sportsman, cyclist, and avid supporter of Mac's Farm.

Lisa became a councilwoman in the small town near her ranch. Increasingly worried about water contamination by run-off from the ranches along the river, she persuaded the city to take more responsibility in monitoring water quality and use of pesticides and fertilizers on local ranches. She and her sister, Sally, took their first trip out of the country in the summer of 2010. They spent two weeks in London, and they mapped ideas for such trips in coming summers.

Robert finished law school at the University of Texas in Austin and is practicing environmental law in Houston. He married a woman he met in law school, and they work *pro bono* a month each year in Mexico with a law firm dedicated to protecting the rights of small farmers.

Richard now runs the family ranch, and he has become the manager of the youth theatre in town and the lead drummer with a jazz band. Several times each year, he and his mother develop a joint project between the youth theatre and other arts groups in the region.

Sally's daughters, Ellen and Anna, are following in their parents' footsteps. Ellen completed law school in Minnesota and is a prosecutor in St. Paul. Her sister, Anna, married just after completing her Bachelor's degree in secondary education, and she gave birth to twins in the spring of 2011. She hopes to return to teaching in the autumn term of 2013.

Dana remains single, struggling with Cordelia, who comes to stay with her each weekend. Cordelia and her dad have their difficulties as well, and Cordelia does not yet show signs of moving easily through the end of her teenage years. She plays truant, has started smoking, and her grades have slipped each of the past two years.

Catherine visits her sister Dana as often as possible, and she has offered several times to keep Cordelia for a weekend, so Dana can get away for a brief vacation. However, Cordelia and Martha, Catherine's daughter, have little in common, and Martha appears self-righteous and hard-hearted to Cordelia, who uses family visits as opportunities to show her worst characteristics. Martha is moving ahead at Johns Hopkins in biology and botanical illustration. She traveled to Sri Lanka in 2011 with a team of students hired for her professor's research team. She says she will earn a doctorate in biology and then establish internships in environmental sciences and botanical illustration within a network of botanical gardens in the eastern US. She is a strong spokeswoman for making gardens and parks year-round learning environments for young people.

All members of the third generation of Roadville and Trackton descendants grew up in the care of intimate strangers in daycare programs, after-school activities, and community organizations. When they went to school, many of them struggled, but most came to understand the essential role of formal education and the many ways school coursework complemented the skills and interests they were developing in their informal learning environments beyond the school day. The most fortunate among these children were those whose parents or close associates from the neighborhood or church stepped in to promote their talents and interests. Others fueled their curiosity and childhood passions by finding like-minded peers, as well as expert mentors from whom they gained critical social, linguistic, and self-management skills. Some children like Mark, Robert, and Bernardo had parents who shared their interests. Some like Marcello and Melvin, Richard, and Martha found mentors in caring adults who viewed their talents as resources. For many, the ways they chose to spend their out-of-school time during much of their childhood influenced their higher education choices and expectations for careers. Socializing with peers in technology-mediated interactions, they developed propensities for specific ways of creating and using visual representation, ways of speaking, and creating genres of written materials filled with their own photographs and sketches. Rebecca and Mark, Jerome, Bernardo, Denny, and Tameka take pride in being bilingual. In law school, Robert took a year away from his studies in the United States to spend a year in Mexico with an environmental sciences research group. He works primarily with Spanish-monolingual clients involved in agriculture.

Working their way through and with each new source of information and inspiration, those within the third generation keep renewing and stretching their early interests to propel them forward with hopes and plans to benefit them and their families and to contribute to their communities.

The Epilogue written for *Ways with words* in 1996 foreshadowed many of the trends and directions illustrated in the stories here. As I step back and read that epilogue, I am surprised by the forecasts I made there. Ethnographers and social historians have no more special talents for predicting the future than other social scientists. However, my long-time immersion in the habits of communication and interaction afford ample possibilities for speculating about the future of social practices and language development in families and communities. The truth that every end is a beginning encourages me to take a chance and use this current epilogue to forecast how the third generation of Roadville and Trackton descendants will push forward in their families and communities.

The third generation of Roadville and Trackton descendants will have several careers, the success of which will be determined primarily by their adaptability and willingness to keep learning. The study and practice they undertake voluntarily through informal learning will make them keenly attuned to their immediate physical context. They will seek out and generate collaborative groups of like-minded individuals who wish to be drawn into the work of projects. They will place a premium on direct face-to-face interactions, and they will expect more service and connection as consumers and citizens. When neither businesses nor bureaucracies meet these expectations, they will look for ways to make change. Though comprehensive changes will usually lie beyond the range of their influence, they will continue to seek collaborative projects. They will be inspired from time to time to respond to felt needs in their own communities and, in some cases, for the broader society and the planet. They will not be discouraged by those who advocate only for systemic change, for they will hear this idea as rationale for doing nothing. In some of their pursuits within their families as well as communities, they will practice relentlessly and guide their children toward having special interests they develop with their parents, friends, community organizations, and on their own.

The third generation will encourage their children's social lives, knowing that the young will need to have more information and skills than any single source or method can provide. They will encourage the young to want to learn more than is explicitly taught by someone else. Social and intellectual capital will be very much part of their plan to help prepare the next generation. Of special appeal to them will be ways to come together in small groups and to network in order to multiply what they know.

Some say that never in the history of economically advanced societies has self-initiated learning on the part of individuals and small groups had such widespread effects and promising potential. Such industrious creativity on the part of citizens is likely to be a major stimulus for technological invention, innovative participation in political processes, and involvement in ever-widening communication networks. This energetic initiative is already being acknowledged as interdependent with the exploratory play of early childhood. As parents, the third generation will do their best to encourage in their communities the idea that families with young children play more often, explore the outdoors, and encourage creativity with visual arts, music, science, and technology. The ill fortune of premature births, babies with birth defects, and children on the autism spectrum will hit this third generation randomly, as was the case with their parents. But this generation of parents will come together with other parents at the local level to find collaborative ways to work for more research and resources for their children. They will enlist existing organizations, such as museums and hospitals, to take these children into account in better ways, and they will investigate new living circumstances for these children as they mature and move into adulthood. In doing so, they will bring together legal forces, scientific information, and technical and artistic experts.

Learning that lies outside formal instruction and designated experts will increasingly characterize everyday experiences as well as planned voluntary efforts in which individuals gain expertise in specific skills and bodies of information. Governments, particularly those at the municipal level, are likely to be less able than in the past to provide special services for those in need. This aspect of political life in the coming decades will be a major impetus for communal projects of collaboration, bringing back an idea from the Vietnam era of "let a thousand flowers bloom." As young parents, many of those in the third generation of Roadville and Trackton descendants will need to find time and motivation for civic commitments and voluntary pursuits to supplement services that formal institutions of government, schools, religion, and medical personnel can no longer provide. Religious organizations will increasingly feel compelled to advance the outreach service work of their members, feeding the hungry, distributing surplus food, providing transport to the elderly and sick for medical appointments, and tutoring children who fall behind at school. Such undertakings will range from on-the-job to recreational, from spiritual to civic, and bring generations together in more ways. Mid-sized towns and rural areas, as well as specific urban neighborhoods, will lead the way in these transformations, in large part because habits of face-to-face communication there have been more steadily maintained than has been the case in metropolitan areas.

Individuals will pursue informal communal project development in spurts across the life span. Some will give the "10,000 hours" of persistent practice in deed and thought that merit leadership positions as experts or specialists. Others will give up on communal projects when they feel that voluntary work has become positive thinking run amuck. If told over the next three decades, the stories of their learning in work and play will give a sense of how this kind of learning is vital to democracies.

The vast separations of possibility, personality, and place between Roadville and Trackton parents and the next two generations illustrate truths today that would have been inconceivable three decades ago. Primary among these is the essential need that children have to fill the learning gaps that neither schools nor parents can manage alone or in combination. This kind of learning remains invisible to most adults; however, society will increasingly value the informal learning that comes through special interests, peer relationships, and mentors who inspire young people to play roles beyond those of child or student and to take on increasing levels of responsibility.

Stories in this book demonstrate the extent to which both individual and group learning without direct pre-designed curricular and instructional direction shapes the lives of learners. Such learning never stands still. It cuts back and forth across all kinds of situations in which experts and less experienced and knowledgeable learners come together in projects of both play and work. Some of these projects are *transitional*, in that individuals move from one status, situation, or stage to another and do so through altering skill sets and increasing stores of information.[2] In Teen Court, Robert had to transition across roles delineated hierarchically by specific requirements of language and behavior. The demand Teen Court made for his transitional learning did not come with sharp and clear demarcations, but with the expectation that by observing and listening, he would decide what was needed and work toward achieving the skills required for him as prosecuting attorney. Martha did not have even the vague guidelines of Teen Court to mark her transitional learning. She seemed to slip unawares into the learning needed for her to move into botanical illustration. Yet as she took each step, she saw the next possibilities opening for her.

Other instances of informal learning erupt as *transformational*. Donna's experience behind bars transformed her thinking about herself, her mother, and what she had to do to salvage her life. Transformational learning tests the core of relationships, making it difficult for parents, partners, children, and friends to adapt and learn what is needed during these times. Bernardo's loss of his mother and the structure she provided transformed him into a difficult child his father, Jay, was not sure he could handle. Jay and Bernardo learned together through the combination of community resources in the Catacombs, the environmental sciences club, and their outdoor lives together in a new place. Life transformations sometimes bring desperate need for skills and knowledge available only beyond the usual institutional resources. Denny and Tameka had in Red a strong and steady parent, but they needed also the challenge of outside guidance and trust that came through their work at the YMCA. Sharp and radical changes in the normal or hoped-for course of lives come with accidents, illness, divorce, and loss that force individuals to recognize that their attitudinal, informational, and skill base has to change.

Transmissive learning that comes within formal learning works both within and alongside the informal learning that comes in transitions and transformations. Individuals throughout the life course need the information and skills that come in direct instruction with codified text materials. Zinnia Mae's move to the church community enabled her to take advantage of the formal classes available there and to adapt habits she learned there into her daily life at home. All the children of the third generation of Roadville and Trackton descendants drew heavily on the resources of formal education in their lives. In building their businesses and preparing for new jobs, the second generation found their way to the classes and training courses they needed. A central goal of all transmissive learning is effective interdependence of codified information and skill sets with the other paths of learning. This means that every learner will bring to transmissive learning and take away from it all that has come from the transitions and transformations of life. When these latter paths of learning have a high degree of compatibility with that of direct instruction, greater comfort and satisfaction in learning generally result. Emotional commitment to seeing oneself as on-going learner taking in broader reaches of information and skill sets opens a vista of positive possibilities.

Individuals within the third generation of Roadville and Trackton descendants take for granted a can-do attitude about learning what they need to know. They are likely to continue to be drawn to both work and play they feel fits their talents, personalities, and needs. They see themselves as needing to take every possible advantage of transitional, transformative, and transmissive learning opportunities in their lives. They take pride in being drawn to out-of-the-ordinary interests, whether auto detailing, botanical illustration, dance, or organic gardening. They keep giving their parents information and encouraging them to try new things, stay fit, and look forward. In some cases, they are persuading members of their family to go along with them toward goals related to childhood interests and dreams. The stories in this volume breathe life into how the current generation is learning in its own ways and is likely to continue to do so.

Appendix A Ethnography as biography and autobiography

> The storytelling that thrives for a long time in the milieu of work – the rural, the maritime and the urban – is itself an artisan form of communication, as it were. It does not aim to convey the pure essence of the thing, like information or a report. It sinks the thing into the life of the storyteller, in order to bring it out of him [*sic*] again. Thus traces of the storyteller cling to the story the way the handprints of the potter cling to the clay vessel.
>
> (Benjamin 1969, p. 91)

In the span of decades this book covers, debates about the "authenticity" of genres have frequently appeared in book reviews, editorials, and opinion pieces.[1] Memoirs later discovered to have been doctored with incidents that did not really happen to the writer have been widely discredited by critics while sales figures for these disputed genres have gone up. Autobiographies thinly masked and elaborated as fiction have stimulated speculation regarding the true identities of fictional characters, places, and corporate enterprises. The key question often raised in these debates has surrounded the kind of knowledge a writer has. To what extent has a writer seen and heard or directly experienced what is filtered through the writer's language to the page or screen?

ANTHROPOLOGY AND SCIENCE

For ethnographers, most especially those who have undertaken long-term field-work or near-continuous tracing of families or groups, the nature of social *science* in the storytelling complicates questions of what was "really" there. In the 1980s, postmodernism, critical theory, hermeneutic philosophy, and narratology chal-lenged objectivity and any claims for the neutrality of science. Postmodernism shook the foundation of notions of objectivity in social science and highlighted the writer's subjectivity and positionality. Anthropologists looked with intense scrutiny at their own writing, from fieldnotes to final stylized texts, and ques-tioned classical ideas of "distanced normalizing description" (Rosaldo 1993, p. 48). The "interpretive" imperative of social science from entry into the field through final editing of manuscripts slated for publication could no longer be hidden beneath affirmations that the science of anthropology could lay bare

174

distinctions between the "primitive" and the "civilized" according to fixed rules of fieldwork. Reinvention was needed (Hymes 1969).

These critiques by anthropologists of their own claims to validity led scholars outside the discipline of anthropology to lay claim to ethnography as a balance to the distancing quantitative work in their particular fields – corporate life, education, ethnic studies, marketing, and nursing. This new group of advocates for ethnography often embraced their own subjectivity and that of those whom they were studying. Hence analyses and reflections of data collected included not only those of the researcher but also the researched. Though some anthropologists working in distant environs explored the power of reflections from those being studied, the idea took hold particularly among ethnographers who studied situations and slices of institutional life within advanced economies, often settings in which they had grown up or been employed.

Sometimes termed "autoethnography" or "reflexive ethnography," and often making evident a clear association with "critical ethnography," many of these works, especially those within classrooms and schools, have more often than not been carried out by young scholars who have not lived for long periods of time outside their own native comfort zones. Few have worked in languages not their own. They have spent no time with native translators or become immersed as an "other" within societies distant from their own in miles and manners.[2]

These scholars viewed their work in ethnography as a way of "practicing" anthropology in order to apply their ethnographic findings to situations in need of change and reform.[3] In their "applied" studies, these ethnographers brought to selection and analysis of their data the interpretive filter of their own prior professional roles. Former nurses undertaking doctoral programs returned to nursing units to do their ethnographies. Former teachers who enrolled in doctoral programs in graduate schools of education returned to classrooms as sites of their ethnographic work. Their publications kept debates about the humanistic and/or scientific character of "qualitative studies" swirling. Such works consisted primarily of reportage of interviews, case studies of target students or situations, and contextualization of the current study within the need for reform. Professional journals and conferences were outlets for a steady stream of questions surrounding definitions, funding sources, and relative need for "basic" research vs. "applied" studies.

In 2010, the American Anthropological Association revised its long-range plan in such a way as to lead constituents to address this issue once again. The plan noted that, in attempting to "understand the full sweep and complexity of cultures across all of human history, anthropology draws and builds upon knowledge from the social and biological sciences as well as the humanities and physical sciences. A central concern of anthropologists is the application of knowledge to the solution of human problems." The plan further noted the holistic and expansive nature of anthropology and its reliance on "the theories and methods of both the humanities and sciences" (www.aaanet.org/about/WhatisAnthropology.cfm). Central in the plan was an openness to "the application of knowledge to the solution of human problems" that are expansive and unpredictable in their origins and course of development. The plan further acknowledged the reliance of anthropologists on other disciplines, especially those typically termed the "hard sciences," as well as the humanities. Anthropologists, particularly those within the academy, responded by fiercely challenging what they interpreted as their professional organization's deprecation of science.

Unstated in either the plan or the majority of responses was specific acknowledgment of the evolving dependence of humanities research on these same sciences, as well as the social sciences, including anthropology, psychology, and sociology. Added to this list in the first decade of the twenty-first century have been the neurosciences and new technologies linked with the development of medical diagnoses, use of laser surgery, and recruitment of robotic technologies. Hard sciences and their applications came in this decade to figure centrally in humanistic texts ranging from philosophical treatises in medical ethics to science fiction novels and autobiographies and biographies recounting the course of illness, medical treatment, and dying.

All such works tracing the history or course of individuals or phenomena cannot avoid exhibiting features of Benjamin's storyteller and of both scientific orientation and literary artistry. This reality does not, however, address the issue of how the autobiography of the storyteller has contributed to choice of *problem*. Here *problem* refers to that definition used by scientists as the pivotal center of an hypothesis and also to the definition that literary theorists use to convey the driving force of the narrative plotline. Observational acuity, degree of interpretive insight, and facility in bringing to bear theories of behavior have always been central to both scientists and humanists. Decision rules apply throughout the processes of both from beginning to end. Though derived from knowledge of theories of behavior – whether of particles and planets or of human beings – these rules still emerge from the imaginative powers of the writer for selecting and organizing data as well as for choosing tools of analysis.

AUTOBIOGRAPHY

In his well-known essay "The storyteller," philosopher Walter Benjamin raises issues that apply to every writer of the "long time," whether biographer, historian, or ethnographer. Shaping of the vessel of what is observed, heard, selected, and crafted will of necessity leave not just traces of fingerprints, but the imprint of the entire hand.

Knowing all of this, we may still wonder about what the story might be that tells us how individual scientists and humanists came to pursue the particular problem at the center of their work. That question becomes especially relevant when the pursuit has extended for decades. These cases arouse curiosity about the back story – that of the storyteller and how he or she has come to the kind of knowledge in the story now being told.

Benjamin recommends "chaste compactness" in any story (1969, p. 91). His advice seems particularly appropriate for back stories, most of which begin in childhood. My story will as well.

In *Ways with words*, my autobiographical story as ethnographer and biographer was largely absent. When I wrote the book in the early 1980s, I took the objective stance that was then the norm of social-science reporting. Only in the Prologue, occasional transcripts, and Epilogue do fragments of my own life story appear. In this current volume, however, I figure as a character and change agent. My relationship with each individual in the cast of characters in these pages is evident, as are my struggles to manage the conflicts that emerge from being both insider and outsider. For many families, I knew more about their history and that of their grandparents and great-grandparents than they did. I also knew secrets that had to remain untold.

My own story before *Ways with words* I have kept quiet if not secret. In recent years, as genres have broken their bonds and spilled into one another, I have grown more comfortable with social science that blends memoir, report, and analysis in a mix of objective and subjective.[4] The unusual nature of the current work and of my long-term association with the families and children whose stories are told here seems now to call for some autobiographical explanation.

I grew up on my grandmother's small farm in rural southeastern Virginia. Our farm, located sixty miles from the nearest town with as many as 10,000 residents, was surrounded by tobacco farms, most of which were owned by black families. Our nearest neighbors were black, and the black church was across the road from my grandmother's house. The first school teachers I ever knew were black. They lived just down the road from my grandmother and me. Critical to my eventual pursuit of linguistics and anthropology is the fact that I grew up, a white girl, listening and looking, fitting in, feeling no difference. I learned by watching others and being expected to do what they wanted me to do. Books, reading, and academic expectations had no role in my early life.

Granny never learned to drive. She had finished only eight years of school and "read" the only book we had, the Bible, by telling stories as she held the Bible open to books of the Old Testament. I was an only child, born to parents who found work and adventure far away from the farm. Their lives and livelihoods benefited from the absence of a young child who clearly felt very much at home running free on her grandmother's farm. To me, life was normal, full of play and work, devoted companionship, and the joy of creating stories from my own imagination. My grandfather died when I was five years old, and my grandmother sold the farmhouse and most of the acreage. She kept a corner of the old farmland,

and the two of us moved there into a two-room temporary house covered in tarpaper (sheets of black insulation) and fronted by a dirt road. We had a barn, hen house, large garden plot, and a small orchard. Within a year or so, neighbors built a little cinder block house for us, and eventually our temporary housing was torn down to make way for a small garden area close to the new house.

Most important about this back story is its starting location. The farmers around us raised and cured tobacco they sold at tobacco auctions held in nearby towns every September. Pulpwood, the other major product of the area, was cut and hauled to the railroad stop where farmers loaded the wood on to cargo trains that hauled it to paper manufacturing plants in another part of the state. Before my grandfather died, Granny had run the general store at the railroad stop.

I grew up looking ahead to the summers when I was hired as a "hand" on the large tobacco farms that surrounded us. Black and white adults and teenagers worked in the fields pulling the tobacco leaves and laying them in the burlap-sided slides that mules pulled from the fields to the shade of the tobacco barn. From the slide, we children gathered bundles of three tobacco leaves at a time to hand to adults who tied these into tidy double-sided lines of bundles arranged along a four-foot pole. Once filled, the pole was lifted into the rafters of the barn in preparation for curing. Each fall, school started only after the tobacco crop had been harvested and taken to auction.

Down the road from my grandmother's house lived two sisters, teachers at the local black school, a handsome, well-stocked building attended by all the neighboring black children who rode the bus to school. Both teachers came from historically black colleges and teacher-training institutes. They lived in brick houses close by the big farmhouse in which their parents, Aunt Berta and Uncle Freja, lived. The big house had a huge kitchen and large pantries, filled each summer with canned bounty from family gardens. Whenever my chores at home with Granny had been completed, I begged her to let me go see Aunt Berta. I would run down the road and burst into the back door and into the kitchen. Aunt Berta's welcome was a bear hug that swooped me into her big white apron made of flour sacks. Fresh cornbread and buttermilk were the prelude to my being sent to the garden to help her grandchildren pull weeds and gather vegetables. Whenever I headed out the door to go home, she produced a parcel of food carefully wrapped and tied with string. Granny and I made a ceremony of opening the packet at dinner each night.

Along with the other white children in the area, I walked to a three-room primary school that hired each year three teachers from outside the area. They rarely lasted more than a full year. Students had little interest in books or lessons, and few of us had ever known any white person who finished secondary school. Printed materials in most homes consisted of the family Bible and Sunday School materials given out by the two small white churches that held services once a month. Once we completed six years of primary school, we walked to the intersection of a paved road where a bus took us to the county seat, location of the consolidated school for white children.

Several years into secondary school, my mother returned and announced that Granny and I should go with her to southern Florida where she now had a job as a seamstress. Each fall, and every year thereafter until I completed secondary school, we loaded into the car and headed south. In the town where my mother worked, blacks lived on the other side of the railroad tracks, had their own schools, and almost never crossed the tracks. The house where Granny and I stayed with my mother was very near the tracks on the white side. On Sundays, I rushed home from our church to ride my bike to the end of our street at the railroad tracks. From there I could hear singing from the black churches. Back at home, Granny and I had lived just across the road from the black church, and I had learned to read hymnals, find scriptures, and recite the Lord's Prayer sitting with Granny in the back of that church.

At the secondary school in south Florida, I met my first Puerto Ricans, Cubans, Filipinos, Jews, and self-proclaimed atheists. Entirely unprepared for academics, I found myself in a strange new world where other students laughed at my accent, sneered at my clothes, and marveled at all that I did not know. I studied all the time and spent hours at the homes of other students who for one reason or another defined themselves as outsiders. We struggled together, none of us doubting that context dictated behavior. We fell in line with other students and worked hard to learn. Having never heard a language other than English, I found Spanish a total mystery. My Cuban and Puerto Rican friends immersed me in their conversations, tutored me in the daily lessons in our textbook, and gave me comic books to read in Spanish. I began to catch up and then some, graduating near the top of the senior class.

The school's guidance counselor realized in the spring before graduation in June that I had probably entertained no thoughts of going on for university study. She was right. She called in my mother, whose primary interest seemed to be in whether or not colleges would feed me if I went there. When I learned that one of my friends had applied to the University of Chicago, I announced to my mother that I would go there too. My father, who weighed in from afar at that point, adamantly declared that I would attend no university that was north of the Mason–Dixon Line, the cultural boundary between the Northern and Southern states.

The final choice was Wake Forest College in North Carolina, a school affiliated with the Southern Baptist Church. My mother and father approved. The school banned dancing, allowed only double-dating, had compulsory chapel attendance, and required that all women wear hats to Sunday church services.

This back story centers on an event that took place during the summer before I was to enter Wake Forest in September. A Filipino friend, Thomas Mendoza, who had been one of my closest friends in the south Florida secondary school, was driving through Virginia on his way from Florida to the Northeast to begin his university studies. He and I corresponded all summer, and when I learned he would be coming through Virginia, I invited him to come by my grandmother's farm where I was spending the summer. When my parents learned of my invitation, they issued the firmest possible refusal. Their explanation: his dark skin proscribed such a visit.

In this denial, the accumulated observations of exclusion and discrimination I had observed but never acknowledged as racism came down on me with life-altering force. I had played and worked my individual life without questioning patterns of separation for black and white. I attributed the exclusion I felt at the secondary school in Florida to my own inadequacies in academic know-how and experience. The structural demarcation that kept black students from my secondary school of brown and white students had not struck me as unusual. Back at my grandmother's in Virginia, I had known black family members only as teachers, employers, and landowners. I had grown up immersed in the music, worship services, and stories of their church and homes. Their children were my playmates and fellow "hands" during tobacco season. We spoke the same dialect, knew the same proverbs, and told the same jokes. Their schools were better, they had buses, and they had books in their homes.

That fall, I left for college restless, uncertain, and confused. The next year, I left college, ran away to Mississippi, and lived in the world of exclusion and deprivation that was generating the Civil Rights Movement. I entered black households, living on their generosity of spirit even in the midst of their privations. I heard their stories of the violence they had met when they came too close to the world whites claimed as theirs alone. I worked in black schools and took part in protests and meetings. I listened to the stories Mississippi grandmothers told and heard preachers and congregation members plead with and sing to the god who knew their sufferings and who would provide them a leader to the promised land.

Work in southern California with migrant children followed my years in Mississippi. Though my Spanish provided me with some qualifications for helping out several days each week in the special needs classes into which non-native English speakers were often placed, I had no other credentials. Taking courses as a part-time student meant careful timing. In one semester, a course in cultural anthropology and another in linguistics fell into slots that matched my schedule. I had no idea what either course title meant or that this duo would set the direction of my professional life. Somehow the unique circumstances of my early life and my naïve blindness during those years had brought me to the disciplines of anthropology and linguistics.

I was a woman who had grown up nurtured by strong women. I wanted to study with strong women. Columbia University took me in for doctoral study. There I came to know Margaret Mead and Ruth Bunzel, who worked in the same cubicle in the Anthropology Department. Because I chose Latin American studies, Ruth Bunzel was my guiding advisor, along with Charles Wagley, both of whom had worked in Guatemala and wanted me to go there for my fieldwork. I side-stepped that option in favor of an immediate choice of immersion in linguistic anthropology and child language socialization.

But soon enough I turned back to Latin American studies and went to Guatemala. There both the random violence and forbidden entry into the areas in which I wanted to work turned me to Mexico. I stayed on to complete my study of the history of language policies from the arrival of Hernán Cortés until the twentieth century. My dissertation and first book told the story of the Castilian determination to make language the instrument of empire. The Church and the conquistadors sent from the Castilian empire fiercely initiated what would be centuries of successive policies and practices designed to diminish uses of indigenous languages and to establish Spanish as the language of everyday interaction. Independence and the creation of a new nation only ramped up efforts to make clear that the cultures and identities of indigenous groups would have no official place in the new state. I completed my dissertation on the social history of these policies and their effects on indigenous groups of Mexico. Once the book was published, first in Spanish and then in English, I returned to the States.

My thoughts turned to questions about how US laws and policies had been shaped by attitudes that had come from the British empire. How were these influences continuing with regard to indigenous languages, tongues of immigrant populations, and the varieties of English? I was sure that all New World nations, regardless of source of initial conquest and settlement, must not have left behind discriminatory policies and practices that were still marginalizing the powerless.

I went to live in the Piedmont Carolinas where the initial decade of research for *Ways with words* took place. The rest is history.

I taught at two branch universities in the southeastern part of the United States, one on the South Carolina side and the other just across the border into North Carolina. This region, known as the Piedmont, was the heart of the textile manufacturing economy. A nepotism law was in effect, and my spouse was teaching at the women's college of the University of South Carolina, making it impossible for me to work full-time in any state institution. Part-time teaching in two universities, separated by a state border, was the answer.

My children were starting their schooling in desegregated schools (my son in the first grade with the only black teacher in a white school). My university students had come from segregated schools and were entering freshly desegregated higher education. The course I taught most often was entitled "Language and Culture." Talk turned easily and often to what was happening all around us. Teachers who were students in my classes rerouted my thinking about US language discrimination. They all reported that black and white students and teachers could not understand one another.

I asked myself: How could this be? These people had grown up in the South side by side, perhaps not in and out of one another's houses as I had, but surely in some forms of public commerce, hardware stores, feed stores, downtown department stores, and tobacco auctions. As I met and grew to trust white and black teachers and students, ministers and choir leaders, I listened. In their interactions with individuals of the other race, speakers of both races changed their dialect and register and used words outside their everyday way of talking. In most instances, however, especially in the midst of classroom debates, church meetings, and regional choir councils, communication flowed with no hitches.

"It starts in the home." This mantra came to mark teachers' talk about how actual uses of language interfered with communication more than pronunciation and lexical differences. These teachers conjectured that child language socialization practices in some homes must be sufficiently different to instill in these children ways of talking that would not match those of the classroom. When children went to desegregated classrooms, they took their ways of using language at home with them to lessons, playground life, and relationships with books. Some black as well as white children had no difficulties either playing with one another or performing in classroom work. Others, generally from farms and mills, did not talk easily with their teachers or with many of the other children in their classrooms. Differences in ways of talking did not align with racial membership but rather with class status and life experiences.

Thus begins the story of the next decade of my fieldwork. In communities and schools in the Piedmont Carolinas, I settled in to learn all that I could about child language socialization. Leaders from both black middle-class families and their white counterparts across town had many ideas, and they also reported having good relationships with each other in public commerce and the business of the county and small towns. The troubles in communicating came, they conjectured, from children of the black and white working poor. On farms and in textile mills, in domestic work and menial labor, relatively little communication of substance took place outside of social greetings and the give-and-take talk necessary to get the work done. What was happening in the homes of the neighborhoods in which the children of these workers were growing up? Were they the children who gave black and white teachers, all from the middle class, the sense that some children could not communicate effectively in their classrooms? Class and educational background of the middle-class teachers had given them little preparation for the fact that some children would not have had the intense and varied kinds of oral and written communication needed to get the work of school done.

In the decade of the 1970s in the Piedmont Carolinas, I spent as many hours as possible in Trackton, a black working-class neighborhood, and Roadville, its white counterpart only three miles away. My relationships with black and white teachers in desegregated schools meant that I could also go along to school with the children. My book *Ways with words: Language, life, and work in commun-ities and classrooms* (1983/1996) recounts the stories that resulted. The full back story of that book is told elsewhere and need not be repeated here.[5]

It is important, however, to note that *Ways with words* reflects the tensions between basic and applied research in anthropology. The book is divided into two parts. The first, "Ethnographer learning," provides the basic research on child language development in Roadville and Trackton homes. In particular, the first part is an ethnography that results from the methods and theories of linguistic anthropology. Little attention goes to my roles and relationships in Roadville and Trackton. I worked hard to try to ensure that any demands of data collection would not alter daily habits of life.

The second part, "Ethnographer doing," takes readers with me into class-rooms where I worked closely with the teachers in the schools attended by the children of Roadville and Trackton. In this portion of the book, I describe ways in which the basic research on children's oral and written language generated classroom practices which teachers and I tried, observed, and assessed. Our goals were to respect language differences and to enable children to learn more ways of using oral and written language that could widen their access to worlds beyond the agrarian and manufacturing life of the local region.

It should be clear that both that book and the current volume bear the strong influence of my own childhood and adolescent experiences with gender, racial, and linguistic discrimination.

Other ethnographers also have long autobiographies evident in the words and images they give us in their ethnographies. George Foster was perhaps the first anthropologist to acknowledge the urge to return to the original site of one's first fieldwork. His volume includes his story of that return as well as accounts from others who made their way back years later to the place where their professional careers began (Foster, Scudder, Colson, and Kemper 1979). Others, such as Jack Goody (2010), have returned to their original fieldsites or sought out individuals with whom they became acquainted in the course of doing their first research stints in foreign lands. Patricia Greenfield, who began studying weaving among the Maya of Chiapas, Mexico, in the 1960s, returned to see how the children of descendant families were learning to weave (2004). Barbara Rogoff returned to Guatemala to capture the ongoing traditions of midwives still working in the region Barbara first studied nearly thirty years earlier (2011). These returnees could not forget the people from whom they first learned about local habits and values. Knowing that none of the groups with whom they first became acquainted decades ago could remain as they had been, social scientists have returned to study habits and values in adaptation. The world has shrunk, while the reach of the global economy has grown more intrusive. We all want to find out what happens to those who will forever be part of our lives. We want to understand how they develop new roles, economic alignments, and rearrange their ways of socializing the young in the ever-evolving frameworks of time and space. We want to learn from their processes of adapting, improvising, and creating.

For those of us whose storytelling has thrived for a long time, Benjamin advises us to ensure that "the wick" of our own lives "be consumed completely by the gentle flame" of the stories we tell (1969, p. 108). My hope is to have done just that.

Appendix B On methods of social history and ethnography

In this volume, social history and ethnography have been inseparable. Recounted here are three decades of the experiences of ordinary people since the double-dip recession of the early 1980s. In the Piedmont Carolinas, where they lived, the textile mills, which had been their primary means of employment, disappeared. They scattered to find work and to adapt their lives to new locations, forms of work, schools, and housing situations. The political and economic dynamics of the next thirty years reached deep into their everyday habits and beliefs, particularly those affecting relationships between parents and children. Place and time keenly shaped how individuals aligned themselves in their families and communities and shifted their self-identities.

Though definitions of the sub-disciplines of social history and ethnography have never been firmly established, most scholars would agree that those who set out to work within either tradition have much in common, particularly the obligation to make as clear as possible their methods of data collection and interpretation.[1] Both genres have put language and other symbol systems at the center of new viewpoints and theoretical approaches. Both social historians and ethnographers have considered language especially in relation to their efforts to identify the degree to which ordinary people have been conscious of larger meanings of their daily experiences.

Social historians, in particular, have searched their documentary data for evidence of how aware at certain points in time individuals have been of how daily habits shifted in relation to political or economic forces or to circumstances of class, work, and a sense of the future. For example, to what extent have individuals reflected not only on their own lives but also on ways their lives were mirrored in the lives of others? Such questions have kept the matter of audience, circumstances, and time of life for any such reflections the focus of attention for social historians. Left primarily with artifacts and documents, some with information that is readily quantifiable, others less so, social historians have had to address the extent to which accidents of preservation and discovery have made their work possible. In the case of those social historians who explicate a societal phenomenon through the animation of individual characters, the pursuit of ancient documents and their interpretation has been a central aspect of such portrayals. The rationale for works that bring readers into the lives of servants, millworkers, and peasants has been to provide a bottom-up perspective on what happened to individuals living through notable events within a span of years altered by institutional reforms issued by church or state (e.g., the Inquisition, the English Poor Laws). "Ordinary folk" (generally illiterate and lacking legal or economic means to escape the effects of political and religious dictates) have had no individual voices in the works of social historians, who quantify public records in order to look into the influence of specific laws, movements, or sweeping economic changes (Steedman 2007; Thompson 1963).

Ethnographers have similarly tried to elucidate individual lives of those who do not record their own voices. They have also attended to what has been termed the "culture" of situations and settings (such as schools, workplaces, and markets) in terms of their adaptation to historical specifics. In contrast to social historians, ethnographers have had the decided benefit of being able to observe, listen, and participate directly with individuals. Most make every effort to explain the decision rules that guided their work.[2]

In addition, ethnographers have been able to see artifacts in use and documents produced and interpreted within the everyday lives of those they portray. Such was the case in *Ways with words*, whose first chapter used primary documents to recount the beginnings of textile manufacturing in the Piedmont Carolinas. In that volume, as well as this current work, contemporary documents and artifacts (ranging from texts to toys to technologies) have revealed the texture of daily life for children and their parents and peers, primarily in relation to activity type and oral and written language uses. To the extent possible, I also documented purposes and amount of time young and old spent with electronic technologies.

Both *Ways with words* and *Words at work and play* sit within the tradition of ethnography of communication, the genre that anthropologist Dell Hymes first delineated in the 1960s (1962, 1964) and that in my writings I have tied closely to social history (Heath 1982). The genre termed *ethnography of communication* came to be closely associated with methods of data collection and analysis that linguistic anthropologists have used to describe the embeddedness of language in the social life of speech communities. Topics such as language socialization, language shift, everyday mathematics, and literacy events and social practices have benefited from their contextualization within the full round of daily life across contexts (Barton and Hamilton 1998, 1999; Bayley and Schecter 2003; Duranti, Ochs, and Schieffelin 2011; Kulick 1992; Philips 1983; Schieffelin 1990; Schieffelin and Ochs 1986; Street 1984; Zentella 1997).

COLLABORATIVE TRACKING

This current volume brings us fast-forward through the next decades of that history. Though deeply informed by principles of long-term ethnographic fieldwork and multi-year accounts of the language development of individual children, this book may be a unique genre that has no ready social-science label. It covers more than three decades, encompasses many sites, and tracks a cast of characters confronting radical economic changes and creation of new social norms surrounding marriage, family, race and ethnicity, and sexual identity.

By the mid 1980s, the flight of the families of Roadville and Trackton from the demise of the textile mills scattered them geographically. Fieldwork through participation and observation within fixed spatial locations – the usual primary means of data collection for ethnographers – became impossible as 300 families multiplied and splintered, redistributed and redefined themselves over thirty years. Methods of data collection I had followed from the late 1960s into the early 1980s had meant spending large blocks of time on a regular basis immersing myself in the daily life of Roadville and Trackton neighborhoods. There I joined household tasks, helped care for infants and young children, and spent after-school time with older children and adolescents during their homework, chores, play, and errands. My field methods matched those of most cultural and linguistic anthropologists at work in their fieldsites: making field-notes in every possible situation. supplementing them with audio- and occasional videorecordings, and asking appropriate questions of clarification and interpretation of local residents.

Following 300 families when they scattered from their original home places called for new methods of data collection. I had to keep track of families as they relocated, changed jobs, added to their families, or gave up on relationships. Now not only geographic dispersal but also new types of alignments gradually absorbed into general definitions of family made impossible close attention to individual nuclear families. Collaboration with family members of different ages who helped me combine several types of data proved to be highly effective, if often problematic and marked by inconsistency. By 1985, on my visits with most families, the fact that I had been a presence in their lives for so many years helped me step into whatever was going on when I arrived. On these occasions, I could usually fall right into the pace of daily life. I cooked, shopped, cleaned, transported children, took pets to the veterinarian, helped with homework, and did a lot of listening. With one or another family member, I managed to squeeze in time to go over data each individual had collected, and while doing so, I could catch up on their lives.

For all but a handful of the original 300 families of the two neighborhoods, I knew before they scattered in the first wave (1981–1990) where each member intended to relocate and circumstances in which their aging parents remained or changed their living arrangements. Children who had been under the age of eight in the 1970s during the decade of original fieldwork for *Ways with words* were ready to start their own families by the end of the 1980s. Many of those who were teenagers in the 1970s had grandchildren by the turn of the millennium.

Many patterns of life of Trackton and Roadville descendant families over the years lay well outside my own experience. As indicated in Appendix A, I spent my early life and years of primary and secondary education in a niche of southern culture in which black farmers managed monocrops such as tobacco and hired local whites who had either no farmland or much smaller landholdings. Though certainly still present in many parts of the Southeast well into the 1980s, monocrop black farms dedicated to tobacco, for example, attracted no newcomers from families whose breadwinner lost employment in textile mills. Over the years as I followed the families of Roadville and Trackton, I often had to remind myself that as ethnographers we study topics such as language socialization without applying our own values, drawing unfounded conclusions, or intervening to shape the choices made by those from whom we are learning. As social scientists, our job starts with delineating the phenomena of human language and surrounding behaviors for particular groups of speakers in specific situations. We then do our best to develop grounded and testable theories.

Such work differs in its degree of contextualization from the majority of studies by psycholinguists and child language experts attuned to how early language development may affect academic trajectories of children. These studies of early child language development have appeared in multiple genres and through a range of disciplinary lenses. Most of those published in flagship journals such as *Journal of Child Language* and *Journal of Verbal Learning and Behavior*, and increasingly in neuropediatric journals, have concentrated on very early language development. Child development centers associated with universities (e.g., University of Kansas, University of North Carolina at Chapel Hill) began in the 1960s to track longitudinally the linguistic and cognitive development of children in their daycare programs and preschool intervention programs for children from poverty neighborhoods. These studies indicated language growth as well as changes in scores on a variety of tests of cognitive skills in relation to various socioeconomic factors as well as home and preschool environmental features.

Language development in the first years of schooling has, for the most part, been measured in terms of vocabulary development, reading skills, and writing abilities. Later language development, or that of the later primary grades, middle school, and adolescence, has received far less attention in terms of oral production, breadth of vocabulary range, register and genre variability, and fluency in the use of specific syntactic constructions in relation to topic domains. Literacy skills in reading and writing have been of primary importance in relation to academic performance, while oral language fluency and range have received relatively little attention. Since 2000, social scientists have given much attention to children's creation of other symbolic systems and written genres such as graphic novels.[3] Some studies have examined how older children learn during their playing of videogames and considered how such activities contribute to children's literacy development and competencies with multimodal literacies.[4] These studies have been carried out in a single home or a handful of homes.

Longitudinal studies of groups or individuals learning in a range of situations, contexts, and across roles beyond that of *student* present insurmountable difficulty in the collection of naturalistic data. Therefore, those studies of oral language use among speakers between the ages of eight and eighteen have tended to focus on specific stylistic, identity, and regional features of youth speech.[5] Emphasis has been placed on situations of oral language interaction in terms of specific lexical, syntactic, and genre features across the years both in families and in non-familial/non-school settings. These latter works have been carried out with acknowledgment that few values and behaviors lie closer to the heart of family life than their uses of language and other symbols marking their identities.

However, because many studies of early child language development have been tied to later academic success or failure, some educators have judged home language contexts in dichotomous terms: on the one hand, deprived, restricted, or inadequate; or on the other hand, advantaged, rich in school readiness, and promising likelihood of academic success.[6] It has been hard to find studies that include the talk of families and their children and that avoid judging such vital issues as discipline, trust, respect, and academic preparation. Thus some studies have concluded that because this or that kind of oral and written language interaction does or does not take place in the home, consequences will follow for children.

Cultural and linguistic anthropologists have tried to avoid these tendencies by focusing on what does happen and not on what may be absent or amiss. Throughout this book, I have tried to encourage readers to avoid assuming that certain presences or absences during childhood confine children to particular lines of destiny. The range of optional environments of learning increases as children grow older, have more independence, can go where their friends are, and learn to recognize and express their particular likes and dislikes in terms of adult caregivers, activities, and schedules. Children grow less and less dependent on their parents as models and interlocutors.

FINDING LANGUAGE

In following the families of Trackton and Roadville, I kept their uses of language across the children's age span as the focus of my data collection. As I set out to devise means of collecting data with family members, the theories of learning language that emerged from *Ways with words* (1983/1996, p. 344) guided my long-distance and close-up mapping of families' daily activities, events, and transitions.

To keep up with the talk and texture of families as they scattered after the recession of 1981, I put in place a plan of regular contact with the original families. Initially I did so through telephone calls, letters, and as many visits as possible each year. Since most families in the first wave of moves relocated within 500–1,000 miles (800–1,600 km) of Roadville and Trackton, this plan worked well except in those cases where turns of fortune of families meant that either they did not want to be found or they could not manage to continue our collaboration.

During the 1990s, new types of employment opened far beyond the radius of geographic locations to which families had migrated in their first wave of exodus after the collapse of textile manufacturing. More young people sought higher education around the country. Their parents could advance their professional careers in government jobs in the nation's capital and within the rapidly expanding fields of information technology and finance in the northeast corridor from Boston to New York. They could move farther south to take advantage of careers in real estate and the aerospace industry. The second wave of moves took them farther west to California, Washington, Oregon, and Idaho.

In increasing numbers after the mid 1980s, infants born into family units of two working parents or a single parent working full-time were placed in daycare before they reached their first birthday. Until they entered kindergarten or first grade, these children were dropped off early in the morning and picked up before six p.m. A few families had live-in caregivers. Some had friends who stayed home with their own infants or toddlers and earned money by taking in the children of a few friends. Older children and adolescents spent time in school-sponsored after-school activities or with youth organizations or teams and activities organized by national or grassroots youth groups, such as YMCA or local community centers. These opportunities meant they could be with their peers, even though adults were generally around to coach, direct, and supervise. Young people sought to be with their friends during their discretionary time.

During this period, some older children and teens were willing to use their cassette taperecorders in the early years and later digital recorders to capture their talk. These recordings made it possible for me to compare their peer language with their talk in interaction not only with their parents in the home but also with their coaches, youth choir directors, or camp counselors. Many of the adolescents who had known me as long as they could remember took advantage of my offer to pay them for completed pages of activity logs they kept at random intervals on one day of the week and one weekend day. On my visits, these partner-researchers listened with me to audiorecordings and analyzed transcripts I had made of peer talk they had recorded.

We sometimes talked together about the value of their work, for they knew that my presence, or that of any adult, cut off the natural flow of talk within groups of children or teenagers. Most of them thought that my doing interviews with young people about their own language use and structures would be pointless. Interviewees could not spontaneously give me a sense of the nuanced interactive flow of peer talk that I needed in order to look at language change over time. I could get this kind of material only by depending on young people as partners in both data collection and analysis. Furthermore, because I had known so many of the children of the families for many years, formally interviewing them had no place in our relationships.

Older family members, usually the mother, often kept activity diaries for preschoolers when adult and child were together at home, in the car, and on a play date with another preschool child. Mothers collected most of their data on preschoolers by leaving the audiorecorder in the home space of their child for one forty-five-minute stretch of time on two days randomly selected in each month. When I got these tapes, often of poor sound quality, I tried to determine: (a) extent of talk and identity of interlocutors within interactional talk; (b) actions and objects present within and during the talk; and (c) presence of multiple and overlapping sources of sound input (e.g., television, videogame, music, radio, "talking" toys). I logged these recordings by major categories, randomly selecting portions to transcribe, and then analyzing emerging themes.

The late 1990s and first decade of the twenty-first century brought new technologies that boosted the amount of data I received from family members, young and old. Children, adolescents, and parents were happy to write to me about their new pieces of technology and to show off their skills of recording. My visits with adolescents often centered on their teaching me new ways of looking simultaneously at different types of data and of arranging verbal and visual materials from prior years. Our joint recording and analysis sessions gave my adolescent partner-researchers documentaries of their lives as toddler, elementary school child, pre-teen, and teenager at various points from the mid 1980s forward. In general, they had more interest in these documentaries than their parents did.

Parents with new technological toys seemed more comfortable recording babies and toddlers than in reviewing the visual and verbal lives of their older children. Almost all the families lost interest in documenting their children beyond the first year or two of school. When I asked parents why this was the case, they explained that, when their children were very young and in the early years of primary school, they could keep track of and often take part in special school events as well as the pace of acquisition of reading and mathematics. Over time, however, as school subjects became more challenging and after-school activities more frequent, parents felt there was little point in recording, because no one had time or interest for viewing the material. Moreover, their recordings were less technologically sophisticated than those their children made on cell-phones. Older children preferred their own computer-generated self-portraits layered with multiple images, special effects, and background music.

As families scattered, they used email with me and with their families in other parts of the country. Children and adolescents sometimes relished writing to me and sending photographs of their friends, athletic achievements, and perform-ances in community organizations. When Skype became available and video calling soon followed, my contacts with teenagers and young adults surged in regularity.

On visits during each year, I fell into the local pace of life to the extent possible, but visits were short and the day-to-day rhythm hard to capture. At times,

I lost track of some children and entire branches of families. However, the adults and children of the households I visited on a regular basis gave me generous chunks of their time, taking me to their favorite places, telling stories, and filling me in on their lives since my last visit. These intermittent occasions, though, fell short of providing the rich texture that came from living in the midst of family and community life. By the mid to late 1980s, as two-working-parent families became more common and infants and toddlers spent the bulk of their time in daycare facilities, the amount of data available for these youngest children diminished rapidly.

As the neighborhoods of Roadville and Trackton emptied, families relocated in distant places among strangers. There they found no counterparts to the familiar dirt plaza of Trackton or the safe backyards of Roadville. Parents and children adapted. No longer did mothers talk of "neighbors." Now they talked of "my neighbor," usually the one nearby person who could be called on "in a pinch to help out or watch the kids." Young children's time away from their parents was generally spent with someone who was paid to take care of them or in fee-for-service activities. In such circumstances, recording the language of a child from a particular family was impossible.

Some families kept up a steady stream of activity diaries for their pre-schoolers. Across the years, some families showed remarkable tolerance for my frequent pleas and explanations of how important it was for me to be able to compare transcripts and activity logs of children of the same age in households across the decades. Analysis of language recordings along with activity log data on participants, material goods, location, and time of activities opened windows into the life of a toddler, elementary school child, pre-teen, or teen in these families at various points in any year from 1969 forward.

Valuable incentive for keeping these records developed as new technologies enabled parents to download my audiorecordings and diaries of their young children into computer data bases. In all instances, however, families lost interest in this kind of archiving of everyday life in their homes as children moved beyond the first year or two of school. Older children grew more independent. Parents sometimes settled into the role of a supportive audience member for school events and occasional questioner about outcomes of school testing. Even those parents most focused on school became less involved, except in spurts of monitoring the production of school projects and volunteering at the school or on fieldtrips.

As the children moved into their fourth or fifth years of school, I came to depend more on the children themselves than on their parents for the collection of data. On my visits, I spent most of my time with older children and adolescents in community sites where they gathered for sports and arts practices, service-learning projects (school-required service commitments in community organizations), and general social gatherings of their friends.

By the mid 1990s, young people became my primary co-researchers and interpreters of data.

I was most successful in tracking adolescents who were dedicated to after-school sports and community organizations filled with arts activities, community service, and environmental projects. Thus after the early 1980s, the collection from older children and teenagers skewed markedly toward these activities. By the 1990s, children over the age of eleven spent far more time with their peers in one another's homes or in group activities than at home with their own families. Older children wanted to be involved in some creative project or just "hang out" with their friends without the presence of an adult. When there were no peers around, then adult company of the right sort could be okay with them, particularly if being with an adult provided a means of transportation otherwise unavailable. However, once children could negotiate a way to be with their friends, they made themselves scarce around adults including me.

In recording the talk of young people, I was greatly aided by university graduate students, "guerrilla anthropologists" who could "hang" with young people unobtrusively. Their presence did not significantly curtail the natural flow of peer talk, for they came to be accepted in the work and play of community youth activities. I greatly benefited from their work, and several of them have become prominent academic researchers as well as leaders in shaping and building community youth programs across the US.[7]

With older children and teenagers, collecting and analyzing language data became an opportunity for them to earn money and to have food, primarily pizzas, with their friends. When I sat down with young people, we had conversations, not interviews. In my years of fieldwork, they have made clear their general regard of interviews as a suspect genre, used by adults to collect information that may be incriminating for young people. Asking any speaker to analyze or theorize about language use is of little purpose to linguistic anthropologists. Young speakers, in particular, either shrug off such questions or provide answers that have little basis in actual structures and uses familiar in their daily lives. I have found language data collected through question-and-answer interview-like situations particularly subject to false introspections and deceptive performances having little to do with ordinary language use. Young people, adept imitators of language they hear but do not themselves use, have always found pleasure in mimicking and fabricating a range of discourse forms that report a collection of "facts" they believe interviewers want to hear from them (Heath 1997).

RECIPROCAL RELATIONSHIPS AND MAKING CHOICES

What kept the young people involved? Why did so many of them stick to some form of data collection and long conversations with me? The answer is hard to determine. No doubt, their interests were often self-serving. From 1985 forward, whenever I was around, they had transport. I drove them where they wanted to go. If they had cross-town subway rides or out-of-town bus rides with team members, I went along. I got to know their friends, favorite music, pop stars, foods, and fun activities. I spent more and more time in community locations of youth activities in cities across the nation, studying not only young people there but also the organizational structures and modes of operating that local young people judged most effective.

The give-and-take necessary to sustain relationships over three decades of ethnographic research relies on reciprocities of all kinds. With approximately 85 percent of the descendants of the original families, I maintained contact from 1981 forward, but the quality of data provided by families varied considerably, as did the consistency of my contact with children of different ages in these families.

How then did I select from the descendant families of Roadville and Trackton those individuals featured in this work? None is a character composite; each one is a real individual. The first level of choice had to depend on the extent and quality of data available on each individual in the data base. By 2001, I determined that about 250 individuals would be appropriate, but they were, of course, of different ages and reflected a range of cross-generational pathways.

As one dramatic security and economic event after another took place around the globe in the first decade of the new millennium, individuals coming into young adulthood seemed to me to be most affected. Hence, I decided that the book's featured characters would be individuals coming into adolescence or young adulthood during this decade. For those in this age-range, future prospects for jobs, health benefits, retirement packages, and home ownership bore little relationship to what had been possible for their parents. Educational quality and content in many of their middle and secondary schools remained unresponsive to employers' increasingly urgent call for creative collaborative workers trained in mathematics, technology, and the sciences. Young blacks and Latinos moved further and further to the back of those in line for advanced placement courses, guidance counseling, part-time or full-time jobs, student loans, and supportive higher education opportunities that could help compensate for the poor quality of secondary schools in under-resourced communities.

In the early 1980s, I had developed a list of twenty-eight characteristics that guided for three decades my interpretation of data collected from descendant individuals and families of Trackton and Roadville. These characteristics cluster around three domains of behavior: (1) language and other symbol structuring in social interactional and sociotechnical activities; (2) curiosity, creativity, and manual dexterity in manipulation of tools and materials used in play and work; (3) personal qualities of memory, self-management, empathy, moral reasoning, and responsiveness and responsibility. Over the years, I came to appreciate the extent to which these characteristics reflected values and observations from my years of teaching and working with children and adolescents. In the 1990s, I especially noted that characteristics in the three sets of behavioral patterns closely paralleled skills and competencies identified as essential for workers in modern economies by national labor and education leaders (SCANS 1991).

By 2006, I selected thirty-two individuals whose behaviors in these domains over the years represented a median course – neither exceptionally successful and noteworthy nor especially damaged by failed efforts or persistent bad luck. Individuals also had to come from a range of patterns of family and community situations. Four quite distinct groupings of such patterns emerged from the amassed data, and I chose from each grouping one or more individuals as characters in the book. The socialization pathways of each had come through one of the following: (1) a relatively stable family and community context during childhood and adolescence (e.g. Mark and Rebecca; Denny and Tameka); (2) an early childhood of considerable deprivation and chaos followed by stable guided opportunities through which individuals developed character and talent (e.g., Robert and Richard; Donna and Marcello and Melvin); (3) a childhood in which the individuals displayed sharp changes in ways of relating to authority and an adolescence of defying parents while simultaneously being drawn into new and positive learning environments where they interacted with experts in fields distant from their parents' interest or expertise (e.g., Donna, Bernardo, and Martha); and (4) a childhood and adolescence filled with sharp twists and turns of fate that called forth survival instincts and pragmatic self-reflection that brought the individual to safety (e.g., Jerome).

As indicated in Chapter 1, neither these characters nor I claim that the ways their strengths and weaknesses or personalities and talents enabled them to navigate the pathways of their life reflect typical choices and chances. Taken together, however, their lives and those of their parents and grandparents do present a spectrum of experiences in the three decades from the double-dip recession of the 1980s to the threat of a repeat double-dip recession in the second decade of the new millennium. My hope is that the level of detail given for each of these individuals shows readers both the truth of the characters and the types of reciprocity I had over the years with them and their families.

This is not a work whose methods, sketched out as they are throughout the book and in its appendices, are likely to be taken up by other social scientists. As is the case with other publications that look back on the opening years of the twenty-first century, this book can carry many descriptions: non-fiction, autobiographical biography, part-memoir/part-ethnography. Throughout the long years of writing this book, I have wanted readers to feel that all that happens here either could or did happen to them or someone they know. I trust that this recognition will lead readers to believe that they hold some responsibility now and into the future for the lives of individuals whose stories resemble those told here.

Notes to text

PROLOGUE

1. Terminology referring to levels and types of schooling differs around the world. The most widely known distinctions are those referring to formal education in the Americas and those encompassing schooling in the United Kingdom and many nations of the former British empire. This volume uses terms common in the United States and in most locations throughout North and South America. Terms such as *classes*, *courses*, and *school* refer to formal instructional environments in which an expert teaches, and students pursue a set sequence of lessons toward some demarcation of their completion of a particular level of achievement. For the young, the mark of achievement is usually a diploma or certificate. For adults in vocational and other types of specialized training, stages of progress are usually marked by the awarding of a license or certificate. In American usage, any place of formal education from preschool (usually referred to as kindergarten) through graduate study for a doctorate or professional degree (such as a J.D., *juris doctor*, a doctorate in law) may be referred to simply as a *school*. In the United States, institutions of higher education that offer post-secondary-school courses of study are generally referred to as *colleges*. The term *university* is reserved for those institutions that include not only four-year courses of study in the liberal arts (usually leading to either a Bachelor of Arts or Bachelor of Science degree) but also graduate-level courses of study leading to a Master's degree or doctorate. Two-year colleges offer no residential dormitories and generally serve primarily students who live in the region and wish to save the costs of living away from home while attending college. They offer not only vocational courses leading to a professional license or certification (in fields ranging from dental hygiene to X-ray technology) but also liberal arts courses. These, if successfully completed in two-year colleges, can be transferred for credit to four-year colleges or to a university, where students live in a dormitory or rented accommodation shared with other students. In the United States and Canada, completion of schooling from grade one (with entry at age six) through grade twelve is generally required, though students may leave school at age sixteen and thus become 'dropouts' who have not completed twelve years of formal schooling. The term *middle school* (generally grades six through nine) refers to the transition years between *primary school* (generally grades one through six) and *secondary* or *high school* (generally grades nine through twelve). At the tenth grade, students are referred to as *sophomores*, at the eleventh grade as *juniors*, and in the final year as *seniors*. This same terminology applies in college and university to students in their second, third, and final year of study toward a college diploma. However, the majority of students who enter some institution of higher education stretch out their time of study toward a Bachelor's degree beyond four years of consecutive coursework.

1 ON BEING LONG IN COMPANY

1. Details of the methods used in tracing the lives of these families may be found in Appendix B. Reviewed there are the collaborative strategies families and their older children used with me in collecting and interpreting data, as well as the process I used to select the families featured in this book. Appendix A offers my perspective on autobiography and long-term ethnography and explores how my childhood living as a white child immersed in a predominantly black rural community set my course for staying close to the lives of Roadville and Trackton families as their children grew into adulthood.

2. President Harry Truman signed the order in 1948 to desegregate US military services. Within the next two years, by the opening of the Korean War, most of the branches of the military included black soldiers. Many chose to serve twenty years and were eligible for retirement in the late 1960s and early 1970s. As desegregation took hold and Civil Rights legislation opened civic and educational opportunities in the South, many veterans returned to the small towns and rural communities from which their parents and grandparents had come.

3. For several decades after the 1920s, blacks living in the South migrated to northern cities. Migrants from specific regions of southern states tended to head for the same cities that had previously drawn their neighbors and relatives. South Carolinians settled in Philadelphia. Migrants from Mississippi and Louisiana preferred Chicago or headed to Oklahoma first and then California. Those from Georgia, Florida, and Alabama went to Harlem. Wherever they went, these migrants took their music, food, and religious devotion, but they also brought to their new locations an ethos of fairness, hard work, and discipline. High on the list of what they most wanted was education. They were convinced that success in school would enable them to fulfill their ambitions. Wilkerson 2010 immerses the lives of three individuals of the "great migration" in the history of race relations and economic swings that triggered the exodus of nearly six million blacks from the South.

4. Some items and topics on these tests, as well as those the children took, were unfamiliar to Southerners who lived far from a major city, had studied social studies texts covering different aspects of history, and were taught to judge style in writing more by appropriateness to occasion than to a standardized norm. For example, items such as *apartment*, *walnuts* (pictured with smooth shells), and names of famous battles that had been fought in the Northeast might not have been familiar to Southerners.

5. Since 1980, several studies by child developmentalists, sociologists, and anthropologists have documented interactions, verbal and otherwise, in homes and classrooms of children (Hart and Risley 1995; Lareau 2003). However, none has provided a social historical accounting of the lives of children and families for more than a year or so. Cross-cultural studies of children's development have given comparative accounts of families (Foster, Scudder, Colson, and Kemper 1979; Greenfield 2004; Tudge 2008).

6. Tyack and Cuban 1995.

7. As a postscript to *Middlemarch*, George Eliot lets her readers in on what befalls the characters they have come to know in the novel. I have leaned on her rationale that humans do want more than the fragments of beginnings and that they find satisfaction in knowing about the webs of life that snare individuals (Eliot 1871–1872/1963, p. 810).

2 A BOY FINDS HIS MAMA(S)

1. These "guerrilla anthropologists" were graduate students trained in linguistic anthropology and comfortable working and learning for a year or more with adolescents living in under-resourced communities across the United States. Carried out under a grant awarded by the Spencer Foundation to Heath and Milbrey W. McLaughlin, the research centered in 120 youth organizations that involved approximately 30,000 adolescents between 1987 and 2000. Sites included urban regions, mid-sized towns, and rural communities across the continent, plus one site in a mid-sized town in Hawaii. For further detail on the research, see Heath and McLaughlin 1993; Heath, Soep, and Roach 1998.
2. Worthman (2002) examines the process of writing, editing, and creating play scripts used by Liberty Theatre and similar theatres who base their plays on materials from the writings of their young actors.
3. Social scientists, as well as community artists, have documented the process of editing and curating the voices of adolescents across numerous contexts. Negotiations around this process have become increasingly difficult as popular culture admits more and more profanity, nudity, and blasphemy. Thus, delineating for young people the difference between being a public organization reliant on grants, donations, and audience development and being a commercial business is essential for organizational leaders (Soep and Chávez 2010, Chapter 2).

3 THE CLOSENESS OF STRANGERS

1. Information on the social interactions of young people working on Mac's Farm was collected by Michael Prentice, who served as crew chief on the farm in the summer of 2006.
2. The concept of "intimate strangers," though, so far as I know without use of this term, has been addressed by several scholars who maintain that nurturing neighborhoods need to provide strong role models in order to support resiliency and aspirations of adolescents (Harrington and Boardman 1997; Schorr 1997). See also McLaughlin, Scott, Deschenes, Hopkins, and Newman 2010 for an analysis of the extent to which community organizations, advocating for and with youth, model awareness and attention, imitation and learning, and interdependence in their modes of operating. They do so in order to advocate effectively and to build coalitions to support youth living in low-income communities. Biographies of "pathmakers," highly successful individuals from under-resourced homes and communities, often point to the multiplying positive effects of such resources in the lives of these individuals (Wideman 1995). In Lareau's (2003) account of "concerted cultivation," organized activities, such as sports and arts, figure centrally in the lives of the nine- and ten-year-olds she studied.
3. Anthropologists have provided studies of apprenticeship and the role of public performance associated with learning by observation, demonstration, and trial and error. Self-transformation develops through the uncertainty involved in the state of liminality or transition phase that apprenticeship offers (Coy 1989; Handelman 1990).
4. Numerous studies of art and science reiterate the nature of craftwork and its relation to curiosity, community connection, and emotional experience. Sennett (2008) provides a history of craft from the Middle Ages through the latest advances in software development. Art historian Barbara Stafford argues for the return of an oral–visual culture over

the text-centered learning that formal education and the division of disciplines have brought since the Enlightenment. She elaborates on the cognitive similarities in the crafts of art and science (1999). In his history of "the scientific life," Shapin (2008) argues that in order to understand how scientific and technological knowledge come about, we need to appreciate the highly personal aspects of trust, familiarity, and personal virtues that go into the production of technoscientific knowledge. His descriptions of the role of uncertainties and risks in scientific work match in many ways those characterizing youth organizations committed to art or science. All feature ephemeral contingently emerging spaces of inquiry, trial and error, and the need to welcome serendipity.

5. The philosophy of viewing young people as resource and as developing expert in a particular field (agronomy, visual art, theatre, music) creates the need and desire of adults to direct individual attention to young people. Adults want to learn with them and to guide them. Young people whose backgrounds in their homes or schools have not fostered this view of them often meet this individual attention with suspicion and belligerence. Many community organizations, therefore, offer a period of four to six weeks in which young people can "try it out" before they agree to commit to the organization (Heath and Smyth 1999).

6. These views parallel in several ways analyses from social scientists who have long associations with youth organizations. See especially Halpern 2003.

4 EMBRACING TALK

1. When children and adolescents undertake tasks in which adults work side by side with them, they inevitably joke, laugh, and tease. The supervision of adults in the "work" of baking cupcakes, cleaning out horse stalls, and planting gardens helps the young learn some of the rewards of meaningful work in which they feel some ownership. The practical work of daily life benefits the self and others and indicates shared responsibility as a member of an intimate unit. This kind of "goodness" depends in large part on perceptual awareness of environmental surroundings and the needs of others or of the unit as a whole. It is within this kind of *work* that the young develop a sense of reciprocity and moral responsibility. See Gardner 2011 and Ochs and Izquierdo 2009 for philosophical considerations related to the development of empathy and responsibility through the everyday interactions of practical work. Youth organizations struggle to keep a balance between the work of their projects and productions and playfulness throughout the process. Halpern 2003 provides a history of the views of play that created playgrounds throughout the US and shaped the goals of some after-school organizations. By the end of the first decade of the twenty-first century, parents, educators, and child developmentalists, along with museums and parks, felt an urgent need to revitalize play in children's lives. The US was suffering from "play deficit," according to organizations that took on the label of "pro-play." In early 2011, when lay proponents organized the "Ultimate Block Party" in Central Park in New York City, the National Science Foundation worked at the side of organizers who wanted to teach parents the science and educational value behind games such as "I Spy" and "Capture the Flag" (Stout 2011).

2. In the periodic national debates surrounding "welfare mothers" and "welfare to work," social scientists consistently confirm the importance of factors that moved Zinnia Mae off of welfare and into a sense of respect for herself as employee, mother, and community member. Hamilton (2002) provides a summative analysis of these studies.

5 LINES OF VISION

1. Narrative theorists have repeated in many ways the idea that readers and listeners feel they benefit from the struggles of the strangers they meet in stories. Kierkegaard regarded irony as the freedom that the audience for stories wants in a continuation of possibilities opening against the certainties that endings bring (1968); see also Miller 1998. Benjamin's essay on "the storyteller" eloquently cautions against "magical escapes" (1969). Bruner 1986 also points out the trap of gaps between the "actual" and the "possible."

2. Details of this first visit with Zinnia Mae and the children may be found in Heath 1990. The account there is a comparative analysis of Zinnia Mae's urban life with that of Sissy, a friend who remained in Trackton for several years after Zinnia Mae left.

3. Details of the early language development of Sissy's oldest child, Denny, along with an account of the alterations in community cohesiveness and church life of the family after their move from Trackton, are included in Heath 1990.

4. The 1980s and early 1990s produced numerous accounts of teenage urban life and the efforts of community organizations to keep these children alive and away from the innumerable hazards and temptations of underground economies. Particularly evident in works published from data collected in the late 1980s was the concern authors expressed for the future of America's children. These volumes did not blame parents for failing to keep their children under control. Instead, these works illustrated the complexities of life for young people struggling to adapt to what some writers saw as "two nations," black and white, that faced one another in inner cities of poverty and violence. The increasing numbers of incoming immigrants led to tensions surrounding the view that the bounties of US opportunities would not be sufficient to go around. Outcomes would surely be unequal and would derive from separateness in the paths ahead. There could be no way of "makin' it." Insecurities fed hostilities and generated fateful choices for many young people. See Anderson 1990; Freedman 1993; Kotlowitz 1991; Kozol 1991; McLeod 1987; Moore 1991. Some writers focused on prevention and ways that community organizations could help the young overcome the problems around them. See Dryfoos 1990; McLaughlin, Irby, and Langman, 1994. But more writers pointed to the inevitable draw of the underground economy for young people growing up in a decade of few models who looked like them. Their parents' backgrounds had given them few strategies for guiding their children through what some called the "epidemic" of crack cocaine and the rising acceptance of early sexual encounters even in the face of growing fears of AIDS. See Wilson 1987. For a take on the continuation of that underground economy for youth throughout the 1990s and first decade of the new millennium, see Venkatesh 2006. During these years, the landscape of hope for young black men growing up poor in urban life had changed in the particulars of its dangers. However, the general topography of inequities of education, justice, and employment remained. By 2010, twenty-four states had some form of "habitual offender" statutes, many of which originated during the 1990s when "three-strikes" laws had been set in place. Such laws required mandatory incarceration of those convicted of serious criminal offenses on three or more separate occasions. Disproportionately affected by these laws were black males (and increasingly black females). See Rich 2009.

6 THE HAND OF PLAY

1. "Scientists in the crib" is a term developmentalists have used to capture the intensity of very young children's visual attentiveness to detail (Gopnik, Meltzoff, and Kuhl 1999). Looking initiates meaning construction: "seeing it" goes a long way toward "getting it" (Heath 2011; Kosslyn 1995).

2. Sutton-Smith (1997) provides a comprehensive interdisciplinary analysis of play that emphasizes its ambiguity and biological functionality. Child developmentalists have consistently advocated the cognitive, emotional, and linguistic benefits of play for young children. For a comparative perspective across two decades of these arguments, see Moore 1986 and Hirsh-Pasek, Berk, Singer, and Golinkoff 2008. Brown 2009 provides an analysis of the special need for play within contemporary families, but Stromberg (2009) offers an anthropological perspective on how difficult it is for families living in a "culture of entertainment" to step back and relearn how to find joy in play. Some social scientists stress the critical scarcity of opportunities for children to play outdoors and to experience the discovery and exploration possible in the natural world (Louv 2005).

3. Lareau (2003), especially Chapters 1 and 9, delineates how families of the middle class value structured activities for their children. As competition for entry into the most selective US colleges has increased, parents have sought after-school and summer experiences likely to bolster the merits of their children's applications for entry into university study.

4. Meltzoff, Kuhl, Movellan, and Sejnowski 2009 and numerous other examinations of young children's responsiveness to human interaction in relation to electronic images affirm the thoroughly social foundation of human learning. The eye and hand are intimately involved in moving language along and in helping children and parents indicate turns, roles, next steps, and strategies in their joint play (Wilson 1998). Between 2005 and 2010, studies from cognitive scientists and neuroscientists who examine visual cognition have exploded in number to push understanding of how visual and haptic learning relate to memory, creativity, and conditional thinking; see Burnett 2004; Pfeifer and Bongard 2007. The role of design, including mental models, planning, and sketching, had been described in Roskos-Ewoldsen, Intons-Peterson, and Anderson 1993 and Roth 1996. Scientists and artists, joined often by art historians, have provided historical perspectives on similarities of laboratories and studios as learning environments (Lynch 1985; Mallgrave 2010; Stafford 1999, 2007). The "artful mind" and the "scientific mind" create in similar ways (Donald 1991, 2001; Turner 2006). Social scientists have documented the ways in which the collaborative work in the learning environments of both scientists and artists relies heavily on gestures, visual representations, and calls to mutual attentiveness and to envisaging beyond immediately accessible knowledge (Goodwin 1994, 1995; Latour 1986, 1987; Latour and Woolgar, 1979; Lynch 1985). Greenfield 2004 provides a textual and photographic account of young children and adults attending closely with eye and hand in their weaving practices across three generations of Maya women and girls.

5. See, for example, Tomasello (1999) and especially Pallasmaa (2009) for explorations of ways that touch enhances vision and hapticity.

6. By 2010, numerous research studies from neuroscientists were reporting the detrimental effects on attention span and visuospatial attentiveness of long hours in front of television and computer screens. Multi-tasking in the use of cellphones and multiple

computer screens with simultaneous functions came in for repeated examination and condemnation. Warnings surrounding the detrimental effects of multi-tasking on brain development, memory, attentiveness, and productivity came not only from neuro-scientists, but also from child developmentalists, business executives, and educators (Carr 2010; Lehrer 2009; Salvucci and Taatgen 2010). Particularly appealing to the public media was the idea that the "teenage brain" was "wired" for multi-tasking (Feinstein 2009).

7. Long-term studies of young children who choose their visual-arts play over passive spectatorship of commercial entertainment point out the strong preference of such children for demonstrating what they know through visual arts rather than written compositions. Anning and Ring 2004 provides case studies of children free at home to do their art work but constrained once they went to school. Matthews (1999, 2003) describes in detail the case of a young male artist from childhood through adolescence and includes rich analyses of the young artist's assessment of what learning through his art work during his time outside school meant to him.

8. The ability of children to create theories regarding the minds of others and the operations of the natural world has long been studied by developmental psychologists (Gopnik and Meltzoff 1998; Gopnik, Meltzoff, and Kuhl 1999).

9. See the essays in Gilbert, Reiner, and Nakhleh (2005). The hand as heuristic figures centrally in the evolutionary history of primates. Under circumstances when action is relevant to visual imagery, the motor system becomes engaged to support the grasping action of the hand. Fixed representations do not sit in the brain; rather, learners undertake perception, action, and cognition simultaneously to bring about representations. This grounded cognition is especially pronounced when the learner is engaged in motor-dependent production of visual representations. The hand, as investigator and manipulator of the environment, calls on all these modal systems, particularly when the hand is shaping, grasping, drawing, modeling, or molding materials. Some neuroscientists have the view that a story results from "force patterns" exerted on the fingers, hand, and arm. See Donald (1991, 2001) on the hand in the evolution of human cognitive abilities. DiSessa and Sherin 1998 provide an overview of processes of conceptual change in relation to conditionals and prediction (see also Dancygier 1998).

10. Ferguson (1983) examined the grammatical and genre differences in the register of sports talk. Within this register, the talk of sportscasters differs from that of sports narrators. Children as young as six years of age can distinguish between the two types of registers almost instantly, even if they know little or nothing about the type of ballgame being played. Productive and receptive competence with both styles of the register of sports talk has been found among young people across social classes and geographic regions of the US (Heath and Langman 1994).

11. The feature of replay in narratives has been much debated in terms of its structures and functions (Heath 1994; Mushin 2000). Its popularity with older children and adolescents grew in the period portrayed in Figure 6.2.

7 WAYS WITH TIME AND WORDS

1. The idea that "It's on the internet" created general problems in academic institutions from 2001 when Wikipedia first became available. Cases of plagiarism escalated. At least two factors may have contributed. The first is that the internet gives the impression that everything on the internet is there for taking. Downloading from YouTube and

copying images and music seem to differ little from downloading texts someone else created and using any of these for one's own purposes. The concept of intellectual property is not easily conveyed to a generation that has little sense of *original*. Today's adolescents and young adults think less about what is *original* than they do about *style*. The latter term means creating a unique twist or take on something others also do, so the creation of *new and original* in reference to text means simply taking what someone else has done, rearranging it a bit into "my own style and submitting it as my own thing." A second factor that may be contributing to plagiarism's rise is the pressure of time the young feel to do everything. Selecting, focusing, and excelling in only a few activities receives little encouragement in the broad social context of youth. Again exceptions come for those who remain within youth organizations for more than a year or so. There they have through this commitment selected and agreed to focus and excel. See Blum 2009 for an ethnographic study of undergraduates and their views and practices related to plagiarism.

2. Numerous origins of aphorisms having to do with salt exist across cultures. In the southern United States, Biblical or religious origins were most common. Judas spilled salt at the Last Supper; hence, spilling salt is bad luck. The devil lurks just over the shoulder; thus throwing salt over the shoulder into the eyes of the devil may send the devil away and thereby temporarily improve your luck.

3. In the Language Technologies Institute at Carnegie Mellon University, computational linguists analyzed tweets and found specific regional features of orthography and usage; the lead investigators were Jacob Eisenstein, Eric P. Xing, Noah A. Smith, and Brendan O'Connor: www.sciencedaily.com/releases/2011/01/110106171011. htm. See also Crystal 2008 for similar analysis of text messages.

4. Perspectives on the roles that retellings play among adolescents who restyle the same stories for different purposes appear in Bucholtz 2011; Eckert 1989; Green 2011; Mendoza-Denton 2008; Tannock 1999.

5. These general statements are based on audiorecordings made by young people working with me as co-researchers in the years between 1998 and 2010. Random samples of audiorecordings of approximately 124 hours of interactive talk in segments lasting at least thirty minutes among teenagers were used to tally counts and to develop the classifications of specific grammatical and stylistic features noted in the summative discussion listed here.

6. Between 2000 and 2010, "smaller is better" became a mantra of education reformers. This movement, funded largely by the Bill and Melinda Gates Foundation, advocated small primary schools and the break-up of large secondary schools into internal units of small schools. This move to smaller schools kept alive in many schools the cooperative learning movement that Robert Slavin had introduced in the 1990s. Within this movement, learners talked and worked together in discussion groups and in joint creation of ideas, written work, and projects. For overviews of these education reform movements and their relation to collaborative authorship, see Lunsford and Ede 1990, 2011. The education reform movement of cooperative learning is summarized in Slavin 1983. The small school reform movement and its relationship to collaborative learning have been locally analyzed in locations where it has been initiated. For a general summary, see Darling-Hammond 2010.

7. As early as the 1980s, librarians, publishers, and lawyers grew concerned about the meaning of "true" authorship and "original" ideas. See Carpenter 1981 for the

perspective of librarians on this issue and an overview of the categories of "writing out" and "writing up," as well as "writing down," "writing in," and "writing over."

8. See Heath 2011 for a summary of studies from the neurosciences and social sciences on envisionment. Slingerland 2008 reviews neuroscience and philosophical debates regarding embodied understanding. Langer 2011 provides classroom-based projects that take into account ways of enabling students to embody and envision their learning across disciplines. Dutton 2011 illustrates through case studies of science fair competitors the commitment of young people designing and developing projects for these fairs. For a treatment of the role of both visual attentiveness and envisionment in reading and of notions of time in consciousness, see Libet 2004; Wolf 2007.

9. In *Rhetoric*, Book 1, Aristotle argued for the vital role of deliberative discourse in sustaining democracy and ensuring the flourishing of freedom (Gutmann and Thompson 1996). Since the 1990s, "deliberative democracy" has been a much debated topic, with numerous studies arguing that citizens living in democracies owe one another mutually acceptable reasons for laws and policies. Reciprocity, openness, and reliable informed judgments characterize deliberation, a dynamic joint linguistic process that aims to bring forth decisions that will bind group members to conjoined action and to caring about what happens in the participation that must follow deliberation (Dryzek 2000; Elster 1998; Mutz 2006).

10. Numerous studies of language within science laboratories confirm uses of relational, referential, and extensional language (Heath 2011; Latour 1986, 1987; Latour and Woolgar 1979; Ochs, Gonzales, and Jacoby 1996).

8 SHAPING THE MAINSTREAM

1. Institute for Children, Poverty, and Homelessness 2010; Wright, Chau, and Aratani, 2011. Hartigan 2010 reviews the US conversation on race.

2. Scholars in psychology and the neurosciences have given considerable attention to whether or not it is possible to identify sources of extraordinary resilience, particularly in young adults. The consensus by 2010 of scholars in the United States and Canada was that those who had experienced a moderate number of crises and setbacks in their young lives were those most likely to weather future crises. Those with too many crises and those who assessed their early lives as generally without crises had the greatest difficulty when they had to face crises beyond childhood (Masten 2009; Reich, Zantra, and Hall 2010; Ungar 2004).

3. The determination that comes with leaving one's home in the hope of something better has singled out emigrants around the world as willing to work and to stay clear-headed about their goals. On the success of Southerners who went to northern areas and the resourcefulness of black families and communities, see Tolnay and Crowder 1999 and the cases recounted in Stack 1973/1997; Wilkerson 2010. For accounts of the entrepreneurial spirit of those who became self-employed and business owners, see Bates 1999; Grossman 1989; Light and Rosenstein 1995.

4. The accounts provided by Anderson 1990; Levitt and Venkatesh 2000a and 2000b; and Spergel 1995 make evident the destructive force of the underground economy for young inner-city blacks. See also Venkatesh 2006.

5. The level of knowledge some of these young adults had concerning drug chemistry and the world drug market during the 1980s is suggested in narratives given in Heath 1994.

6. See, for example, Wideman 1995.
7. In 2011, reports from the nation and individual states on the effects on racial and ethnic groups of the economic recession and unemployment rates hovering between 9 and 15 percent (depending on geographic location) emphasized the growing wealth disparity between blacks and Hispanics, on the one hand, and whites on the other. Just under 10 percent of Americans held approximately 90 percent of the wealth in the United States by 2011. See Kochhar, Fry, and Taylor 2011.
8. Hogan 2011 develops the idea that literature now provides otherwise unavailable insights into ways that emotions are experienced and enacted in social life. His argument has special merit for young people who have increasingly rare opportunities to talk with adults in extended conversations about topics such as jealousy, pity, guilt, and romantic inclinations. Young adult novels, often written as direct conversational narratives, appear to be filling this role for some young people (Heath and Wolf forthcoming).
9. The analysis of Williams 2010 leaves little doubt regarding the effects on women and families of women's full-time participation in career development. Williams details aspects of the "cultural" and "style" differences that professional career women bring to family life; see especially her Chapters 5 and 6.
10. The essays in Tannen and Goodwin 2006 illustrate these features of adult–child interactions in households with two working parents.
11. Connerton 2009 views memory as dependent on stability. When the status of home or family becomes unsettled for young people, and consumerism and entertainment develop as central foci, the sharing of memory is diminished in habit and valuation.

EPILOGUE

1. Ingold 2007 examines cross-cultural fascination with lines and reflects the ways in which societal norms can shape expectations as well as behaviors and the punishments and rewards that surround these. Psychologists, more than anthropologists, tend to hold monolineal perspectives on child development, labeling as "delays" an individual's failure to fit into the succession of points toward specific milestones of development. School curricula, particularly those most directly related to reading, writing, and mathematics, take a similar view when they judge individual student progress on the basis of criteria linked with predetermined benchmarks of scope and sequence.
2. These ideas are further developed in Banks 2007; see also Finnegan 2005 on an "ethic of knowledge for today" and Heath and Heath 2010 on "free spaces" for social movement.

APPENDIX A: ETHNOGRAPHY AS BIOGRAPHY AND AUTOBIOGRAPHY

1. The primary difficulties come in sorting out the facts of the story reported to the best of the teller's ability from reflection and creative or critical compression and expansion. Social scientists complicate this sorting in that they are expected to explain and amplify their storytelling as well as their methods or ways of knowing what they report. Theories and analysis of works that compare or contrast with the current story also have to find their way into the telling. No assignment as a "pure" genre of any sort

will come easily for this mongrel book with its mix of autobiography, biography, ethnography, memoir, and narrative social history (see Miller 2007 for a comparative point of view).

2. Re-examinations of fixed definitions and standards for determining what is literature and what is art parallel in numerous ways those throughout the history of American and British anthropology. Since the days of Franz Boas at Columbia University in the early twentieth century, Americans have been particularly anxious over the extent to which the four-field approach (physical anthropology, cultural anthropology, linguistics, and archaeology), cherished in many departments of anthropology well into the 1970s, defined the field (see Kuper 1996, 1999, 2005). The work of Raymond Williams (1966/1985) strongly influenced ethnographers, who turned a critical eye on their sense of themselves and their writing in the 1980s just as Williams had done on art and literature (Clifford 1986; Rosaldo 1993). These works led the way for arguments in support of interdisciplinary work as necessary replacement for claims of objectivity and the singular contribution of anthropology (see especially Greenhouse, Yngvesson, and Engel 1994; Watkins 1998).

3. See Eriksen 2006 for an analysis of the need for anthropology to have a public presence.

4. This initial breaking of genre boundaries appears in Heath 2010, which provides my personal "literacy history." Told there are stories of life with my grandmother and my eventual foster family. This work illustrates the need for family literacy enthusiasts to acknowledge the interdependence of early literacy experiences with many factors other than the presence of books in the home. Primary among these are space, time, deliberative talk, and patterns of play and household work.

5. The Prologue and Part II of *Ways with words* (1983/1996), describe my close work with black and white teachers and the findings from my comparative analysis of language socialization in homes and classrooms.

APPENDIX B: ON METHODS OF SOCIAL HISTORY AND ETHNOGRAPHY

1. Kuper (1996, 1999) has provided accounts that reveal the linkages between British social anthropologists working as ethnographers and social historians. The tradition of social history has been somewhat stronger in Europe and Great Britain than in the United States. However, see Stocking (1992) for a history of ethnography in the United States that reveals some parallels to the work of social historians. Social historians such as Natalie Zemon Davis have been influential for anthropologists working, in particular, on gender, ethnic groups, urban life, and literacy. Anthropologists have only rarely used a single character to portray an historical phenomenon. The story of Ishi (the last Native American in northern California, who lived most of his life entirely without exposure to European American contact) is the most notable exception (Kroeber 1961). Social historians, however, have used to great effectiveness the strategy of portraying a particular period of history through the life of a single ordinary character (see Davis 1983 on the case of imposture created by the disappearance of the sixteenth-century peasant Martin Guerre, and Davis 1995 on the lives of three women of the seventeenth century; and Steedman 2007 on Phoebe Beatson, an early-eighteenth-century servant who bore an illegitimate child that Steedman links with a character in Emily Brontë's (1841/1965) novel *Wuthering Heights* of the same period).

2. See Chapter 3 of Heath and Street 2008.
3. See chapters on videogames and graphic novels in Flood, Heath, and Lapp 2008, as well as studies of individual children (Dyson 1997; Gee 2003).
4. Kress (2003, 2010) provides comprehensive contextualized analyses of multimodal systems of symbolic structuring.
5. Studies by linguists have been particularly revealing about the fine distinctions in language that young people use to assess one another in terms of racial and ethnic identity and social clique membership (Bucholtz 2011; Eckert 1989; Green 2011; Mendoza-Denton 2008).
6. Hart and Risley 1995 and 1999, and Lareau 2003 reveal the significant ways in which time and financial resources within households influenced extent and range of lexical input to children as well as coverage of topics.
7. The studies by Fleetwood 2005; Tannock 1999; and Soep 2005a, 2005b, and 2006 reflect the work of these guerrilla anthropologists.

References

Alter, R. 2010. *The wisdom books: Job, Proverbs, and Ecclesiastes. A translation with commentary*. New York: W. W. Norton.

Anderson, E. 1990. *Street wise: Race, class, and change in an urban community*. University of Chicago Press.

Anning, A. and Ring, K. 2004. *Making sense of children's drawings*. London: Open University Press.

Banks, J. 2007. *Learning in and out of school in diverse environments*. Seattle, WA: LIFE Center and Center for Multicultural Education, University of Washington.

Barton, D. and Hamilton, M. 1998. *Local literacies*. London: Routledge.

1999. *Situated literacies: Reading and writing in context*. London: Routledge.

Bates, T. 1999. *Race, self-employment, and upward mobility*. Baltimore, MD: Johns Hopkins University Press.

Bayley, R. and Schecter, S. R. (eds.). 2003. *Language socialization in bilingual and multilingual societies*. Clevedon: Multilingual Matters.

Benjamin, W. 1969. "The storyteller," in *Illuminations*. New York: Schocken Books, pp. 83–111.

Blum, S. D. 2009. *My word! Plagiarism and college culture*. Ithaca, NY: Cornell University Press.

Brontë, E. 1847/1965. *Wuthering Heights*. Harmondsworth: Penguin.

Brown, S. 2009. *Play: How it shapes the brain, opens the imagination, and invigorates the soul*. New York: Penguin.

Bruner, J. 1986. *Actual minds, possible worlds*. Cambridge, MA: Harvard University Press.

Bucholtz, M. 2011. *White kids: Language, race and styles of youth identity*. Cambridge University Press.

Burnett, R. 2004. *How images think*. Cambridge, MA: MIT Press.

Carpenter, M. 1981. *Corporate authorship: Its role in library cataloguing*. Westport, CN: Greenwood.

Carr, N. 2010. *The shallows: What the internet is doing to our brains*. New York: W. W. Norton.

Clifford, J. 1986. "Introduction: Partial truths," in J. Clifford and G. F. Marcus (eds.), *Writing culture: The poetics and politics of ethnography*. Berkeley, CA: University of California Press, pp. 1–26.

Connerton, P. 2009. *How modernity forgets*. Cambridge University Press.

Coy, M. W. (ed.). 1989. *Apprenticeship: From theory to method and back again*. Albany, NY: SUNY Press.

Crystal, D. 2008. *TXTNG: The gr8 db8*. Oxford University Press.

Dancygier, B. 1998. *Conditionals and predication: Time, knowledge and causation in conditional constructions*. Cambridge University Press.

Darling-Hammond, L. 2010. *The flat world and education: How America's commitment to equity will determine our future*. New York: Teachers College Press.

Davis, N. Z. 1983. *The return of Martin Guerre*. Cambridge, MA: Harvard University Press.
   1995. *Women on the margins: Three seventeenth century lives*. Cambridge, MA: Harvard University Press.

DiSessa, A. A. and Sherin, B. 1998. "What change in conceptual change?" *International Journal of Science Education* 10.10: 1155–1191.

Donald, M. 1991. *Origins of the modern mind: Three stages in the evolution of culture and cognition*. Cambridge, MA: Harvard University Press.
   2001. *A mind so rare: The evolution of human consciousness*. New York: W. W. Norton.

Dryfoos, J. 1990. *Adolescents at risk: Prevalence and prevention*. New York: Oxford University Press.

Dryzek, J. 2000. *Deliberative democracy and beyond*. Oxford University Press.

Duranti, A., Ochs, E., and Schieffelin, B. 2011. *Handbook of language socialization*. London: Blackwell.

Dutton, J. 2011. *Science fair season: Twelve kids, a robot named Scorch . . . and what it takes to win*. New York: Hyperion.

Dyson, A. 1997. *Writing superheroes: Contemporary childhood, popular culture, and classroom literacy*. New York: Teachers College Press.

Eckert, P. 1989. *Jocks and burnouts: Social categories and identity in the high school*. New York: Teachers College Press.

Eliot, G. 1871–1872/1963. *Middlemarch*. New York: Washington Square Press.

Elster, J. 1998. *Deliberative democracy*. Cambridge University Press.

Eriksen, T. H. 2006. *Engaging anthropology: The case for a public presence*. Oxford: Berg.

Feinstein, S. G. 2009. *Secrets of the teenage brain*. Thousand Oaks, CA: Corwin.

Ferguson, C. 1983. "Sports announcer talk: Syntactic aspects of register variation," *Language in Society* 12: 153–172.

Finnegan, R. 2005. *Participating in the knowledge society*. London: Palgrave.

Fleetwood, N. 2005. "Authenticating practices: Producing realness, performing youth," in S. Maira and E. Soep (eds.), *Youthscape: The popular, the national, the global*. Philadelphia, PA: University of Pennsylvania Press, pp. 155–172.

Flood, J., Heath, S. B., and Lapp, D. (eds.). 2008. *Handbook for literacy educators: Research in the visual and communicative arts*. Vol. II. New York: Lawrence Erlbaum.

Foster, G., Scudder, T., Colson, E., and Kemper, R. (eds.). 1979. *Long-term field research in social anthropology*. New York: Academic Press.

Freedman, M. 1993. *The kindness of strangers: Adult mentors, urban youth, and the new voluntarism*. San Francisco, CA: Jossey-Bass.

Gardner, H. 2011. *Truth, beauty, and goodness reframed: Educating for the virtues in the twenty-first century*. New York: Basic Books.

Gee, J. 2003. *What video games have to teach us about learning and literacy*. New York: Palgrave.

Gilbert, J. K., Reiner, M., and Nakhleh, M. (eds.). 2005. *Visualization: Theory and practice in science education*. Guildford: Springer.

Goodwin, C. 1994. "Professional vision," *American Anthropologist* 96: 606–633.
   1995. "Seeing in depth," *Social Studies of Science* 25: 237–274.
Goody, J. 2010. *Myth, ritual and the oral*. Cambridge University Press.
Gopnik, A. and Meltzoff, A. 1998. *Words, thoughts, and theories*. Cambridge, MA: MIT Press.
Gopnik, A., Meltzoff, A. N., and Kuhl, P. K. 1999. *The scientist in the crib*. New York: Perennial.
Green, L. J. 2011. *Language and the African American child*. Cambridge University Press.
Greenfield, P. M. 2004. *Weaving generations together: Evolving creativity in the Maya of Chiapas*. Santa Fe, NM: School of American Research Press.
Greenhouse, C., Yngvesson, B., and Engel, D. 1994. *Law and community in three American towns*. Ithaca, NY: Cornell University Press.
Grossman, J. 1989. *Land of hope: Chicago, black southerners, and the great migration*. University of Chicago Press.
Gutmann, A. and Thompson, D. 1996. *Democracy and disagreement*. Cambridge, MA: Harvard University Press.
Halpern, R. 2003. *Making play work: The promise of after-school programs for low-income children*. New York: Teachers College Press.
Hamilton, G. 2002. *Moving people from welfare to work*. Washington, DC: US Department of Health and Human Services.
Handelman, D. 1990. *Models and mirrors: Towards an anthropology of public events*. Cambridge University Press.
Harrington, C. and Boardman, S. K. 1997. *Paths to success: Beating the odds in American society*. Cambridge, MA: Harvard University Press.
Hart, B. and Risley, T. 1995. *Meaningful differences in the everyday experience of young American children*. Baltimore, MD: Paul H. Brookes.
   1999. *The social world of children learning to talk*. Baltimore, MD: Paul H. Brookes.
Hartigan, J. 2010. *What can you say? America's national conversation on race*. Stanford University Press.
Heath, C. and Heath, D. 2010. *Switch: How to change things when change is hard*. New York: Broadway Books.
Heath, S. B. 1982. "Ethnography in education: Toward defining the essentials," in P. Gilmore and A. Glatthorn (eds.), *Ethnography and education: Children in and out of school*. Washington, DC: Center for Applied Linguistics, pp. 33–55.
Heath, S. B. 1983/1996. *Ways with words: Language, life, and work in communities and classrooms*. Cambridge University Press.
Heath, S. B. 1990. "The children of Trackton's children: Spoken and written language in social change," in J. Stigler, R. A. Shweder, and G. S. Herdt (eds.), *Cultural psychology: The Chicago symposia on human development*. New York: Cambridge University Press, pp. 496–519.
Heath, S. B. 1994. "Stories as ways of acting together," in A. H. Dyson and C. Genishi (eds.), *The need for story: Cultural diversity in classroom and community*. Champaign, IL: National Council of Teachers of English, pp. 206–220.
Heath, S. B. 1997. "Culture: Contested realm in research on children and youth," *Applied Developmental Science* 1.3: 113–123.
Heath, S. B. 2010. "The book as home? It all depends," in S. A. Wolf, K. Coats, P. Enciso, and C. A. Jenkins (eds.), *Handbook of research on children's and young adult literature*. New York: Routledge, pp. 32–47.

Heath, S. B. 2011. "If you don't see it, you don't get it!" in W. Tate and C. C. Yeakey (eds.), *Research on schools, communities, and neighborhoods: Toward civic responsibilities*. Washington, DC: American Education Research Association.

Heath, S. B. and Langman, J. 1994. "Shared thinking and the register of coaching," in D. Biber and E. Finegan (eds.), *Sociolinguistic perspectives on register*. New York: Oxford University Press, pp. 82–105.

Heath, S. B. and McLaughlin, M. W. (eds.) 1993. *Identity and inner-city youth: Beyond ethnicity and gender*. New York: Teachers College Press.

Heath, S. B. and Smyth, L. 1999. *ArtShow: Youth and community development*. Washington, DC: Partners for Livable Communities.

Heath, S. B., Soep, E., and Roach, A. 1998. "Living the arts through language-learning: A report on community-based youth organizations," *Americans for the Arts Monographs* 2.7 (Entire volume).

Heath, S. B. and Street, B. 2008. *On ethnography: Approaches to language and literacy research*. New York: Teachers College Press.

Heath, S. B. and Wolf, J. L. forthcoming. "Brain and behaviour: The coherence of teenage responses to YA literature," in M. Hilton and M. Nikolajeva (eds.), *Contemporary adolescent literature and culture: The emergent adult*. Farnham: Ashgate.

Hirsh-Pasek, K., Berk, L. E., Singer, D., and Golinkoff, R. M. 2008. *A mandate for playful learning in preschool*. Oxford University Press.

Hogan, P. 2011. *What literature teaches us about emotion*. Cambridge University Press.

Hymes, D. H. 1962. "The ethnography of speaking," in T. Gladwin and W. Sturtevant (eds.), *Anthropology and human behavior*. Washington, DC: Anthropological Society of Washington, pp. 15–53.

  1964. "Introduction: Toward ethnographies of communication," in J. Gumperz and D. H. Hymes (eds.), *The ethnography of communication* (Special publication, *American Anthropologist*, 66.6 (2): 1–34). Washington, DC: American Anthropological Association.

  1969. *The reinvention of anthropology*. New York: Random House.

Ingold, T. 2007. *Lines: A brief history*. London: Routledge.

Institute for Children, Poverty, and Homelessness (ICPH). 2010. "American family experiences with poverty and homelessness," *Uncensored*, Vol. II.1 (Entire issue). New York: ICPH. [www.ICPHusa.org, accessed January 2011].

Kierkegaard, S. 1968. *The concept of irony*. Bloomington, IN: Indiana University Press.

Kochhar, R., Fry, R., and Taylor, P. 2011. *Wealth gap rise to record highs between whites, blacks, and Hispanics*. Washington, DC: Pew Research Center.

Kosslyn, S. M. 1995. "Visual cognition: Introduction," in S. M. Kosslyn and D. N. Osherson (eds.), *Visual cognition*, Vol. II. Cambridge, MA: MIT Press, pp. xi–xii.

Kotlowitz, A. 1991. *There are no children here*. New York: Doubleday.

Kozol, J. 1991. *Savage inequalities: Children in America's schools*. New York: Crown.

Kress, G. 2003. *Literacy in the new media age*. London: Routledge.

  2010. *Multimodality: A social semiotic approach to contemporary communication*. London: Routledge.

Kroeber, T. 1961. *Ishi in two worlds: A biography of the last wild Indian in North America*. Berkeley, CA: University of California Press.

Kulick, D. 1992. *Language shift and cultural reproduction: Socialization, self, and syncretism in a Papua New Guinean village.* Cambridge University Press.

Kuper, A. 1996. *Anthropology and anthropologists: The modern British school.* 3rd edn. London: Routledge.

1999. *Culture: The anthropologists' account.* Cambridge, MA: Harvard University Press.

2005. "Alternative histories of British social anthropology," *Social Anthropology* 13.1: 47–64.

Langer, J. 2011. *Envisioning knowledge: Building literacy in the academic disciplines.* New York: Teachers College Press.

Lareau, A. 2003. *Unequal childhoods: Class, race, and family life.* Berkeley, CA: University of California Press.

Latour, B. 1986. "Visualization and cognition: Thinking with eyes and hands," *Knowledge and Society* 6: 1–40.

1987. *Science in action.* Cambridge, MA: Harvard University Press.

Latour, B. and Woolgar, S. 1979. *Laboratory life: The construction of scientific facts.* Beverly Hills, CA: Sage.

Lehrer, J. 2009. *How we decide.* Boston, MA: Houghton Mifflin.

Libet, B. 2004. *Mind time: The temporal factor in consciousness.* Cambridge, MA: Harvard University Press.

Light, I. and Rosenstein, C. 1995. *Race, ethnicity, and entrepreneurship in urban America.* New York: Aldine de Gruyter.

Louv, R. 2005. *Last child in the woods: Saving our children from nature deficit.* Chapel Hill, NC: Algonquin Books.

Lunsford, A. and Ede, L. 1990. *Singular texts/plural authors: Perspectives on collaborative writing.* Carbondale, IL: Southern Illinois University Press.

2011. *Writing together: Collaboration in theory and practice.* Boston, MA: Bedford St. Martins.

Lynch, M. 1985. *Art and artifact in laboratory science.* London: Routledge.

McLaughlin, M., Irby, M., and Langman, J. 1994. *Urban sanctuaries: Neighborhood organizations in the lives and futures of inner-city youth.* San Francisco, CA: Jossey Bass.

McLaughlin, M., Scott, R., Deschenes, S., Hopkins, K., and Newman, A. 2010. *Between movement and establishment: Organizations advocating for youth.* Stanford University Press.

MacLeod, J. 1987. *Ain't no making it: Leveled aspirations in a low-income neighborhood.* Boulder, CO: Westview Press.

Mallgrave, H. F. 2010. *The architect's brain: Neuroscience, creativity, and architecture.* Malden, MA: John Wiley.

Masten, A. 2009. "Ordinary magic: Lessons from research in resilience in human development," *Education Canada* 49.3: 28–32.

Matthews, J. 1999. *The art of childhood and adolescence: The construction of meaning.* London: Falmer Press.

2003. *Drawing and painting: Children and visual representation.* 2nd edn. London: Paul Chapman.

Meltzoff, A., Kuhl, P. K., Movellan, J., and Sejnowski, T. J. 2009. "Foundations for a new science of learning," *Science* 325: 284–289.

Mendoza-Denton, N. 2008. *Homegirls: Language and cultural practice among Latina youth gangs.* London: Wiley/Blackwell.

Miller, J. H. 1998. "Coda," in *Reading narrative*. Norman, OK: University of Oklahoma Press, pp. 227–230.

Miller, N. 2007. "The entangled self: Genre bondage in the age of memoir," *Publications of the Modern Language Association* 122.2: 537–548.

Moore, J. 1991. *Going down to the barrio: Homeboys and homegirls in change.* Philadelphia, PA: Temple University Press.

Moore, R. 1986. *Childhood's domain: Play and place in child development.* London: Croom Helm.

Mushin, I. 2000. "Evidentiality and deixis in narrative retelling," *Journal of Pragmatics* 32.7: 927–957.

Mutz, D. C. 2006. *Hearing the other side: Deliberative versus participatory democracy.* Cambridge University Press.

Ochs, E., Gonzales, P., and Jacoby, S. 1996. "'When I come down I'm in the domain state': Grammar and graphic representation in the interpretive activity of physicists," in E. Ochs, E. Schegloff, and S. Thompson (eds.), *Interaction and grammar.* Cambridge University Press, pp. 328–369.

Ochs, E. and Izquierdo, C. 2009. "Responsibility in childhood: Three developmental trajectories," *Ethos* 37.4: 391–413.

Pallasmaa, J. 2009. *The thinking hand: Existential and embodied wisdom in architecture.* Chichester: John Wiley.

Pfeifer, R. and Bongard, J. 2007. *How the body shapes the way we think: A new view of intelligence.* Cambridge, MA: MIT Press.

Philips, S. 1983. *The invisible culture: Communication in classroom and community on the Warm Springs Indian Reservation.* New York: Longman.

Reich, J. W., Zantra, A. J., and Hall, J. S. (eds.). 2010. *Handbook of adult resilience.* New York: Guilford.

Rich, J. A. 2009. *Wrong place, wrong time: Trauma and violence in the lives of young black men.* Baltimore, MD: Johns Hopkins University Press.

Rogoff, B. 2011. *Destiny and development: A Mayan midwife and town.* New York: Oxford University Press.

Rosaldo, R. 1993. *Culture and truth: The remaking of social analysis.* Boston, MA: Beacon Press.

Roskos-Ewoldsen, B., Intons-Peterson, J. J., and Anderson, R. E. 1993. *Imagery, creativity, and discovery: A cognitive perspective.* Amsterdam: Elsevier.

Roth, W. M. 1996. "Art and artifact of children's designing: A situated cognition perspective," *Journal of Learning Sciences* 5: 129–166.

Salvucci, D. D. and Taatgen, N. A. 2010. *The multitasking mind.* New York: Oxford University Press.

Schieffelin, B. 1990. *The give and take of everyday life: Language socialization of Kaluli children.* Cambridge University Press.

Schieffelin, B. and Ochs, E. 1986. *Language socialization across cultures.* Cambridge University Press.

Schorr, L. 1997. *Common purpose: Strengthening families and neighborhoods to rebuild America.* New York: Doubleday.

Secretary's Commission on Achieving Necessary Skills. 2000. *What work requires of schools. A SCANS report for America 2000.* Washington, DC: US Department of Labor.

Sennett, R. 2008. *The craftsman.* New Haven, CN: Yale University Press.

Shapin, S. 2008. *The scientific life: A moral history of a late modern vocation*. University of Chicago Press.

Slavin, R. 1983. *Cooperative learning*. New York: Longman.

Slingerland, E. 2008. *What science offers the humanities*. Cambridge University Press.

Soep, E. 2005a. "Critique: Where art meets assessment," *Phi Delta Kappan* 87: 38–40, 58–63.

　　2005b. "Making hardcore masculinity: Teenage boys playing house," in S. Maira and E. Soep (eds.), *Youthscapes: The popular, the national, the global*. Philadelphia, PA: University of Pennsylvania Press, pp. 173–191.

　　2006. "Critique: Assessment and the production of learning," *Teachers College Record* 208.14: 748–777.

Soep, E. and Chávez, V. 2010. *Drop that knowledge: Youth radio stories*. Berkeley, CA: University of California Press.

Spergel, I. A. 1995. *The youth gang problem: A community approach*. New York: Oxford University Press.

Stack, C. B. 1973/1997. *All our kin: Strategies for survival in a black community*. New York: Basic Books.

Stafford, B. M. 1999. *Artful science: Enlightenment, entertainment and the eclipse of visual education*. Cambridge, MA: MIT Press.

　　2007. *Echo objects: The cognitive work of images*. University of Chicago Press.

Steedman, C. 2007. *Master and servant: Love and labour in the English industrial age*. Cambridge University Press.

Stocking, G. 1992. *The ethnographer's magic*. Madison, WI: University of Wisconsin Press.

Stout, H. 2011. "The movement to restore play gains momentum," *New York Times*, p. 1 (January 5).

Street, B. 1984. *Literacy in theory and practice*. London: Routledge.

Stromberg, P. 2009. *Caught in play: How entertainment works on you*. Stanford University Press.

Sutton-Smith, B. 1997. *The ambiguities of play:* Cambridge, MA: Harvard University Press.

Tannen, D. and Goodwin, M. H. 2006. "Family discourse, framing family" (Special issue), *Text & Talk* 26.4/5: 627–634.

Tannock, S. 1999. "Working with insults: Discourse and difference in an inner-city youth organization," *Discourse and Society* 10: 317–350.

Thompson, E. P. 1963. *The making of the English working class*. Harmondsworth: Penguin.

Tolnay, S. E. and Crowder, K. 1999. "Regional origin and family structure in northern cities: The role of context," *American Sociological Review* 64.1: 97–112.

Tomasello, M. 1999. *The cultural origins of human cognition*. Cambridge, MA: Harvard University Press.

Tudge, J. 2008. *The everyday lives of young children: Culture, class, and child rearing in diverse societies*. Cambridge University Press.

Turner, M. (ed.). 2005. *The artful mind: Cognitive science and the riddle of human creativity*. New York: Oxford University Press.

Tyack, D. and Cuban, L. 1995. *Tinkering toward Utopia: A century of public school reform*. Cambridge, MA: Harvard University Press.

Ungar, M. 2004. *Nurturing hidden resilience in troubled youth*. University of Toronto Press.

Venkatesh, S. A. 2006. *Off the books: The underground economy of the urban poor.* Cambridge, MA: Harvard University Press.

Venkatesh, S. A. and Levitt, S. 2000a. "Are we a family or a business? History and disjuncture in the urban American street gang," *Theory and Society* 29.4: 427–462.
2000b. "The financial activities of an urban street gang," *Quarterly Journal of Economics* 115.3: 755–789.

Watkins, E. 1998. *Everyday exchanges: Marketwork and capitalist common sense.* Stanford University Press.

Wideman, J. E. 1995. *Fatheralong: A meditation on fathers and sons, race and society.* New York: Vintage.

Wilkerson, I. 2010. *The warmth of other suns: The epic story of America's great migration.* New York: Random House.

Williams, J. C. 2010. *Reshaping the work-family debate: Why men and class matter.* Cambridge, MA: Harvard University Press.

Williams, R. 1966/1985. *Keywords.* New York: Oxford University Press.

Wilson, F. R. 1998. *The hand.* New York: Vintage.

Wilson, W. J. 1987. *The truly disadvantaged: The inner city, the underclass and public policy.* University of Chicago Press.

Wolf, M. 2007. *Proust and the squid: The story and science of the reading brain.* New York: HarperCollins.

Worthman, C. 2002. *"Just playing the part": Engaging adolescents in drama and literacy.* New York: Teachers College Press.

Wright, V. R., Chau, M., and Aratani, Y. 2011. *Who are America's poor children?* New York: National Center for Children in Poverty (NCCP) [www.nccp.org, accessed July 2011].

Zentella, A. 1997. *Growing up bilingual.* London: Blackwell Publisher.

Index

216

career: choices, 18, 93, 155, 169; planning, 18
Carolinas (Piedmont): as location of Roadville
    and Trackton, 1, 8, 9, 181–183; return visits
    to, 130; and textile industry, 8
Catherine (Turner): as an adult, 105, 120–122,
    128, 168
cellphones: *see* phones
Census of 2010: 154
checking account: 5, 13, 14, 102
child language: stages of development, 89
childcare: broad changes in, 9, 20, 190; in
    daycare facilities, 90, 113–114, 190; by
    live-in nanny, 44
church: black, 8; Catholic, 25, 40; decline in
    attendance, 156; as family support, 5, 103;
    for mainstreamers, 14, 16; in Roadville, 41;
    in urban renewal programs, 76, 77–83, 95
Civil Rights: leaders, 8, 152; legislation of, 10,
    93, 150–152; Movement, 1, 15, 164, 180
coaches: in college negotiations, 98; as
    disciplinarian, 47, 51, 161; as intimate
    strangers, 19, 47, 48–49
cognitive mapping: 102
collaboration: in play, 116; in research, by
    adolescents, 190–193; in youth
    organizations, 38–39, 45–46
college (university): black, 15, 16; community,
    39, 100; in family identity, 14, 131; loans, 6,
    39, 94, 101; technical, 89–92; time to
    complete, 100, 101
college students: diversification among,
    153–154; first-generation, 68, 98–100
comics: as an art form, 54, 120, 125; Manga,
    120; in Spanish, 54
computer: as deterrent to family conversation,
    157; learning to use, 83, 103; as source of
    entertainment, 108–109. *See also* digital
    media; electronic gear
concerted cultivation: definition of: 114;
    practices of, 114–115, 161–162, 198 n. 2. *See
    also* parenting
conjunctions: coordinating, 29; temporal and
    causal, 141, 147, 158
consequences: pathways of, 121; unintended,
    103; within sports, 127
conversation: and academic discourse, 99–100;
    among adolescents, 29, 32–37; adult–child,
    86–87, 205 n. 10; family, 15–17, 45, 69, 72,
    75–76, 131–132, 136, 158; peer-to-peer,
    128–129; within community, 83
Cordelia (Turner-Bailey): in middle childhood,
    128–130; in secondary school, 168; as
    struggling writer, 142
creative projects: critical role of, 103–104; in
    play, 105–107, 110–120

credit card: 5; debt, 6, 130
critique: technical terminology of, 37
CSA (community-supported agriculture): 46, 58
cultivation, concerted: *see* concerted cultivation
cultural capital: 48–50
curricula: 18

Dana (Turner): as an adult, 128–130, 168
dance: 78–79
Danny (Brown): as an adolescent, 43; as an
    adult, 106–107; as a child, 41–43, 106–107
daycare: *see* childcare
decision rules: in social science research, 176, 186
decision-making: consequences of bad, 96;
    growth in power of, 82–83, 134
deictic: 146. *See also* gestures
deliberation: in dramatic arts, 37–38; in family
    talk, 162–163; in sustaining democracy,
    204 n. 9; in youth talk, 33–36
Denny (Clark): as a child, 88–90, 96, 103, 169;
    as an adolescent, 90–91, 96, 143; as a college
    student, 91; as a young adult, 167
desegregation: 15, 16, 17, 18; in classrooms,
    92, 181
dialect: accent in dialect, 23, 24, 26; in Twitter
    language, 203 n. 3. *See also* African
    American English Vernacular
digital media: in consumerism, 159. *See also*
    Facebook; multi-tasking; phones; YouTube
dinner: Sunday, 24, 40, 41, 72, 164. *See also*
    conversation
documentary evidence: 185–186
Donna (Green): as an adolescent, 80, 91–92; as
    a child, 27–28, 76–78, 84–88; as a young
    woman, 40, 92, 103, 166
dramatic arts: 19; Children's Broadway Theatre,
    128–129; problem-solving within, 37–39,
    76; and role change, 68; and technical work,
    71; as topic of family conversation, 75, 131;
    in youth organizations, 23–24, 28, 31, 32
drinking and alcoholism: 67, 71, 74
drugs: as allure for teenagers, 48; in public
    housing projects, 33, 92–93; and trafficking,
    151, 204 n. 5

Eduardo: as an adolescent, 23–24, 39; as a
    young adult, 40, 164
education: 196 n. 1; policies, 18; reform, 18,
    203 n. 6; segregated, 8. *See also* childcare;
    college; desegregation
electronic gear: failures of, 144; iPhone, 135;
    iTouch, 135; reading directions for, 119. *See
    also* computer; digital media; multi-tasking
Ellen (Dobbs-Ryan): as a child, 70; as a young
    woman, 168